Model Based Environment

A Practical Guide for Data
Model Implementation with
examples in PowerDesigner

Vladimir Pantic

Order this book online at www.trafford.com
or email orders@trafford.com

Most Trafford titles are also available at major online book retailers.

Printed in the United States of America.

ISBN: 978-1-4669-7967-3 (sc)
ISBN: 978-1-4669-7968-0 (e)

Library of Congress Control Number: 2013902607

Trafford rev. 02/08/2013

 www.trafford.com

North America & international
toll-free: 1 888 232 4444 (USA & Canada)
phone: 250 383 6864 ♦ fax: 812 355 4082

Contents

. . . to my daughter Iva

Colleagues that experienced the Model Based Environment said . . .

The concepts presented within this book provide the necessary steps to fundamentally change the way that you design, implement, and maintain all varieties of database. My experience with the MBE approach is that it leads to an increase in the overall success of projects by reducing risk and improving the maintainability of the final product.

Anthony Jones—Senior Risk Technologist

From a build, release management and deployment perspective, model based database development has significantly reduced errors, improved quality, reduced cycle time and simplified deployment. The true power of model base database development will be abundantly evident when refactoring a complex data model. Refactor to deployment in hours instead of weeks. This book is an indispensable resource to those seeking to bring quality and agility to enterprise database development projects.

David Needs, Software Build and Release Management

There are a number of books about System Development Life Cycle (SDLC), its stages, challenges and about usage of different methodologies and tools to manage its complexity. This book approaches this topic from the different angle—data centric point of view. Data is the core of all and each Information System, yet so little is written about pure data related concepts and their relationship to SDLC. This book will guide you through the whole process, from the conceptual idea, data model based requirement, analysis and design stages, all the way through physical database implementation and maintenance. Model Based Environment will help you understand what did you do wrong in your last project, since you ignored this specific topic while you were creating your last system that was based on database, data warehouse or it was just data centric . . .

Dejan Kecman, Senior Director

PREFACE

Many times I have heard that data modeling is a nice exercise, but real projects have tight time-lines that do not allow for it. Unfortunately many people involved in professional software development do not perceive data modeling as adding value. Frequently you will hear:

"Real developers don't need models, they do development!"

Every project starts with an idea of designing a software solution that will save time and money by simplifying and automating a business process. Most of the time it is not clear what needs to be done, but technical people are forced to predict if the solution is possible and how it is going to be done.

So the project starts . . .

Planning is done at a very high level. Components of the solution are outlined, estimates are done based on a generalized problem definition.

Then the analysis starts. Everyone is busy and business analysts are writing the requirements—binders and binders, hundreds of pages of documentation—for the purpose of articulating the problem.

After the analysis phase is completed, the impression is that we understand exactly what needs to be done, so we move on to the design phase where the architects and modelers start designing the solution. Developers are eager to start coding so the design is usually rushed. The walk-through with developers marks completion of the design phase and coding starts. Frequently the design phase is combined with development to speed up the software development. This results in poor documentation and a solution that can be sub-optimal due to squeezed time-lines.

After the development phase is completed the testing phase begins. Usually the time allocated for testing is insufficient and we go into production with a solution that is (hopefully) working properly.

Following production implementation the maintenance cycle starts. The documentation exists but it is very difficult to use due to its volume, complexity and inconsistency. This becomes very obvious at 2:04 AM when the application crashes and we are called to fix it! At that time, nothing seems to be easy and searching through hundreds of pages in some dusty binders or on-line documents certainly doesn't help.

Sound familiar . . . ?

At least once in our career we have been part of a similar project. Rushing through the phases of System Development Life Cycle (SDLC) usually leads to disastrous outcome but this path is repeated over and over again with everyone hoping for a miracle.

How can this be avoided?

The intent of this book is not to solve all development issues, but to focus on working in a Model Based Environment (MBE) to improve the design, development, validation and maintenance of the database while mitigating database issues. By introducing and maintaining data models using a MBE we hope to achieve:

- standardized documentation as a result of modeling
- automate maintenance of created artifacts and
- a disciplined approach to improve the modeling process

We've all worked with requirements, design documents and code that are difficult to read, follow or understand, simply because of the way it is presented or designed. The proposed solution to the problem creates documentation while modeling the database using standard data modeling techniques and specialized data modeling tools.

This book concentrates on a methodological approach using data models to interpret data requirements while preparing the design for the purpose of database implementation. The model will also be used to validate database implementation and maintain the database in a production environment.

* * *

ACKNOWLEDGMENTS

I would like to express gratitude to my friends and colleagues that helped me with their comments, suggestions and guidance with this project. Without help and contribution from my colleagues *Eli Fine, Goran Zugic, Martin Zimmer* and *Fahad Khan*, this project would not be successful.

A special thanks goes to my colleague and dear friend *Fred Dohle* for the exceptional effort editing and collaborating on this book.

I wish also to thank my daughter *Iva Pantic* for her effort in designing the book cover.

✷ ✷ ✷

1. INTRODUCTION

Software development projects may consider using models for various artifacts as a means of abstracting and simplifying a complex set of problems the team is trying to automate by providing a software solution. In this book the discussion is limited to using data models as a technique to analyze and record business data structures to design and implement a database. Furthermore we will formalize the Model Based Environment as *the practice of using models to analyze, design, implement and maintain the database throughout its life-cycle.*

The purpose of this book is not to teach you modeling; there are many excellent books that you can read and learn how to do conceptual, logical and physical data modeling. My assumption is that as a modeler you have an understanding of modeling concepts and database technology. This book will cover the following:

- types of data models encountered in various phases of SDLC
- model components required as a minimum to provide baseline for the next phase in the model life-cycle
- model elements required for code generation and database implementation
- model maintenance processes and procedures[1] required for efficient database maintenance

The assumption that the modeler knows how to complete a model for transition to the next modeling phase is plain and simply wrong! Every modeler has his own definition of *model completeness.* Therefore a good portion of the book deals with the minimum defined set of components required for transition to the next modeling phase.

Without discounting importance of the conceptual and logical data models we will concentrate on the physical data model as the final deliverable required for code generation and implementation in the database.

In the world of physical data modeling your best friend and colleague is a database administrator (DBA). Together you will embark on the task of designing, implementing and maintaining the databases from development to production. Team work is very important in modeling. The physical data modeler and DBA have to be able to understand each other when working together. Believe it or not, this is not always the case. When the modeler starts talking about Third Normal Form (3NF), Star Schema and other common modeling concepts, the DBA starts talking about performance optimization, index types, clustering, and very quickly the team work disappears turning into endless discussions about "good" and "bad" design approaches. This is counterproductive for the project and it should be avoided at any cost. It is mandatory that the modeler and DBA work as a team from the beginning of the project helping each other to create an optimal model and implement it in the database.

---

[1] The process defines **what** needs to be done while the procedure defines **how** its done

Model Based Environment (MBE) is a concept and as such it should be tool-independent. To demonstrate the concepts and their implementation, examples we will use PowerDesigner CASE[2] tool by Sybase. However, principles of the MBE are not specific to PowerDesigner and can be implemented in other products.

Before discussing the specifics of the MBE some basic modeling terminology will be covered to get us on the same page so to speak. This will help the reader relate concepts to a tool-specific implementation.

1.1. Model

We are surrounded by a variety of objects that are involved in constant interaction. *Models* are used to help us simplify and capture important object characteristics. The role of a model is to hide details that are not required for understanding of an object's structure or behavior, at the same time emphasizing important characteristics dependent on the business perspective. This brings us to the following:

DEFINITION: *Model is a simplified, abstract human perception of real-world objects.*

The definition implies the following:

- model represents an abstraction of real-world objects. By eliminating the details that are not relevant and by creating analogies, the goal is to use a model to collect and represent important object features. Having too many details does not improve our ability to comprehend the complexity of objects. That is why, by abstraction, we can conceal the details that we perceive as less important and emphasize what is important
- model is dependent on the perspective the designer has on a real-world object. In other words, the model can be significantly different when two people observe the same object

Models, in general, can capture the structure and object behavior. A data model on the other hand captures data structures and has limited behavioral components.

The following is a simple example that will demonstrate different aspects of a model. We will observe the concept of a *PERSON* and the goal of our model is to capture some attributes that will describe the concept.

For instance if a *PERSON* is observed by a modeler who has a marketing business perspective, the attributes would include elements relevant for marketing. The *PERSON* will be described by attributes such as: *first name, last name, birth date, marital status, education, employment status, salary,* etc.

---

[2] CASE stands for Computer-Aided Software Engineering. CASE tools are a class of tools that provide modeling capabilities for software engineering

On the other hand, if a *PERSON* is observed by a modeler who has a medical perspective, the model might end up with some of the common attributes (first *name, last name, birth date*) but other attributes might be completely different: *systolic and diastolic blood pressure, red cell count, white cell count, height, weight, vaccination history,* etc.

Although the *PERSON* object is the same, the set of attributes is driven by the business perspective of a modeler that designed the model.

1.2. Data model and modeling

Intuitively we are using models all the time by creating analogies that helps us understand a problem. Models of cars, mathematical models, models of buildings, they all represent a simplified version of the real world. In this book we will limit our discussion to data models only. The following is the definition of the data model:

DEFINITION: *Data model is a type of model that represents a simplified abstraction of the data structures with relationships between them.*

The *data model* essentially comprises of data structures and relationships that are linking them. Data structures should not exist by themselves and they should be related to each other through relationships. In rare cases this rule is not applicable[3] but these will be treated as exceptions. A relationship between objects defines the set of business rules that will be further enforced through the database or application code.

There are many different classifications of data models. In this book the ANSI[4] classification is used:

- conceptual schema. Theoretically, business systems could be segregated into seven to nine logical groupings of objects, inter-related with high-level relationships. Each grouping is known as a subject area. The conceptual schema provides a data model that outlines the boundaries of the business problem, further segregating the logically consistent subject areas
- logical schema. These are the models that provide the business perception of data structures and relationships. The level of details is very limited, allowing efficient communication between the business analyst and the data modeler. The most popular logical data modeling technique is the Entity-Relationship Modeling (E/R modeling) technique developed by Peter Chen
- physical schema. These are the models that are used to generate code used for database implementation. A popular technique for the physical data modeling is Relational data modeling

---

[3] For instance data structures required for auditing, performance monitoring, history etc

[4] American National Standards Institute (ANSI) is an affiliate of ISO (International Standards Organization) that maintain standards in North America

This book will focus on the physical data model as an ultimate deliverable of the modeling process. However, this does not mean that other model types are less important. On the contrary, a good physical data model is dependent on the logical and conceptual data models.

Data modeling is a process of analysis and design of data structures and their relationships. The modeling process is performed by the data modelers. Depending on the data model classification we can segregate data modeling into:

- conceptual
- logical
- physical

Data modeling is part of all SDLC phases, playing a crucial role in successful database implementation. Implementation of the database is not the end phase of modeling because the models will continue to be used for production database maintenance.

Depending on the data models class that needs to be created, different skills and knowledge is required from a modeler. While conceptual and logical data models are more oriented to the business analysis and understanding of the business problems, the physical data model deals with the physical database design and a variety of technical challenges imposed by the database itself.

1.3. Data model components

Data models have their development phases and each phase incorporates more details when compared to the previous phase. Ultimately, the physical data model is the final, very detailed and precise model ready for implementation. Building blocks for various model types are different but there is a logical mapping between the model components. The following table provides a cross-reference between the data model components as they pertain to the specific data model class (Table 1):

Conceptual data model component	Logical data model component	Physical data model component
Subject area	Subject area	Schema
Entity	Entity	Table
Relationship	Relationship	Reference
	Attribute	Column
	Domain	Domain
	Definition	Comment
	Business rule	Constraint
		Buffer Pools

Conceptual data model component	Logical data model component	Physical data model component
		Tablespaces
		Stored Procedures
		User Defined Functions
		Sequences
		Permissions

Table 1: Cross-reference between the conceptual, logical and physical data model components

It becomes obvious that, as we progress from conceptual to the physical data model, the number of building blocks increases. The cross-reference table provides a model transition mapping between the object types.

1.4. CASE tools and model repositories

CASE is an acronym that stands for **C**omputer-**A**ided **S**oftware **E**ngineering, it defines a class of tools specifically intended for software engineering. There have been many attempts to automate—or at least help with automation—of various software design components, but the most successful class within the CASE tools is the set of tools for data modeling. There are many popular data modeling tools available on the market and it is very difficult to say which one is better. They definitely provide various options that we might find useful or completely useless depending on how the tool is intended to be used.

Some of the popular CASE tool vendors with their products are listed in the Table 2:

Vendor Name	Product Name
Computer Associates	AllFusion
Sybase	PowerDesigner
Embarcadero	ER Studio
IBM	InfoSphere Data Architect
Grandite	Silverrun

Table 2: CASE tool vendors and their tools

The *Model Based Environment* adopts mandatory use of CASE tools for data modeling. CASE tools are used to create and maintain data models. The final product, the physical data model is used to create a script that will be implemented in the database. Data modeling tools can be used to validate database implementation by comparing the model with the database. This functionality provided by CASE tools is a major advantage comparing to any manual validation process.

5

There is some confusion between capabilities of modeling and graphing tools. Creating boxes and lines that represent data modeling objects (entities and relationships or tables and references) is possible with graphing tools[5], but the intention of a model is not just to graphically show modeled objects. Modeling tools offer functionality that clearly differentiates them from the graphing tools, including:

- model validation
- derivation of the physical data model from the logical data model
- maintenance of meta-data[6] (business and technical)
- ability to perform the model forward engineering to the database
- ability to perform reverse engineering by creating or updating physical data model from a database, script or another model
- ability to derive physical data models for multiple database platforms[7]
- ability to compare:
  - two models
  - model and database
  - model and SQL script

Some CASE tools offer support for a multi-user environment through the model repository—specialized software that allows users to control model versions and use CASE tools for simultaneous model development. A detailed discussion on repositories and their functionality is provided later in this book.

1.5. Roles and responsibilities in the modeling process

Data models play a critical role in the life-cycle of a project. It is important to understand the roles and responsibilities of team members so that expectations are properly set. The data modelers are responsible for the creation, modification and maintenance of data models.

The team of data modelers, DBA and business analysts comprise the *data team*. The illustration 1 provides a typical structure of the data team:

---

[5]   For instance Visio from Microsoft: http://office.microsoft.com/en-us/visio/
[6]   Meta-data is a set of descriptive data that further explains the model components. For instance, every business object should have a definition. The object definition is considered a part of the business meta-data
[7]   For instance the CASE tool can derive new physical data model based on existing one

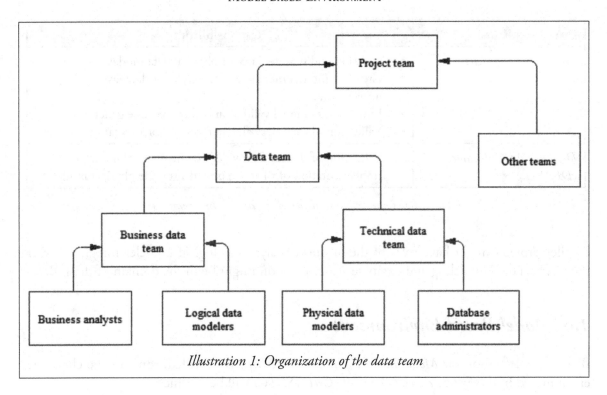

Illustration 1: Organization of the data team

The data team is further divided into two teams:

- *business data team*—responsible for the business aspect of the data including the logical data model
- *technical data team*—responsible for the physical data model and database implementation

Here is a closer look into the responsibilities for each of the data team roles (Table 3):

Role	Responsibilities
Business Analyst (BA)	• Gathering the data requirements • Structure requirements into a document so that each requirement can be cross-referenced to the objects in the logical data model • Validate completeness of the logical data model from a business data requirements perspective
Logical data modeler[8]	• Creation and maintenance of the logical data model • Clarification of data structures and business rules to the physical data modeler • Completeness validation of the "first-cut" physical data model provided by the physical data modeler

---

[8]   Further: logical modeler

Role	Responsibilities
Physical data modeler[9]	• Creation and maintenance of physical data models • Creation and maintenance of the code for database implementation • Physical data model validation before the code generation • Validation of the physical data model implementation
Database Administrator (DBA)	• Validation of the code provided by the physical modeler • Implementation of the code provided by the physical modeler

Table 3: Roles and responsibilities of the data team members

Smaller projects might have roles of the business analyst and logical modeler integrated while the physical data modeling and database administration might be in the domain of the DBA.

1.6. Model Based Environment

Before the definition for *Model Based Environment (MBE)* is provided, some of the challenges encountered in the *System development Life Cycle (SDLC)* will be outlined.

The System Development Life Cycle requires various artifacts created and maintained during the phases of planning, analysis, design, construction, testing and implementation[10]. Efficient artifacts creation and maintenance was always a complex issue for projects of any size. Each project is faced with following challenges:

- *uniformity of artifacts produced by each phase of the project*. This has always been a problem for a project that involves team of people with different experiences, skills and knowledge, resulting in artifacts that have non-uniform content and structure. The goal is to standardize on the level of details captured, structure and look of each artifact before it is created
- *maintainability and synchronization of artifacts*[11] *throughout the project phases*. Tools that we are using to complete tasks are able to produce large documents very quickly. Unfortunately, once on the paper, documents become outdated and there is usually no defined procedure to maintain the documentation. The documentation that is outdated becomes useless very quickly and serves no purpose for personnel involved in maintenance or future system enhancements or modifications
- *transition* from one phase of SDLC to another requires controlled approach and synchronization between different classes of data models. Keeping the lineage between

---

[9]   Further: physical modeler

[10]   It is worth mentioning that different methodologies define different phases of SDLC but essentially every methodology can be mapped to the phases mentioned here

[11]   Artifact is a deliverable that is in the domain of the team's responsibility. The data team will have the data models as their deliverables

the source and target (derived) model components is simply impossible if done manually

- *personnel's ability to acquire and efficiently use various tools, modeling techniques and methods.* It is anything but easy to use sophisticated tools in various phases of the project. Each tool requires the modeler to have both theoretical and practical knowledge. Inexperience and lack of theoretical knowledge can severely impact the quality of deliverables and efficiency of the personnel on the project
- *time to create and maintain produced artifacts.* Doing everything "by the book" is perceived as slow and not acceptable for tight project time-lines. However, there is a good reason why certain processes and procedures are methodologically prescribed as an optimal way of solving the problem. A disciplined and organized development approach will result in an increased chance for successful system design and implementation. Every artifact created in the process has to have a purpose of supporting the final software solution. Processes and procedures must be in place to keep the documentation (created artifacts) synchronized with the target physical implementation

At this point we are ready to define the concept of Model Based Environment:

DEFINITION: *Model Based Environment (MBE) is a concept of efficient utilization of CASE tools to support the System Development Life Cycle[12]. Models and modeling artifacts created and stored in the CASE tool are used to perform:*

- *problem analysis*
- *design, develop, implement the database and*
- *validate database implementation*

Emphasis in MBE is on the CASE tools but it is important to state that tools by themselves will not solve the problem. The CASE tool is an important component of MBE but additional components are also required (Illustration 2):

- repository
- people
- processes and procedures

---

[12] SDLC

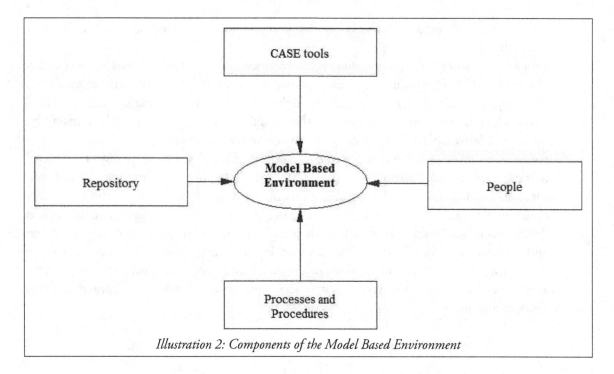

Illustration 2: Components of the Model Based Environment

A main premise of the MBE is that CASE tools are used to create and maintain models as a collection of artifacts created during various phases of the SDLC. Considering that the scope of the book is limited to data model creation and maintenance we are focusing on the CASE tools that support the data modeling process. Without a proper tool set, the MBE would not be efficient and it would lead to an increase rather than a decrease in projects cost.

To establish robust version control and provide multi-user modeling capabilities, models should be stored and maintained in the model repository. Using a specialized repository is more appropriate than using generic repositories because they provide version control at the data modeling object level rather than the file level (typical for generic repositories).

Having CASE tools will not help unless there is an experienced team of people that can efficiently use them to speed up and standardize the modeling process. Theoretical knowledge and practical experience is critical for efficient tool use. Many times the CASE tools are blamed for mistakes created by modelers. The tool will follow the rules and best practices of data modeling but, although very sophisticated, it cannot automatically correct all mistakes done by the modeler.

The last component, important for the success of MBE is the use of the formal methodologies that are the foundation of the SDLC. A methodology clearly defines the steps that need to be performed for completion of a system's analysis, design and implementation. Although formal methodologies are supporting utilization of the CASE tools they are not mandating it. The Model Based Environment puts emphasis on the CASE tools and their utilization in all phases of the SDLC.

2. DATA MODEL DEVELOPMENT CYCLE

Formal methodologies define the phases of SDLC by clearly stating the tasks, deliverables (artifacts) and resources[13]. Each methodology includes a part that deals with data, defining the steps required to create artifacts pertinent to the data layer of a software solution. Creation of data models requires a clear definition of processes and procedures that will guide the data team step-by-step towards successful completion of their deliverables. Failures of the data team have disastrous effects on the overall project success, so special attention has to be devoted to the data model development cycle within the SDLC to avoid potential problems.

Following the notion that every activity has to be planned and prepared, then executed and finally validated, the data model development cycle will be divided into the following modeling phases:

- preparation phase
- conceptual data modeling
- logical data modeling
- physical data modeling
- model implementation
- implementation validation

Each phase will be further elaborated in the next chapters. The following diagram shows the phases of the data model development cycle:

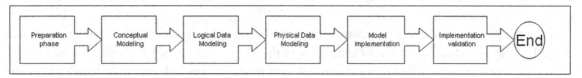

Phases of the data model development cycle

The Preparation phase is the first phase of the data model development cycle. It is focused on preparing the environment for data modeling. This can be the most important phase in the whole process if data modeling is a new discipline in the company! Do not discount the resistance you will encounter when introducing modeling to the project. People tend to continue doing what they were doing before; new advanced techniques usually raise eyebrows and hesitations when introduced to the audience for the first time. Even some advanced environments that are accustomed to modeling are reluctant to accept data models as the driving force for efficient analysis, design and implementation. It is critical to prepare all participants in the modeling process by introducing the modeling concepts that will be

---

[13]   Participants involved in the system analysis, design, development and implementation.

used and explaining why the modeling needs to be done. Every team member has the same question:

"What's in it for me?"

When you start "selling" the concept of MBE and modeling in general, always focus on answering this question and success is almost guaranteed. The data modeling cycle will require heavy involvement of the participants for a lengthy period of time and it is important to highlight the expected benefits so that participants are motivated to participate. Forcing an unmotivated group of people to do something they perceive as having small benefit will not lead to success in the long run.

At the same time, while preparing the team to accept and use models and create an environment driven by Models, it is necessary to prepare the MBE technically by defining the following standards that will be used in the process:

- standard domains for data values
- standard naming conventions
- standard default values

Additionally MBE also includes:

- validation checkpoints in the modeling process
- resources and participants involved in the modeling process
- CASE tool and the repository used in the modeling process

Failing to create standards and define activities and resources required in the process will unnecessarily increase a risk of failing to introduce and implement the MBE successfully.

The second phase in the process is **conceptual modeling**. As a result of the process the artifact created is the *conceptual data model* that depicts the "big" picture of the major business areas within the organization. Without a conceptual data model it would be very difficult to develop a strategy for integrated system development at the corporate level and promote data reuse instead of data exchange between the systems. The conceptual data model serves as a blueprint of corporate data structures defining major data components within the organization.

Logical data modeling is a process of logical model creation which is the artifact created as a deliverable of this phase. This process involves heavy participation of the business' representatives that will work together with the logical modeler to produce the logical data model (LDM). The LDM serves two purposes:

- for the business community, the intention is to create a semi-technical presentation of the business data so that it can be used to validate the understanding of a business problem gained through the analysis process
- once the analysis is completed the LDM is used as a basis for physical data model creation

Physical data modeling is the fourth phase that starts with the transition from the logical to physical data model. This transition is a formal process that involves both logical and physical modelers. Physical data modeling is a process that requires high level of technical expertise while depending on the quality and completeness of the LDM. The purpose of the physical data model is to create an *implementation ready* model that will be used to generate the code for database implementation. The phase is a joint effort between the physical modeler and the database administrator with help from the logical modeler. The team will create a physical data model that is the deliverable of this phase.

The fifth phase is **the model implementation phase** includes fine model tuning and implementation of all modifications required for performance optimization in order to produce the final model version. This phase requires involvement of technical resources responsible for model optimization and database implementation

- physical modeler
- DBA
- developers

The physical modeler is not necessarily a database expert and input provided by the DBA and developers has to be considered before the model is finalized. The database administrators and developers have intimate knowledge of database and application technical details so their input can significantly contribute to the model optimization. The final step in this phase is code generation and implementation in the database.

Successful implementation of the physical data model requires model validation against the database. Detailed discussion of this step is covered in the **implementation validation phase**. The model validation against the database is effectively the ending phase of the data model development. After this phase the model formally enters the **maintenance cycle**.

Each phase brings a new level of complexity to the project. Careful planning and following a disciplined approach to implementation of MBE is a critical component for success. Successful MBE implementation equally depends on the tools, people, methodologies, processes and procedures. Failing to consider any one of them will inevitably lead to challenges with successful implementation of MBE.

3. Preparation phase

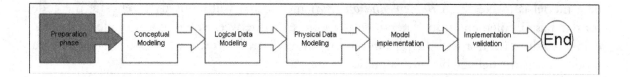

The Preparation phase has to ensure successful start of the data modeling process by establishing the modeling environment. Success of all subsequent phases is directly dependent on successful completion of this phase. The scope for the preparation phase includes the following:

- standardization of:
    - □ definition of standard logical data domains
    - □ definition of the standard naming conventions
    - □ standardization of the default values
- specification of the validation checkpoints in the modeling process
- definition of resources/participants involved in the modeling process
- specification of the CASE tool and model repository

Specification of standards, processes and procedures, resources and tools lay out the foundation for an environment where the models are managed in uniform fashion. Documents that outline standards are vital for the MBE and they will be further explained.

3.1. Logical data domains standardization

One of our goals is to ensure consistency both within each model as well as across the other models in the application domain. Having a team of modelers, business analysts and database administrators can cause confusion in creating and maintaining data models. Once the logical model is transitioned to the physical model, the modeler may find logical domain to data type conversion problems leading to: data truncation, incorrect rounding of numbers or accidental modification of data content. This can be avoided by setting up the stage for controlled and disciplined modeling guided by standards, processes and procedures established early in the process.

DEFINITION: *Logical data domain[14] represents a set of allowed values that an attribute can take.*

Instead of trying to be perfect when defining the initial set of logical domains, we can start with just few of the basic domains:

---

[14]   Further: logical domain

- *numeric*—reflecting the values that can be used in calculations (e.g. amount)
- *number*—a numeric value that cannot be used for calculation (e.g. street number)
- *string*—sequence of characters
- *date*—generic date or timestamp
- *large object*—binary or character large objects (e.g. picture, video or some large document)
- *undefined*[15]—usually this domain is treated as a string allowing any alphanumeric data content

Logical domain standardization should be a relatively simple task. We start with a small set of standardized domains, gradually enhancing it as we go through the modeling process. This is an iterative process and depends on the business problem. New logical data domains are defined in the modeling process and added to the list of standard logical domains.

As the modeling process goes through the analysis phase, segregation of logical domains introduces more refined definitions driven by the business nature of data. The following list is an example of more detailed logical domains that can be used:

- *Numeric:*
  - *Amount (regular)*[16]
    - *Large Amount*
    - *Small Amount*
  - *Rate*
  - *Identifier (regular)*
    - *Small Identifier*
    - *Long Identifier*
- *Number*
- *String*
  - *Code (regular)*
    - *Long Code*
    - *Short Code*
  - *Description*
  - *Name (regular)*
    - *Long Name*
    - *Short Name*
- *Date*
  - *Date only*
  - *Date and time*
  - *Date and time with the time zone*
- *Binary Large Object*
- *Character Large Object*

---

[15] This is a "catch-all" domain for attributes where we cannot explicitly specify the domain. Usually we treat the undefined as a character string

[16] It is difficult to standardize data format and length so the idea of segregating the length to regular, short (small) and long (large) is an attempt to provide three alternative lengths that can be used

Once defined, logical domains have to be reviewed and approved by the data architect to be used as standard domains in the modeling process. Organizations that practice data architecture at the corporate level have very strict approval processes and procedures for new or modified logical data domains. Logical data domains are centrally maintained and distributed to various projects as part of the model's preparation.

Maintenance and dissemination of the logical domains might become an issue if spreadsheets are used instead of CASE tools. Maintaining consistency of logical domains with spreadsheets is an increasingly complex and time consuming effort. The problem is that when the spreadsheet with logical domains has to be used in the model someone has to manually update the model. This activity is prone to errors if the list of standard logical domains is lengthy. Instead, logical domains should be maintained in the CASE tool and distributed to modelers as part of the initial model setup. An example of logical domains defined in PowerDesigner is shown in the Illustration 3:

	Name ▼	Code	Comment	M	
1	Amount	AMT	Monetary value expressed as a numeric.	☐	
2	Code	CD	Text representing a reference value.	☐	
3	Date and time	DATE_TIME	Date and time together.	☐	
4	Date only	DATE	Generic date in standard format.	☐	
→	Description	DESC	Textual explanation.	☑	
6	Identifier	ID	A unique number used for identification of a concept.	☑	
7	Large Amount	AMT_L	Large monetary value expressed as a numeric.	☐	
8	Large Object Binary	BLOB	Multi-media object.	☐	
9	Large Object Characte	CLOB	Large text.	☐	
10	Long Code	CD_L	Text representing a reference value with extended length.	☑	
11	Long Identifier	ID_L	A unique number with extended length used for identification of a concept.	☑	
12	Long Name	NAME_L	Text representing a designation of a concept.	☐	
13	Name	NAME	Text with extended length representing a designation of a concept.	☐	
14	Number	NUMB	Numeric that cannot be used for any type of calculation.	☐	
15	Rate	RTE	Decimal value with extended precision.	☐	
16	Short Code	CODE_S	Short text representing a reference value.	☑	
17	Short Name	NAME_S	Text with short length representing a designation of a concept.	☐	
18	Small Amount	AMOUNT_S	Small monetary value expressed as numeric.	☐	

Illustration 3: List of the standardized logical domains

In PowerDesigner the definition of the logical domain allows for specification of the corresponding physical data type. The physical data type is used to implement the logical data domain when the model is transferred to the physical data model.

Each standardized logical domain should have a clear business definition reflecting the nature of data content it stores. The purpose of the definition is to provide the insights into the data content and specific limitations imposed on the logical domain.

If not properly defined, the logical domain definition can be very confusing. Let's use *rate* as example. The *rate* is defined as a coefficient used in calculation. It is applied as a multiplier to the base value. We are all familiar with the use and meaning of interest rates, the meaning and application of an interest rate of 3.11, expressed as percentage, poses no problems for implementation. The assumption is that the number 3.11 represents the percentage value of the interest rate so the calculation that has to be performed is:

*result value = <some value> * 3.11 / 100*

or

*result value = <some value> * 0.0311*

Now let's assume that the number that we see is 0.000012114. If there is no clear definition specifying that the value showed is actually a percentage value, many of us will get confused about the number. It is not clear anymore what the value represents:

- interest rate of 0.000012114 expressed as a coefficient that can be used directly in the calculation or
- a value of 0.000012114, that has to be divided by 100 before it is used in the calculation

This issue is typical when the user is faced with an unfamiliar system and no definitions are available. Similar problems can cause confusion and inconsistency so the recommendation is to spend some time classifying the data into clearly defined logical domains that can be consistently and uniformly reused in the modeling process.

3.2. Logical data domains and business rules

Logical data domains can be further enhanced by a business rule definition. Assigning a logical domain to an attribute results in a business rule being implicitly applied.

For instance, a logical domain called *large amount* used for monetary value may have a business rule stating that monetary value cannot be negative[17]. Instead of applying this rule to every data element defined as the value, the rule can be defined at the domain level resulting in the specification of a constraint that will be inherited by all data elements where the domain is applied.

CASE tools allow for a definition of the business rules applicable to the domain. When domain is applied to an attribute, the rule is automatically inherited from the domain. The Illustration 4 shows the *large amount* logical domain that will be further associated with the business rule to allow positive values only:

---

[17] This is just an assumption in this example.

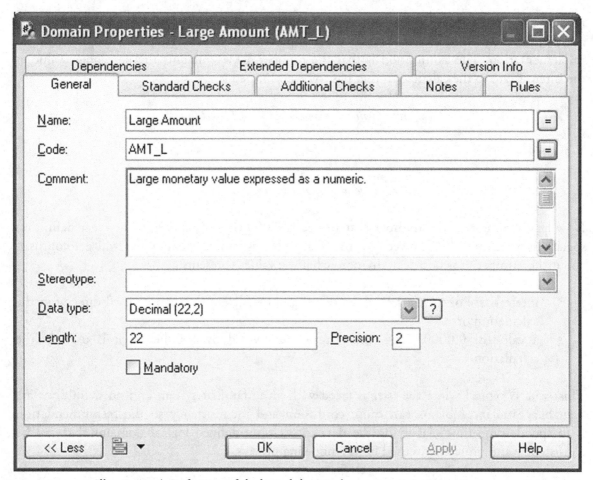

Illustration 4: Definition of the logical domain large amount in PowerDesigner

In this example *large amount* is defined as a logical domain with underlying data type *decimal* and specified *length* and *precision* (22, 2) respectively. Attribute content is optional and the database column will allow NULL values as specified by the *mandatory* box. While the *name* represents full, logical name of the domain, the *code* represents physical name of the database object that will be implemented in the physical data model. The *comment* is where the definition of the domain is provided.

Logical domain definition is the first step in modeling. When a logical data model is used to produce the physical data model, each logical domain is converted into a physical data domain. In our example, the definition of the logical domain *large amount* will result in the creation of a physical data domain *AMT_L* with underlying data type of *decimal* (22, 2) as specified in the model. Table columns defined with this domain will be created as optional (NULL) considering that the *mandatory* box is not checked off.

If required, the logical domain can be enhanced by definition of a business rule. For instance a business rule requiring the amount to be positive can be defined in the tool by specifying the minimum value of zero. The business rule is automatically inherited by all attributes that use this domain. The illustration 5 shows the definition of the business rule to allow positive values for the *large amount* logical domain:

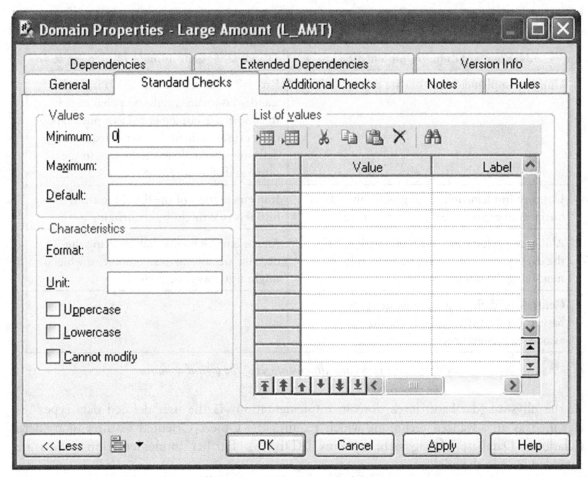

Illustration 5: Business rule definition

The business rule applicable to the *large amount* logical domain states that the *large amount has to be greater than or equal to zero* (large amount >= 0).

Implementation of the business rules in the physical data model does not imply implementation of the constraints enforced by the database. Alternatively the application code or triggers can be used to implement the same business rule. A strategy for business rules in the physical data model will have strong impact on:

- overall software solution maintainability
- performance

Both database and application code can be used for enforcement of the constraints that implement the business rules.

Some of advantages and disadvantages of domain implementation are shown below:

Advantages of domain implementation	Disadvantages of domain implementation
Uniform implementation of data types	Exception to the rule (deviation from the standard domain) might be a challenge if the domain is implemented as a physical object (user defined data type) requiring definition of an alternate domain in the physical data model
Uniform implementation of generically defined business rules applicable to the data type	Implementation of the deviation from the business rule might be challenging
Ability to perform massive modifications of the data types, formats and business rules by modifying the domain	All the data elements that are using the domain are automatically modified which might not always be desired
Centralized definition and maintenance of basic meta-data that describe the domain and associated business rules	

Table 4: Advantages and disadvantages of the logical domains

At the physical (database) level, domain implementation via the user defined data types[18] is classified as an advanced technique which requires the Object Oriented features of modern Relational Database Management Systems (RDBMS). Further implementation details are provided later in the book.

3.3. Standardized default values

Each attribute and corresponding database column allows for an explicit definition of a business rule that states if the data is required (mandatory) or not (optional). The rule is implemented as a NOT NULL constraint at the column level in the database. Standard representation of missing data is the NULL value which literally represents "nothing". The NULL represents an empty set and special comparison rules are applicable to the NULL value resulting from explicit mathematical definition. For instance, the NULL is not comparable to any other value-not even another NULL. From the performance perspective the NULL value can cause problems in some databases because the NULL value is not included in specific type s of indexes[19], triggering a full table scan and causing performance problems.

Performance issues with NULL values and the inability to represent various flavors of missing data[20] require the definition of default values to appropriately represent the missing data.

---

[18] Databases usually use UDT as an acronym for the user defined data type

[19] For instance, Oracle RDBMS does not include NULL value in the B-tree type of index while the NULL value is included in bit-map index type

[20] For instance: not applicable vs. not found or not provided....

DEFINITION: *Default value is a predefined value used when the input data is not explicitly provided.*

Using the business rule implemented as a constraint, the modeler can define two alternate scenarios:

- data must be provided (NOT NULL)
- data is missing (NULL)

Some business situations require definition of various "flavors" of missing data because the missing data can indicate a potential unusual event[21]. To allow multiple flavors of values that represent the missing data specific values can be predefined for each data type. The Table 5 can be used to standardize the values for various types of missing data:

Missing Data Type	String	Date	Numeric . . .	. . .
Not Found				
Not Applicable				
Not Provided				

Table 5: Default values for various data types

Each cell contains a value that has to be used to replace a specific missing data type. The definition of the *default value*s for missing data is not always a trivial task. For instance the following approach can be used to represent missing data for DATE and STRING[22] data types:

- DATE—specific date far in the future (e.g. January 1, 3000). Predefined default value for the data type can be sometimes challenging to define, because the value can accidentally have a business meaning
- STRING—specific character like question mark

The default values for the numeric data types are more complex. Numbers are used in calculations and some aggregate functions (e.g. average, variance, standard deviation) are sensitive to missing values. In other words, missing values are excluded from calculation. If we replace the missing value with some specific predefined value, we can end up with unexpected results. Here is an example:

10
20
NULL
Average is **15**

---

21   Fraud, for instance
22   Alphanumeric set of characters

However, when zero is used as a default value the result of the same aggregate function is different:

10
20
0
Average is **10**

In the first example the NULL value is excluded from the calculation so the total is divided by two giving the result of 30/2=15. Second example treats zero as a number resulting in calculation of 30/3=10. For numeric values involved in calculation the modeler has to asses if aggregate functions are used in calculations, before the default value is specified.

Standardization of the default values will bring the following benefits:

- Instead of only having a single value to represents the missing data (NULL), several missing value flavors are available (as explained). This is important when the database is used for DSS[23] analysis where the missing value requires further classification based on the reason for missing data
- Standard values will be uniformly used so that developers do not need to be "inventive" and provide their own "version" of the default value. This will significantly improve usability of data by introducing uniformity

Standardized default values represent a step towards overall data standardization and require careful planning at the corporate level. Data architects should put emphasis on uniform definition and use of a consistent set of predefined default values enforcing it in the modeling process.

3.4. Principles of the logical data model naming conventions

The business concept names defined in the data requirements document usually lack consistency considering that they represent the business knowledge collected and structured by the business analysts during the analysis phase. The data requirements document allows certain freedom in naming the business concepts later implemented as data modeling objects. The goal for the analysis phase is to extract and structure the business knowledge into a form that can be further modeled. Although the business analyst should make an attempt to streamline the lingo used when naming the business concepts, names are not necessarily structured in a uniform way. The challenge for the modeler is to develop a way to control the names by consistently applying the naming rules in uniform and repeatable fashion.

---

[23]   DSS stands for Decision Support System.

DEFINITION: *Logical data model naming conventions have to ensure implementation of uniform syntactic and semantic rules for the object names in the logical data model.*

CASE tools can implement and enforce naming rules for the names in the model. The business analyst is not a technical resource and their name preference is aligned with the names of the concepts used by the business. Enforcing strict rules for the naming conventions in the logical data model would probably be excessive, causing more problems than benefits. The challenge is to find a balance between the discipline in object naming and flexibility to use full, business friendly names.

The following set of rules will guide the definition of the *logical data model naming conventions*:

- object names in the logical data model should use the words from the list of available business terms from the *Corporate Data Dictionary*[24]
- each *name should be structured* in the following fashion:
  - □ *class word* that defines the main concept, usually an entity (e.g. CUSTOMER)
  - □ *modifier* defines how is the domain being used (e.g. LAST or FIRST)
  - □ *domain* defines the allowed set of values (e.g. NAME, given that the NAME is defined as a domain)
- *acronyms or abbreviations should be avoided*[25]. Although it is common in every company to have the "standard" set of acronyms and abbreviations, the preferred approach is to avoid excessive use of these. It is challenging for new team members (especially if they are coming from another industry) to adopt new terminology if they are not familiar with the meaning of it.

CASE tools use the *corporate data dictionary*[26] to enforce the rules imposed by naming conventions. There are various ways to maintain the *data dictionary* but most of the time, the dictionary is represented in a spreadsheet format or flat file[27] that is easily loadable into the CASE tool[28]. The Illustration 6 shows the phases in which the naming conventions are implemented using the *data dictionary*.

---

[24] Data Dictionary is the list of predefined business terms with their definitions. The business terms will be used as constituents of the object names in the logical data model

[25] Sometimes this is not possible, but we should try to limit usage of these

[26] Further: the data dictionary

[27] Comma separated values (CSV) ASCII data file

[28] Of course, certain formatting of the data is required so that the CASE tool can use and enforce the naming conventions automatically

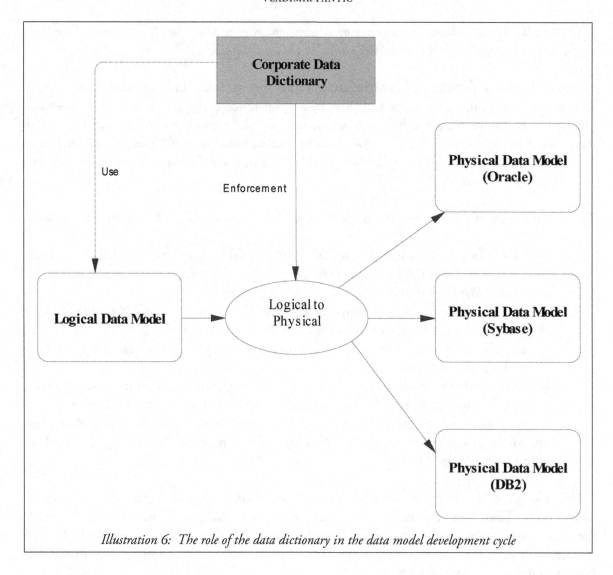

Illustration 6: The role of the data dictionary in the data model development cycle

Implementation of naming conventions[29] starts with the logical data model, however strict implementation in this modeling phase is not strongly recommended to smooth discussions between the modeler and the business analyst. At this stage in the modeling process the model will be under the heavy influence of the business considering that the purpose is to extract the business knowledge and record it in the logical model. Strict enforcement of naming conventions starts with the model transition from the logical to the physical data model. The naming rules are enforced by the CASE tool and they are applied to the object's logical names when the model is transitioned to the physical data model.

---

[29] Naming rules will be used synonymously

The Table 6 shows an example of the *list of allowed words* that are defined as part of the *corporate data dictionary*:

Formal word	Standard abbreviation	Type	Description
AMOUNT	AMT	Class word	Monetary value expressed in currency.
COMPANY	CMPNY	Class word	Legal entity that acts as a Business organization.
CUSTOMER	CSTMR	Class word	Current or potential consumer of products.
NAME	NAME	Modifier	…………..
FIRST	FRST	Modifier	…………..
………….	………….		…………..

Table 6: Example of the corporate data dictionary

The data dictionary should always be maintained at the corporate level by the data architecture team. This team is responsible for maintenance, dissemination and enforcement of the naming conventions. Each word specified in the *data dictionary* must have a standard abbreviation that will be used in the physical data model. While the logical data model allows for lengthy object names, the physical model must conform to the standards imposed by the target database forcing the modeler to use standard abbreviations when necessary.

Recommendations for naming conventions in the physical data model are provided below:

- be consistent in structuring the object names
- avoid using abbreviations (if possible) for the class and modifier words. This will improve the physical model readability
- try not to reach maximum allowed length for the object name. If the object (e.g. column) is involved in formula along with other object with lengthy names, the formula itself might not be readable, spanning multiple lines

The data dictionary also provides the allowed word's definitions, describing the data content classification. The following are examples of how the data dictionary can be used to name the attributes according to defined naming conventions:

COMPANY REGISTERED NAME where:
    COMPANY is a class word
    REGISTERED is a modifier of a
    NAME that is defined as the domain

TRANSACTION AMOUNT where:
    TRANSACTION is a class word
    AMOUNT is defined as the domain

CUSTOMER SEGMENT NAME where:
    CUSTOMER is a class word
    SEGMENT is a modifier and
    NAME is a domain

The data modeler is often asked if the naming conventions should be strictly implemented in the model. The answer is: NO! The goal of implementing naming conventions is to achieve a high level of standardization through uniformity and consistency, but sometimes the modeler is forced to deviate from these simply because the name either has no meaning to the business or has an inappropriate connotation.

3.5. Validation points in the logical data modeling process

The logical data model will go through many modifications while refining and validating data structures, relationships and business rules that have been defined in the model. After the model is finalized and ready to proceed to the physical modeling phase, the logical modeler has to perform model validation to ensure that the model complies with formal modeling rules and industry best practices. PowerDesigner provides model validation functionality for all supported model classes: conceptual, logical or physical.

DEFINITION: *Model validation is a process of verifying that the model complies with formal modeling rules and best industry practices.*

The Illustration 7 describes steps in the logical data model validation.

Formal validation of the logical data model involves validating the model against the rules and best practices of logical data modeling (e.g. compliance to normal forms, proper use of generalization relationships, etc.). While the formal logical data model validation is automated process implemented in PowerDesigner, additional validation against the best industry modeling practices is a manual process.

Model validation for completeness has to ensure that all required elements are included in the model:

- entities with definitions
- attributes with definitions
- relationships with definitions
- data domains with definitions

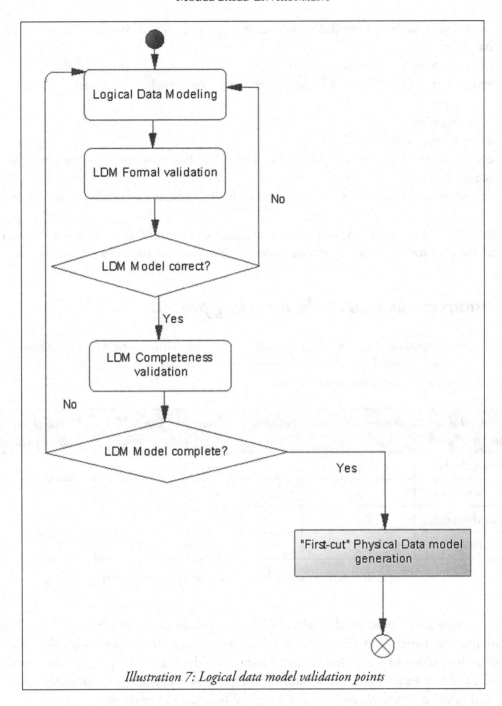

Illustration 7: Logical data model validation points

Enforcement of the naming conventions is an important segment of model validation. The most efficient implementation of the naming conventions is using the CASE tool that provides automated rule enforcement. However, manual implementation of naming conventions is not rare. The model compliance with the best industry practices requires the model assessment against the following principles:

- model should be normalized (assuming that the model supports a transactional[30] database)
- model should avoid excessive normalization
- model has to properly specify the generalization relationship be defining the following:
  - *discriminator*[31]
  - *partitioning*[32] rule
  - *coverage*[33] rule
- each relationships type[34] complies with the business rule stated by the data requirements
- subject areas should be designed to promote logical cohesion of modeling objects included

After the logical data model is validated, the modeler can proceed with creation of the initial version of the physical data model referred to as the "first-cut" of the physical model.

3.6. *Resources involved in the modeling process*

The roles and responsibilities of participants in the modeling process have already being defined. The Table 7 provides a *roles interaction matrix* that shows how the roles work together throughout the data model development cycle:

Role/Role interaction	Business Analyst	Logical modeler	Physical modeler	Database Administrator
Business Analyst		X		
Logical modeler	X		X	
Physical modeler		X		X
DBA			X	

Table 7: Interaction matrix between the roles in the data team

Role interactions are focused on the deliverables to be produced. While gathering the business requirements and structuring the logical model, the business analyst and logical modeler are involved in discussions of a business nature. Frequently, the business representatives have to be consulted to clarify issues encountered during the process. Logical data modeling can be very lengthy and resource intensive process involving the business community.

It should be emphasized that the logical data modeler is not a business expert relying heavily on the analysis and data requirements prepared by the business analyst. The modeler should

---

[30] OLTP—on-line transactional processing
[31] Discriminator performs classification of a super-type into subtypes
[32] Exclusive or inclusive partitioning
[33] Covering or non-covering generalization type
[34] Identifying vs. non-identifying relationship types

not make subjective decisions based on their perspective and understanding of the business problem. Imprecision or incorrect implementation of data structures and business rules in the logical model can have serious consequences in later phases of the data model development cycle when the logical model is used as a foundation for the physical model design.

When development reaches the phase of physical modeling, the discussion turns to be very technical. Various design and performance issues are discussed with the DBA. Database sizing, parallelism, indexing, partitioning, storage optimization etc. becomes prevalent topics.

The modeling process requires a balanced team in terms of skills, knowledge and experience. The business analyst and logical data modeler comprise the part of data team that is predominantly business-oriented while the physical data modeler and DBA make the technical team responsible for model implementation in the database. The ultimate goal for the data team is to deliver the database properly designed for optimal performance while complying with the required set of business rules stated in the data requirements document.

To set expectations for the data team it is necessary to understand the type of skills and knowledge required for each role:

Business analyst:

- knowledge and understanding of data used in the business process
- ability to understand and clearly formulate the business rules
- ability to structure acquired knowledge into the business requirements document
- ability to use examples to explain various scenarios related to the data
- ability to resolve issues and clearly answer the data and business rule related questions
- working knowledge of the productivity tools (text processors, spreadsheets etc.)

Logical modeler:

- experience with logical data modeling concepts and best practices
- working knowledge of the CASE tool and the model repository[35]
- good understanding of the business related concepts
- basic understanding of the physical data modeling concepts

Physical modeler:

- good understanding of the logical data modeling concepts
- working knowledge of the CASE tool and the repository
- basic understanding of the business related concepts
- good understanding of the database related concepts
- working knowledge of the database design principles including the performance optimization techniques (e.g. data partitioning, referential integrity etc.)

---

[35]   If the repository is used

Database Administrator:

- administration experience with specific RDBMS
- ability to read the physical data model
- good understanding of physical data modeling concepts
- experience with database optimization techniques
- experience with the repository

Depending on the size of the organization, responsibilities assigned to the roles might be merged. For instance in smaller organizations it is common to have the following roles integrated into a single role:

- business analyst and logical modeler
- physical data modeler and database administrator

Although limited resources might force the decision to merge roles and responsibilities, it can negatively impact the quality of deliverables due to complexity of knowledge and skills required for each role.

3.7. CASE tools and model repository in the modeling process

Standardization is always a challenge for every organization. It is not uncommon to have multiple CASE tools used at the same time. The choice of tools is sometimes a matter of personal preference as much as functional capabilities offered by the tool. Each data modeling practitioner is frequently asked a question of *what CASE tool is the best?* The answer is very common in the world of Information Technology: *It depends* . . . And it really does! Each CASE tool has its advantages and disadvantages and, when combined with personal preference, it is difficult to avoid a biased answer to this question.

Regardless of the CASE tool or the model repository chosen, try to stick with only one of them and use it uniformly across the whole organization. Selection of a single CASE tool and repository will lead to lower cost of use for the following reasons:

- *licensing for the CASE tool and repository*—CASE tools are not cheap and licensing cost can add-up especially if different tools are used and volume discount is not available due to a limited number of licenses purchased
- *training*—modelers, developers, data architects and other personnel needs training to properly use the tool set. Having more than one tool may lead to an increase in training cost
- *support*—additional expenses are incurred in situations where multiple tools have to be supported internally (within the organization) and externally (by purchasing the maintenance services from the vendor)
- *modeling*—it becomes increasingly difficult and time consuming to manage models in multiple CASE tools

At the same time, by using a single CASE tool and model repository, the data team's efficiency will be significantly improved. Having multiple CASE tools will result in models of various formats stored in different tools. If a model needs to be transferred from one tool to another, the transition process is anything but simple. The functionality of the CASE tool requires a high level of sophistication that is achieved through comprehensive meta-data stored within the model itself. Transferring the model from one CASE tool to another will usually result in problems that need to be handled manually by the modeler. Vendor's help is limited in this case simply because the help is provided for their own tool and the modeler might end up having to resolve the problems on their own. Avoiding the model transition problems can only be possible if the organization achieves standardization in terms of the CASE tool and the corresponding repository used across the enterprise.

When starting with data modeling, modelers are faced with the following situations:

- either there is *no CASE tool* defined in the process or
- the *CASE tool is already given* and the modeler has to work with it

When the CASE tool is already present in the environment where the data model has to be developed and maintained usually nothing can be done to change the tool. The CASE tool is already in place and data models are developed and maintained using it. Changing the CASE tool in this case could cause problems and unnecessary costs within the organization. Many times you will hear data modelers blaming the CASE tools for their failures. Fortunately the tool is rarely the problem! A lack of understanding of the functionality or a specific implementation process imposed by the tool is the real cause of frustrations.

Efficient use of the tools requires understanding of their modeling capabilities listed and briefly explained here:

- **logical data modeling capabilities**
  - □ *standard logical data modeling technique*—widely accepted as a standard for logical data modeling is the *Entity/Relationships (E/R) modeling* technique.
  - □ *formal validation of the logical data model*—CASE tools provide formal model validation functionality. The model is validated against the predefined set of data modeling rules. The goal is to produce a logical model that is capable of successfully transitioning to the physical data model
  - □ *comparison of logical data models*—CASE tools provide reporting capability presenting differences between two models
  - □ *transition from the logical to the physical data model*—moving from the logical to the physical data model requires a formal model transition. Formal model transition methodology is used to perform the transition. CASE tools provide automated model transition functionality hiding complex theoretical details from the modeler
- **physical modeling capabilities**
  - □ *standard physical data modeling technique*—most CASE tools on the market use the *Relational modeling technique* to model the database.
  - □ *formal physical data model validation*—CASE tools provide automated model validation ensuring that elements required for code generation are properly defined

- *code generation (forward engineering) capability*—CASE tools are able to produce various classes of code:
  - *DDL*—the *data definition language* that will create/drop/modify the database objects (e.g. tables, indexes etc.)
  - *DCL*—the *data control language* that will define the permissions (GRANT or REVOKE specific permission)
  - *DML*—the *data manipulation language* comprising of INSERT/UPDATE/DELETE statements intended to maintain the data content while modifying the structure of database objects
- *comparison between two models, model and database, and model and script* This is probably one of the most sophisticated capabilities provided by CASE tools. A model can include large number of elements and it is almost impossible to manually find out what has changed from one model version to another. Although it is theoretically possible to find the differences when objects are compared, it is time consuming and prone to errors. The DBA usually have their own script that helps them compare the database objects. However the deployment validation preformed by script has the following challenges:
  - database versions constantly change the internal structure of the *data dictionary*[36] requiring the DBA to constantly update their scripts. Sooner or later the scripts become outdated
  - having a team of multiple database administrators always brings a challenge of choosing the "standard" script for a certain type of validation given that each DBA will (usually) have their own validation script
  - running the script is time consuming and usually does not produce nicely formatted results[37] making reports produced by the script difficult to use
  - from time to time, the DBA is faced with a challenge of comparing two scripts and analyzing the differences. Manual comparison is almost impossible because the scripts might have the same content but different object locations, the DBA would have to spend time scanning through the script to find corresponding elements. CASE tools provide the reverse engineering capability from the script to the model, allowing comparison of two models based on the underlying scripts
- *reverse engineering capability*—having a script, database or another model allows the modeler to produce the target data model by re-engineering the objects and their relationships

Functionality to compare the model with the database, script or another model, is fully automated process if CASE tools are used. Typically the tool can produce nicely formatted reports that can be analyzed or distributed as a document outlying the differences found by comparison.

---

[36]   Data dictionary that is the heart of the database's related information is changing from one version of the database to another

[37]   DBA like other technical personnel pay more attention to the content rather than the look of the report. Many of the outputs are rather cryptic and not re-usable by others

4. CONCEPTUAL DATA MODELING

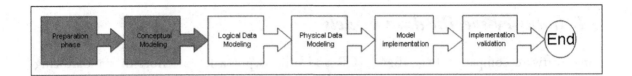

Complexity of business problems require methodical data decomposition into cohesive logical entities linked with major relationships. The goal is to create cohesive logical units that can be further modeled independently. These entity groupings comprise the subject areas. Each subject area delineates a set of entities that describes a part of the business data. The conceptual data model allows better coordination and ability to create independent logical models in parallel work streams.

Coordinated model development is important in every organization and this is clearly a challenge today. Large organizations have many projects that are structured in a way to include parts of existing subject areas. Unfortunately due to a number of ongoing projects, it is difficult to keep track of the modeled data components included in the model leading to the following:

- excessive allocation of technical staff to the modeling process
- creation of disparate data structures and inconsistent business rules. This is discovered later when the data exchange between various systems take place
- difficulties in establishing the data ownership because the data is scattered in various databases

Having a clear definition of subject areas in the conceptual data model allows allocation of data modelers to handle specific subject areas. The complexity of data modeling sometimes lies in the fact that the modeler is not a business expert and has to rely on the business analysts as the information source. If the subject area is not clearly defined, the discussion and therefore the logical data model can drift away from the original topic slowly leading to a scope creep. When the conceptual data model is used as a starting point for logical data modeling, discipline is introduced in the modeling process. Boundaries of the subject area prevent discussions that are not focused on analysis of specific subject areas.

The following is the definition of the conceptual data model:

DEFINITION: *Conceptual data model is a class of data models that depicts the major subject areas with generic relationships among them.*

Subject areas defined in the conceptual data model are used to define boundaries for logical modeling. Hence the details in the conceptual data model are kept at a high level. Each subject area might result in one or more Logical data models that are later integrated.

The relationships between the subject areas are intentionally defined without explicitly specifying the cardinality. The relationship's cardinality between the major entities is always assumed to be M:M (many-to-many).

4.1. Industry-specific data models

Large software companies (e.g. IBM, NCR and others) put a lot of effort in standardizing the industry-specific models. These models define reusable data structures, relationships and corresponding business meta-data so that data modelers can have a solid starting point when creating data models.

Industry-specific data models are used to achieve the following goals:

- speed-up the logical data modeling process by providing industry accepted modeling patterns
- streamline the modeling process by providing the foundation for data integration across the organization
- help modelers to create high quality data models[38]

The starting point for industry-specific data models is a high-level conceptual data model. The model specifies major subject areas that are further enhanced by definition of entities and relationships in the logical data model. The Illustration 8 shows major subject areas in IBM's **Financial Services Data Model** (FSDM)[39]:

---

[38] Industry-specific data models are created and scrutinized by experts in the industry. Models are created using strict modeling standards and best practices which provide a good example of how the modeling should be done.

[39] Reference: http://www.globaldataconsulting.net/articles/technology-platform/ibm-ifw-financial-services-data-model-fsdm-beginners

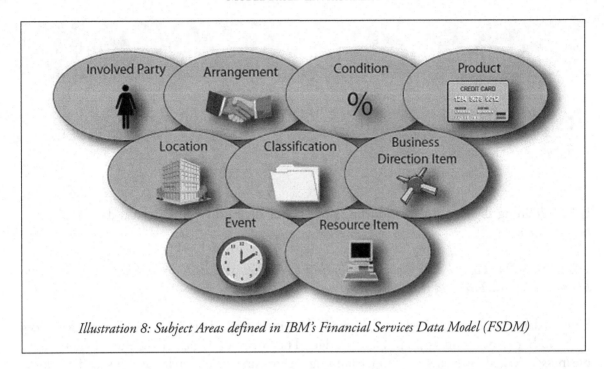

Illustration 8: Subject Areas defined in IBM's Financial Services Data Model (FSDM)

Theoretically business data can be decomposed into seven to nine subject areas. It is interesting to notice that the subject areas are common across the business. Companies that produce these data models basically use the similar set of subject areas across different industries which prove that the definition of the subject areas at the conceptual level is generic. A challenge with Conceptual data modeling is to clearly define the boundaries of each subject area so that there is no overlap[40]. Clear definition of the subject areas in the conceptual data model isolates the cohesive set of related entities to be modeled. Once the subject areas are defined, the modeling continues with defining relationships established among the subject areas.

---

[40] An entity should belong to only one subject area at the time.

5. LOGICAL DATA MODELING

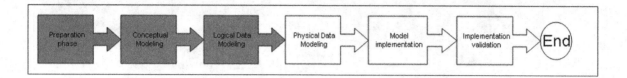

Before defining the logical data modeling process, the definition of the logical data model will be provided:

DEFINITION: *Logical data model is comprised of entities, relationships and attributes depicting business data structures and relationships between them.*

Logical data modeling by itself is a separate data modeling discipline that requires resources with both business and technical knowledge. The focus of logical data modeling is more business oriented, focusing on understanding the business data, relationships and business rules.

DEFINITION: *Logical data modeling is a process of creating the logical data model.*

The deliverable of the logical modeling process is a logical data model created to achieve the following goals:

- record the business data structures (*entities*)
- record the nature of the data stored in attributes (*logical domains*)
- record *attributes* important for each business concept
- record r*elationships* among entities
- record *business definitions for entities, attributes and relationships*

The process is depicted in the Illustration 9:

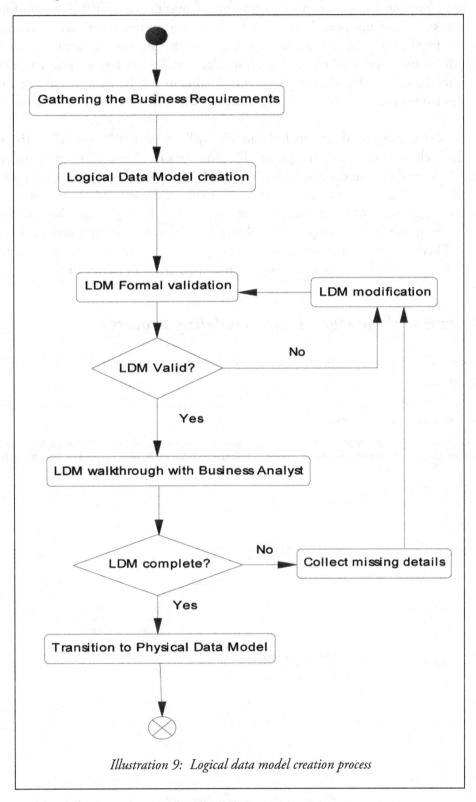

Illustration 9: Logical data model creation process

Logical data modeling starts with gathering the business requirements. Documented business requirements represent a comprehensive definition of overall functional and non-functional requirements stated by business. The logical model concentrates on data structures and relationships stated in the data requirements segment of the business requirements document. After analysis of the data requirements, the modeler and business analyst will work on the logical data model design. The data requirements document will be used to validate and assess the model for compliance with business rules and data structures specified in the document.

Once the model is completed, the logical modeler will create the "first-cut" of the physical data model which officially closes the phase of logical data modeling. The "first-cut" physical data model is defined as a model that is directly based on the logical data model. This model is further used for physical data modeling by enhancing the model with additional data structures and physical components required for implementation. The final physical data model differs significantly from the model marked as a "first-cut" in terms of comprehensiveness and complexity. Theoretically it is possible to always synchronize the logical and physical data models but this generally becomes a challenge from a time and cost perspective.

5.1. Overview of the logical data modeling process

The following diagram represents an overview of the steps and deliverables of the logical data modeling process:

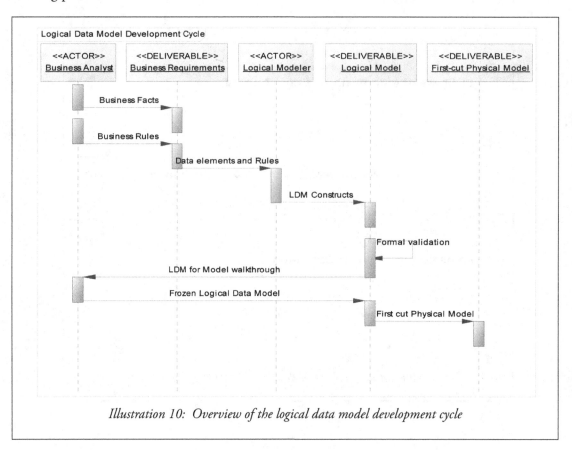

Illustration 10: Overview of the logical data model development cycle

After gathering the data requirements the logical modeling process starts by defining *the business data structures* (data concepts that will be the foundation for the entities and attributes) and applicable *business rules* (rules that will drive creation of the relationships between the entities and constraints at the attribute level).

Logical modeling is a process driven by the conceptual data model. In this process the modeler is concentrating on one subject area at time delving into details limited by logical boundaries defined for the subject area. After completing all of the subject areas in scope, the modeler and business analyst will spend significant time integrating them into a final model by defining the relationships that support the generic relationships established between the subject areas in the conceptual data model.

The logical data model will go through the process of formal validation to verify compliance with rules and best industry practices.

Support of the business requirements from the business perspective is performed by the business analyst during the logical model walk-through. This is the last step before the logical model is frozen, signed-off and ready for transition to the physical data model.

The final version of the logical data model is checked into the model repository formally completing the logical modeling process.

At this point the data model is ready for the transition to the physical model. Model transition from the logical to the physical model is performed by the logical modeler who understands the modeling rules and their physical implementation. However, the best results are achieved when the model transition is done as a collaborative effort between the logical and physical modelers. This collaboration significantly improves the quality of the first-cut of the physical model.

The SDLC is focused on processes and procedures required to create specific deliverables. Logical model is developed based on the conceptual model and the data requirements.

The modeling process produces various data model classes as summarized below:

- *conceptual data model*—high level model that defines subject areas and corresponding relationships. This model is used to define boundaries for the logical data model
- *data requirements document*—part of the business requirements stating the data elements and applicable business rules required in the model
- *logical data model*—the main deliverable of the logical data modeling process. The model properly structure, organize and refine the data elements and applicable business rules into a form that can be later used to derive the physical data model
- *"first-cut" of the physical data model*—initial version of the physical data model derived from the logical data model

5.2. Model development approaches

Logical data model development depends on the modeling approach chosen by the modeler. The following two approaches will be discussed:

- *Project based*
- *Subject area based*

When the model is created for a specific project without taking into consideration company-wide data reuse, the modeling approach is classified as *Project-based*. Being a localized solution, the model provides functionality required by a project without trying to provide data sharing capabilities across the organization. This approach is characterized by the following:

- *data redundancy*—concepts (entities) implemented in the model may also implemented in various other models
- *data replication*—by providing a localized solution this approach requires a significant amount of data exchange between the systems resulting in increased ETL[41] processing between the databases

Having clearly defined data requirements at the project level speeds up the model development because the localized model developed for a specific project, does not need to include additional requirements to be a solution at the corporate level. From the project management perspective this is a very attractive characteristic and difficult to disregard knowing that the time and resources available to the project are limited. However, at the corporate level, the project based approach will increase the costs by redundantly developing models and maintaining redundant data. Over time it is almost impossible to control the allocation of resources because many smaller projects drive the costs up via the redundant data. After realizing that this approach does not work, organizations usually make an effort to switch to more disciplined *Subject area based approach*.

---

[41] Extract, transform and load (ETL).

The Illustration 11 will be used to demonstrate the concept of data redundancy:

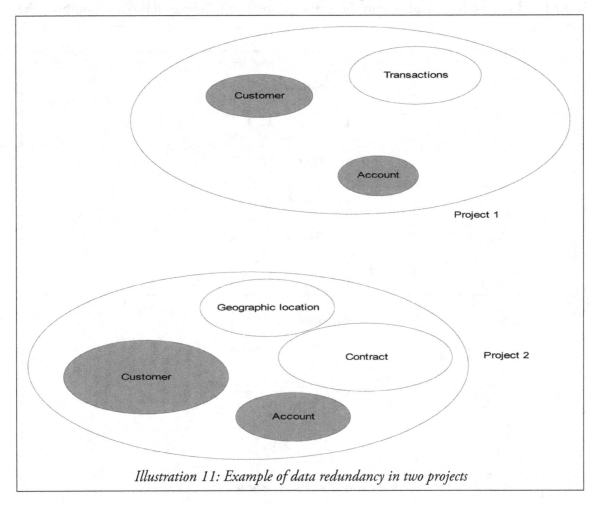

Illustration 11: Example of data redundancy in two projects

The example shows two projects using the *Project based approach*, modeling the same subject areas (customer and account) locally, within each project. In order to provide data synchronization between the project 1 and project 2 databases an ETL process has to be build. Challenges of this approach are outlined below:

- *redundant data structures and business rules* could be implemented with slight differences in two models, inevitably leading to creation of disparate data structures and business rules
- if a new model tries to *integrate the data sourced from these two models*, the data analysis has to be performed to define integrated data structures and business rules
- each project requires separate data models, data modelers and business analysts, increasing the pressure on available resources and driving up the project's costs

Although beneficial, switching from *Project* to *Subject area based approach* is anything but simple and organizations that have to perform this transition usually ask for help from consulting companies. Streamlining the applications portfolio and properly organizing and designing the databases are required to implement the *Subject area based approach*.

The Subject area based approach follows the idea that data is a corporate asset and as such it is used and constantly reused within the corporation. The following illustration outlines the approach.

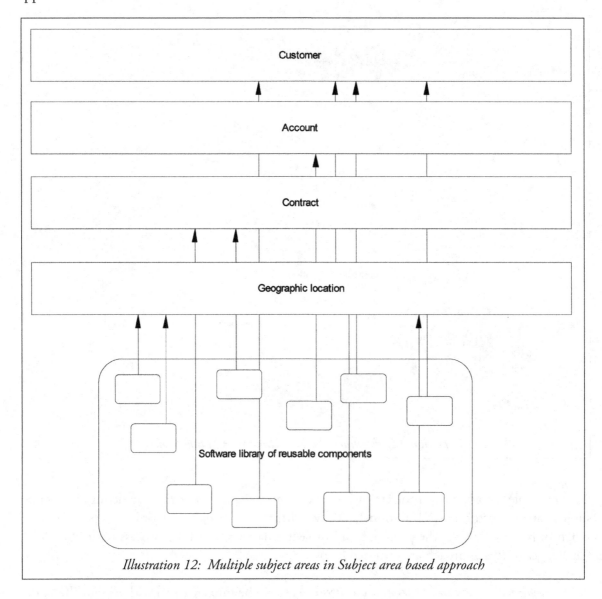

Illustration 12: Multiple subject areas in Subject area based approach

The boundary of each subject area is defined to include entities logically grouped together. The idea is to have each subject area shared across the organization instead of data redundantly modeled and stored. Application development has to support the modeling effort by creating the reusable software components to access each subject area. The data redundancy is minimal due to high level of data decoupling and data concentration into subject areas.

Using the *Subject area based approach* each data model is developed to support a single *subject area* resulting in data models that are highly cohesive with well defined boundaries. The model's physical implementation is usually based on implementation of services that provide specified functionality to the consumers.

The approach recommended in this book is the *Subject area based* model development. It allows controlled model growth and high maintainability combined with inherent data sharing. This approach provides a high level of data integrity, consistency and accuracy combined with well controlled availability.

From a complexity perspective, *Subject area based approach* is more complex than the *Project based approach* for the following reasons:

- *coordinated models development* is required. Although models for each subject area can be developed independently, the model integration requires coordinated development due to inter-dependencies between the models
- as a result of data concentration into reusable components, *implementation of Master Data Management principles* are required to support efficient data sharing within the organization

Implementation of the *subject area based approach* requires corresponding modification in the development of the application layer. The application layer has to be build by creating services that will expose the functionality to the end-user rather than a monolithic project-specific application.

5.3. Data requirements

The Systems Development Life Cycle starts with the process of creating the business requirements document. This is a document that describes the requirements for future system functionality as seen by the end-user. The document has three major components:

- *functional requirements* reflecting the future functionality expected from the system
- *data requirements* reflecting the requirements for data that the system will handle
- *non-functional requirements* represent the requirements that will ensure safe and efficient system operation under various scenarios

The data modeling process focuses on the *data requirements* component of the business requirements. From a project perspective only a subset of subject areas defined in the corporate model are in scope. The focal question for the data requirements can be formulated as: ***what data** needs to be stored and **what business rules** enforced in the future system?*

The intention of the *data requirements* document is not to provide the detailed data structures and business rules, rather it has to provide sufficient details for each of the business concepts along with corresponding major business rules further to be modeled in the logical model.

The document creation is in the domain of the business analyst's responsibility. Later, during the model validation, the data requirements document will be used to asses the completeness of the logical model.

The following is the illustration that shows the life cycle of the *data requirements:*

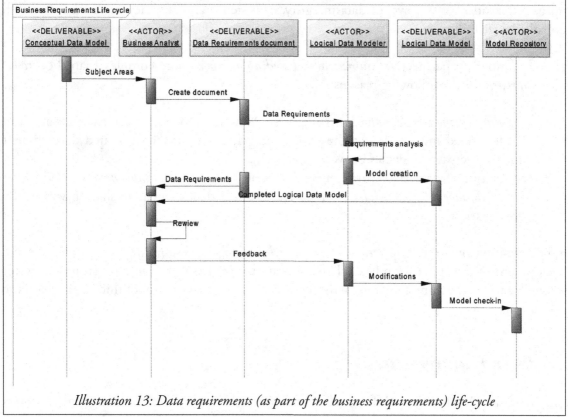

Illustration 13: Data requirements (as part of the business requirements) life-cycle

Based on the conceptual model the business analyst delivers the data requirements document which is reviewed and used by the logical modeler to create the model. Data requirements specify data structures and business rules (relationships) pertinent to the subject areas in scope. The modeler will create a logical model concentrating on one subject area at a time until all the subject areas are completed. The model creation process requires interaction with business analyst who will provide details and further clarification of the data requirements.

The completed logical data model is reviewed by the Business Analyst who provides the feedback to the modeler. After the model is updated to include required modifications, reviewed and signed-off, it is checked into the model repository.

5.4. Segregation of the subject areas

The conceptual data model is comprised of logical entity groupings which are related via the major relationships. The intention of the conceptual model is to isolate entity groupings into logically cohesive subject areas. The challenge for the modeler is how to define the subject area boundaries to minimize overlapping. The conceptual data model is usually created as a first step in the modeling process to outline the scope for a future logical model. However, if a conceptual model exists at the corporate level it will be used as a starting point in the modeling process, driving the logical data model design for each project.

A simple example will be used to demonstrate the approach of subject area segregation. The staring point for the example is a *Legal Entity*. Each *Legal Entity* instance has one or more physical addresses perceived by business as an integral part as shown below:

> *Legal Entity: Company A*
>   *Employees count: 34*
>   *Line of business: Information Technology*
>   …………
>   *Address:*
>   *Country: Canada*
>   *Province: ON*
>   *Postal Code: M4B 2A1*
>   *Street: 123 New street west*
>
> *Legal Entity: Joe Mason*
>   …………

The goal for conceptual modeling is to delineate boundaries between the major concepts creating subject areas with high cohesion and minimal overlapping, so the modeler has to "carve" logically cohesive segments from the provided data structure.

In the example provided it is obvious that two clearly distinct business concepts are hidden:

- *Legal Entity* defined as a company or a person and
- *Geographic Location* (physical address)

Legal Entity, as a business concept, comprises of attributes describing either a person (individual) or a company. Although a Legal Entity has an address, the Geographic Location (address) can be isolated into a separate concept. This segregation will achieve the following goals:

- *Legal Entity* will comprise of attributes that directly describe the concept
- *Geographic Location* will be isolated into a separate concept related to the *Legal Entity*
- *Geographic Location* can be reused by establishing the relationship from other business concepts
- *Legal Entity* and *Geographic Location* can establish a complex relationship (e.g. shipping address, home, address, billing address etc.)

The conceptual model established based on segregation of two separate business concepts is shown below:

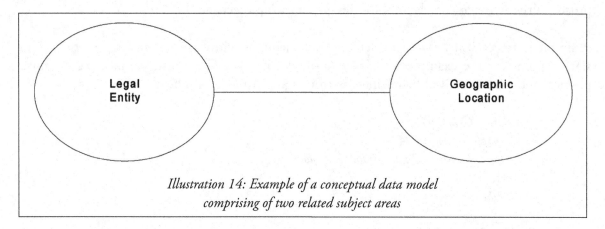

Illustration 14: Example of a conceptual data model comprising of two related subject areas

The conceptual model comprises of two subject areas: *Legal Entity* and *Geographic Location*. The cardinality of the relationship between subject areas is not explicitly defined, assuming it to be *many:many*[42]. The subject area segregation achieved the goal of creating *loosely coupled* groupings of entities with *minimal or no overlap* by defining the *Legal Entity* and *Geographic Location* as the two distinct subject areas.

When modeling a subject area the goal is to position an entity in a single subject area. However, to enhance model readability it is allowed to include entities from other subject areas. Different color or shape should be used to mark each entity in the logical model that belongs to the other subject area.

Once the conceptual model is completed, the modeler can continue building the logical model. Modeling can start with any subject area in scope considering logical isolation from other subject areas.

5.5. *Logical data model creation*

By modeling one subject area at a time, the logical modeler can focus on a relatively isolated, logically cohesive set of objects. Modeling subject areas in isolation helps structuring the entity's attributes and relationships by focusing the design on a very specific subset of data requirements delineated by boundaries of a subject area. The modeling process is repeated for each subject area until completion of all subject areas in scope. Isolation of subject areas into non-overlapping logical units allows multiple data modelers to work in parallel targeting different subject areas.

After completion of the related subject areas, the modeler continues with modeling the *major relationships*. This is the process of *subject areas integration* where the finalized logical model is

---

[42]   One Legal Entity is related to many Geographic Locations and one Geographic Location is related to many Legal Entities

created. The process of *subject area based logical model development* is favored in this book and depicted in the following process schematic shown in illustration 15.

The modeling process assumes that the model is developed following an iterative approach. Each iteration of model development is characterized by adding more details to the model while refining existing modeling constructs. The top-down approach is characterized by the following:

- *modeling starts with identifying and defining the entities within the boundaries of the subject area modeled. The preferred approach is to start with a set of independent (fundamental) entities*[43] *and progress by adding dependent entities*
- *the next step is to define the relationships. Each entity should be related to at least one other entity. In other words an orphan entity*[44] *should not exist in the logical data model. Each relationship specifies a business rule that is defined by its:*
  - □ *cardinality—defined as a number of entity instances involved in the relationship*
  - □ *dependency type between the entities—the relationship between entities is further classified into the following types:*
    - o *identifying relationship type*[45] *that defines the business rule where identification of an instance in the child entity requires parent entity's identifier*
    - o *non-identifying relationship type that defines the business rule where identification of an instance in the child entity does not require parent entity's identifier since it has an identifier of its own*
    - o *generalization relationship type that defines the concept of super and sub-types structure*
- *entities are further defined by specifying the attributes. An attribute is an entity component that stores atomic*[46] *data. However, it should be mentioned that modern database management systems include very strong Object-Oriented features by supporting the structured data types. These constructs allow non-atomic data to be stored. A logical model should not explicitly use the structured data type considering that they are database specific implementation components*
- *logical model development is completed by specifying the business definitions for each object included in the model. The definition specified in the logical model will be propagated to the "first-cut" of the physical model*[47]

---

[43] These are the entities that do not depend on any other entity in the model

[44] An entity without any relationships to other entities in the model

[45] An explicit relationship classification on identifying and non-identifying is not present in all the CASE tools

[46] Data content has a logical meaning to the user. Each atomic piece of data cannot be further decomposed without loosing the information it carries

[47] A physical model created as a result of the transition from the logical data model

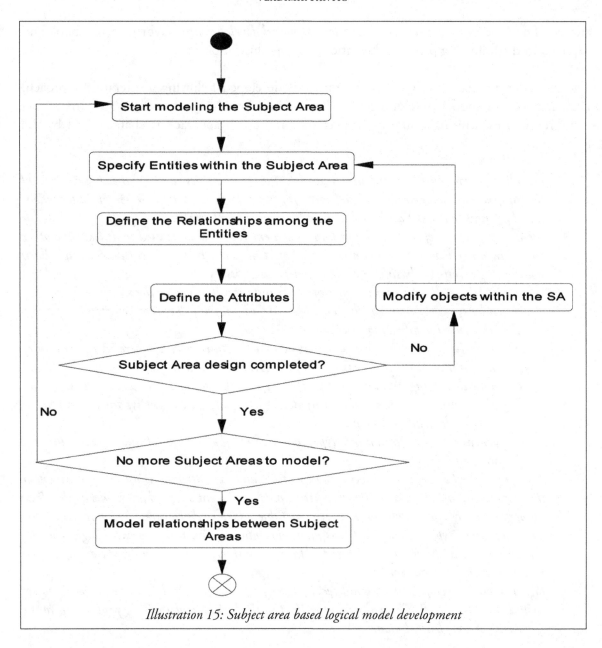

Illustration 15: Subject area based logical model development

Standardizing on uniformity of model content has always been a challenge especially in environments where multiple modelers are working in parallel supporting different subject areas that will be integrated into the final model. To help avoid inconsistencies in the model content, the model check-list is provided later in the book.

Continuing with the conceptual model example we will start developing the logical data model for each of the subject areas in scope. The logical model for the *Legal Entity* subject area is shown in the Illustration 16:

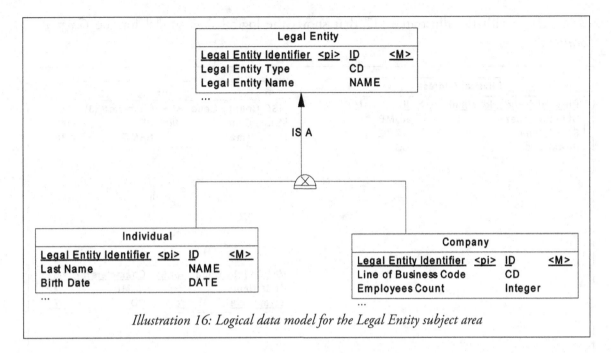

Illustration 16: Logical data model for the Legal Entity subject area

The *Legal Entity*, the central concept in this subject area, is modeled as a generalization relationship. The relationship is *exclusive* (identified by X symbol in the semi-circle) stating that a LEGAL ENTITY must be classified either as an individual or a company.

The physical modeler should pay attention to the generalization relationship type. The model implements the business rules using the type of coverage (covering or non-covering) and partitioning (exclusive or inclusive). The covering and partitioning characteristics of the generalization relationship will define the type of joins between the super and sub-type tables in the database:

- the *fully covering relationship* assumes that each *Legal Entity* has at least on subtype instance related. Therefore the inner join between the super-type and subtype tables is appropriate
- *non-covering relationship* assumes left outer join between the super-type and subtype tables
- *exclusive partitioning* assumes that at any point in time a super-type table record is related to one and only one subtype record
- *inclusive partitioning* implies that a super-type record might be related to one or more subtype records at the same time requiring a super-type table join with multiple subtype tables

It is obvious that the generalization relationship definition in the logical model has strong impact on corresponding physical model hence the modeler should spend some time understanding the nature of the relationship.

We continue with the Illustration 17 that shows the logical data model for the *Geographic Location*:

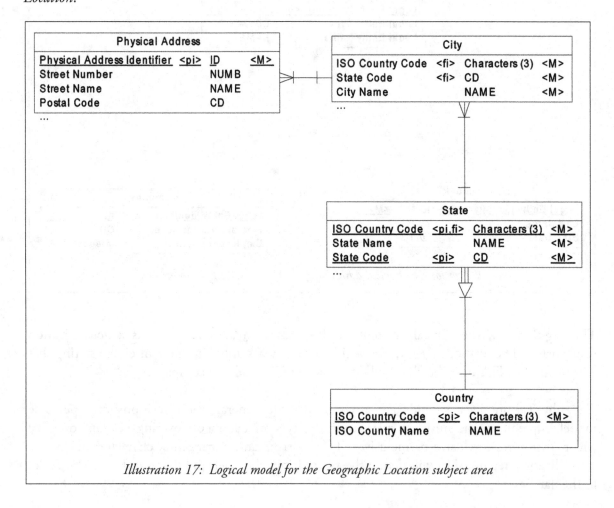

Illustration 17: Logical model for the Geographic Location subject area

The Logical model for the *Geographic Location subject area* shows entities that describe attributes of the Physical Address. The model is normalized but it should be clear that further normalization is possible although not necessarily required. The *country* is the only *strong entity type*[48] in the model stating the rule that *country* is independent of other entities in the model. The *state* is a dependent entity involved in an identifying relationship with the *country*. The business rule implemented by the relationship between the *country* and *state* is that the state cannot exist without an instance of a *country*.

City is an entity that depends on the *state* but it has its own identifier. The same is applicable to the *physical address* that is dependent on the instance within the entity city. Both are involved in non-identifying relationships stating that both entities have their own identifier independent of the parent entity's identifier.

---

48   Strong entity is an entity that can stand alone i.e. an entity with no parent entities

If the subject areas are segregated properly then each logical model, developed for a subject area, stays within the boundaries of the subject area defined by the conceptual data model allowing completely independent and isolated modeling. By following this approach the modeler works with a coherent logical data model keeping the content within the boundaries of the subject area.

The logical data model developed for a subject area always has an entity that serves as a starting point in the modeling process. In the case of the *Legal Entity* subject area, the focal entity becomes the *Legal Entity* modeled as a super-type with two sub-type entities: *Individual* and *Company*.

In the case of the *Geographic Location* subject area, the focal point a concept of the *physical address* entity. A helpful practice is to highlight the focal entity within the subject area to help the modeler focus the discussion with the business analyst on a limited set of related entities.

5.6. Subject area integration

Independent modeling of subject areas creates sub-models that are isolated "islands" of related entities. However, having a set of isolated subject areas does not really comprise a model that describes the business, so the next step in the modeling process is to finalize the model by integrating subject areas into the final logical data model.

DEFINITION: *Subject area integration is a process of using the conceptual data model's relationships to integrate independently modeled subject areas into the final logical data model.*

Based on the definition, the starting point for subject area integration is the conceptual data model. Subject areas are related with major relationships and the integration process will have to focus on them. For purpose of subject area integration our focus will shift from subject areas to the major relationships as they are defined in the conceptual data model. We will use a simplified model comprising of two subject areas to describe the concept (Illustration 18).

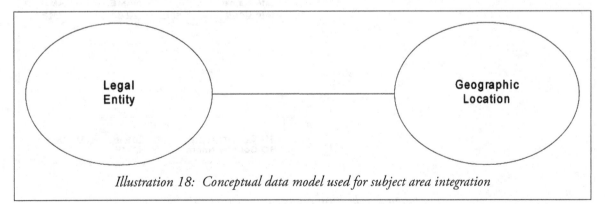

Illustration 18: Conceptual data model used for subject area integration

In each of the subject areas the modeler should choose an entity or a set of entities that are the main representative of the subject area. These entities will most likely be the entities that will take part in modeling the major relationship between the subject areas. Using our example, the focal entities within each subject area are highlighted in the illustrations 19 and 20:

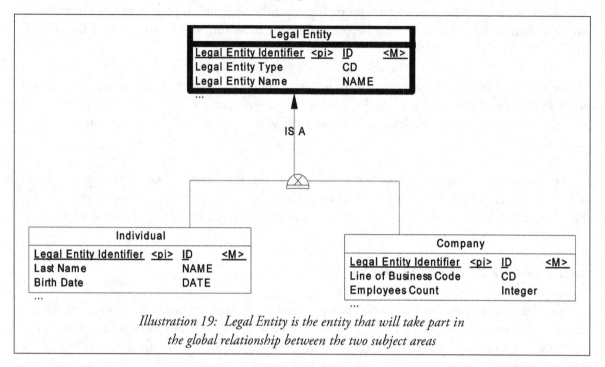

Illustration 19: *Legal Entity is the entity that will take part in the global relationship between the two subject areas*

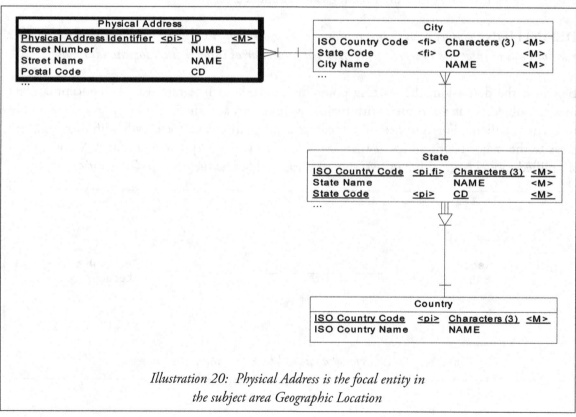

Illustration 20: *Physical Address is the focal entity in the subject area Geographic Location*

As stated previously, both subject areas are developed in complete isolation as independent components of the conceptual data model. Isolation of subject areas allows for enhancement or modification to be done independently, within each subject area.

By looking at the conceptual model, the relationship between subject areas effectively represents relationship between the two focal entities in separate logical models: *Legal Entity* and *Physical Address*. The major relationship, as defined in the conceptual model, assumes M:M cardinality so for the integrated logical data model we could actually leave the relationship between these two entities intact. Contrary to what some data modelers think, it is not detrimental for the logical data model to use relationships with M:M cardinality if the relationship does not need additional attributes recorded. The purpose of the logical data model is to structure the data requirements into a form that is precise and ready for physical modeling. At the same time the logical model has to serve as a vehicle for communication between the business analyst and the modeler so overloading the model with too many entities might actually have negative impact on model's readability from the business perspective.

If a major relationship requires defining attributes then the relationship has to be further modeled. In our case we might need to specify the type of the *Physical Address* related to the *Legal Entity*. As we know there are different types of *Physical Addresses* that can be maintained for each *Legal Entity* (e.g. mailing, shipping, home, billing, contact) so additional classification of a *Physical Address* usage is required. Essentially, the line representing the major relationship between the *Legal Entity* and the *Geographic Location* at the conceptual level will be modeled as an entity as shown below:

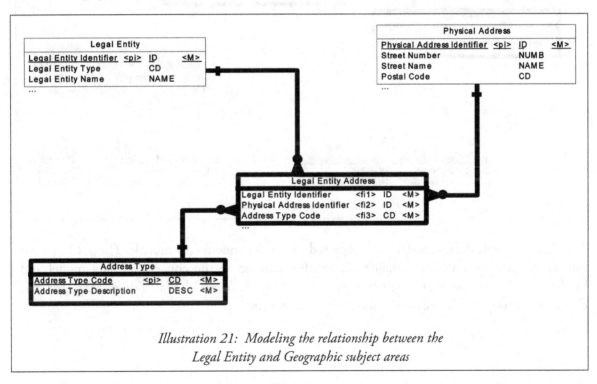

Illustration 21: Modeling the relationship between the Legal Entity and Geographic subject areas

The relationship between the two subject areas is modeled as an *associative entity*[49] type, *Legal Entity Address,* and connects entities from two different subject areas. The entity named *Address Type* is an entity that provides classification of the usage of the *Physical Address* by the *Legal Entity* (e.g. home, mailing etc.). The final version of the logical data model with integrated subject areas is shown in the Illustration 22:

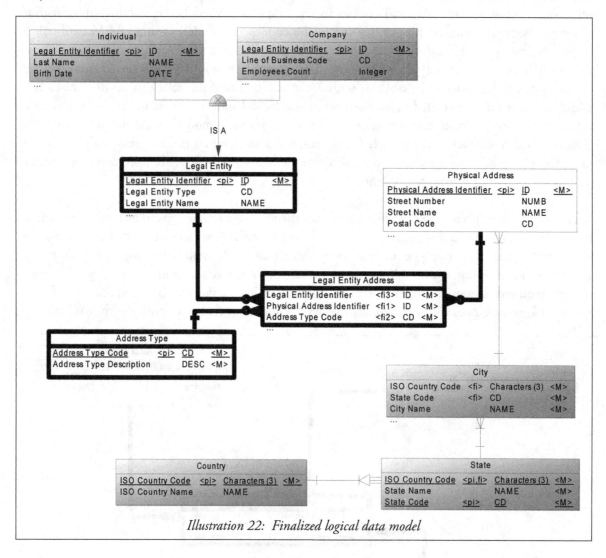

Illustration 22: Finalized logical data model

The finalized logical data model has integrated two independent sub-models. The subject areas integration was driven by the major relationship defined in the conceptual data model and implemented by an associative entity type *Legal Entity Address* with classifier *Address Type* that classifies the usage of the *Physical Address* by the *Legal Entity.*

---

[49] Associative entity is an entity that replaces the relationship with M:M (Many to Many) between the two entities

5.7. Developing a logical data model in a multi-user modeling environment

Large projects are faced with complexity and size of data models requiring multiple modelers to handle the workload. Due to size and complexity of each subject area, modeling may require multiple modelers per each subject area with simultaneous access to the same model.

One alternative is to rely on the locking mechanism of the Operating System (O/S) to prevent accidental change of the model stored in the file. Working with models stored in files controlled by each modeler increases the administration complexity failing to provide a robust solution for multi-user access.

PowerDesigner has a specialized repository that controls the models at the object level. The following is the functionality provided by the **model repository**:

- *locking mechanism* that controls the user access—The locking mechanism is in place to provide concurrent access to the model disallowing accidental modifications. The model repository implements *check-in/check-out* procedure that allows explicit model locking
- *model comparisons*—Models are stored chronologically in the model repository. Functionality to compare different model versions is part of the repository's functionality and report can be produced detailing changes between versions
- *model integration*—PowerDesigner offers functionality to integrate two models by allowing the modeler to specify objects and their components to be integrated
- *robust version control*—Version control is implemented in the model repository allowing various scenarios of chronological model version tracking. PowerDesigner offers a repository with robust version control at both the model and the object level

Assuming the *Subject area based modeling approach* is used, the Illustration 23 shows the logical modeling process involving the model repository:

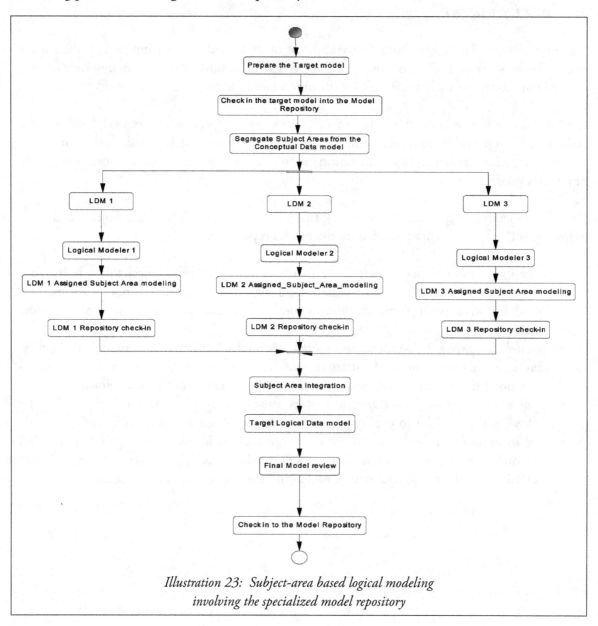

Illustration 23: Subject-area based logical modeling involving the specialized model repository

The modeling process is started by the data architect responsible for initial model set-up. The initial model set-up will have to ensure that modelers start with the same foundation. Minimum requirements for the initial set-up include the definition of the following:

- *naming convention rules* and their enforcement
- *predefined data domains* and *business rules*
- *initial set of subject areas*[50]

Naming conventions define the rules for naming the objects in the model and they are progressively more rigid as the model approaches the physical design. The logical model predominantly uses a business-friendly vocabulary while the physical data model must ensure that the naming rules implemented by the target database are followed. Initial data domains and associated business rules ensure that the model consistently uses appropriate data types and relevant constraints.

The set of subject areas defined in the conceptual data model is used as a starting point for each model however the modeler will target just a limited subset of subject areas based on the data requirements.

Once the logical models for each subject area are complete the model created by the data architect will serve as the target logical data model used for integration of individual subject area models. After the logical model set-up is completed, the model will be checked-in as a new model into the model repository. At that point in time, the model is available to all users authorized to access the repository and retrieve the model.

PowerDesigner's repository is now in full control of the logical data model offering the following functionality:

- *Checking-out without locking*—The model is checked out by the user in *read-only* mode. There are no locks held by the repository allowing other users to modify the model and record modifications in the model repository
- *Checking-out with locking*—The user that is checking out the model will *exclusively lock* the model disallowing any potential modification by another user. Once the model is locked, other users can read the model (read only access) but not modify it

Model development continues by a modeler modeling each subject area in isolation. This allows multiple logical modelers to work in parallel giving them full control of their deliverable. The advantage of this approach is that the model can be segregated into multiple subject areas treated independently of each other. In the case of large projects this approach can decrease the time required to complete the model allowing early start of the next, physical data modeling phase of the project.

The initial data model is created and distributed by the data architect so that each data modeler starts with the same model. Modification of the shared elements has to be coordinated and approved by the architect and all data models have to be subsequently synchronized with the

---

[50] Some CASE tools (e.g. AllFusion by CA) have a concept of subject area while others don't. If the concept of subject area is not present (e.g. PowerDesigner by Sybase), we can use multiple diagrams to mimic the concept.

new version of the initial model. Modelers cannot change the logical data domains as this would complicate model integration.

Assuming that subject areas are modeled based on the conceptual model, the expectation is that they are not overlapping and initial integration, where the subject areas are brought together into the target model, should be relatively straight forward.

5.8. Formal validation of the logical data model

After the logical modeler creates the data model the model has to go through a formal validation step. The goal of validation is to ensure that the model complies with the principles and best practices of logical data modeling and it has sufficient details required for transition to the next phase. Model validation of adherence to the principles and best industry practices is validated by PowerDesigner using an automated procedure.

The following is an example of a formal logical data model validation provided by PowerDesigner:

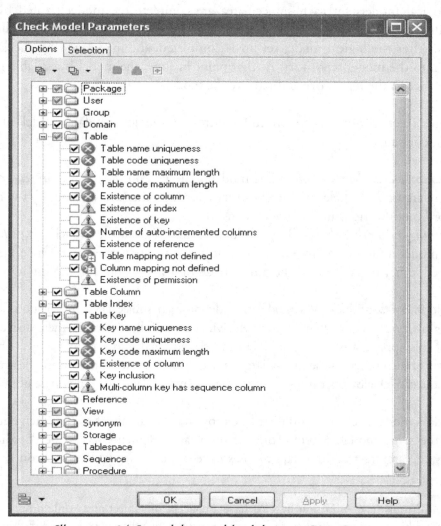

Illustration 24: Logical data model validation in PowerDesigner

Validation rule violations result in either *warning* (marked with an exclamation symbol) or an *error* (marked with circled X symbol). *Errors* are critical rule violations that will result in a model that is not usable for the next phase. Each error must be corrected before proceeding with the transition to the physical data model. For instance, an ENTITY IDENTIFIER must have an IDENTIFIER NAME UNIQUENESS option checked, or the model transition will not be possible.

On the other hand, the *warnings* are violations of rules that negatively impact the quality the logical data model, but the model can proceed with transition to the next phase. The modeler's goal is to eliminate all errors and minimize the number of warnings in the model so the model can progress to the next phase.

Note that the check-mark in the box for each rule allows activation or deactivation of a specific validation option. Be careful when deactivating specific options because if the validation process does not report an error, it does not mean that problem with the model does not exist!

To demonstrate the concept of formal model validation we will use the previously created logical data model (Illustration 25):

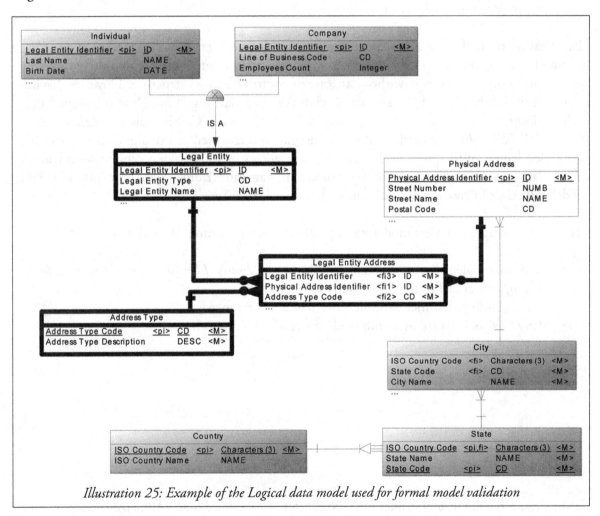

Illustration 25: Example of the Logical data model used for formal model validation

The results of formal model validation are presented in the Illustration 26:

Category	Check	Object	Location
⚠ Entity	Existence of identifiers	Entity 'City'	<Model>
⚠ Entity	Existence of relationship	Entity 'Company'	<Model>
⚠ Entity	Existence of relationship	Entity 'Individual'	<Model>
✖ Entity Identifier	Existence of entity attribute	Identifier 'Legal Entity Address.Identifier_1'	<Model>::Legal Entity Address

Illustration 26: Results of the logical data model validation by PowerDesigner

Validation of the logical data model has reported a few warnings and one error:

- *Legal Entity Address* has an identifier that does not have any attribute defined. It is not allowed to have an entity without attributes
- the *City* entity does not have a primary identifier defined
- two entities involved in the generalization relationship do not have any other relationships. This is not necessarily a problem but it is sometimes appropriate to assess if entities involved in generalization relationship do need a local relationships to support certain business rules

Classification of the findings can sometimes confuse the modeler. What is an error vs. warning is sometimes not that clear! For instance, an entity without attributes is definitely an error because an entity cannot exist without at least one attribute in its structure. However, having a column with UNDEFINED data type is classified as a warning although it is assumed that each attribute must have data type explicitly defined. Generally CASE tools will define a *data domain UNDEFINED* as a catch-all domain (usually implemented as a string of characters with predefined length in the physical data model) that allows us to postpone explicit specification of the data type. If this warning is not corrected, transition from logical into physical data model will result in creation of a column with a generic data type[51].

Before continuing to the next modeling step, all errors and warnings should be handled:

- a primary identifier comprising of the *Legal Entity Identifier* and *Physical Address Identifier* is added to the *Legal Entity Address*
- the *Offending* identifier without any attributes is removed
- *City Code* is specified as a unique identifier of the *City* entity

---

[51] By default the CASE tool defines the UNDEFINED data domain as VARCHAR data type with specified length. This data type allows storing of any type of data (alphanumeric). Furthermore, the definition of the UNDEFIED data domain can be customized by the data modeler

The new version of corrected logical data model is shown in the Illustration 27:

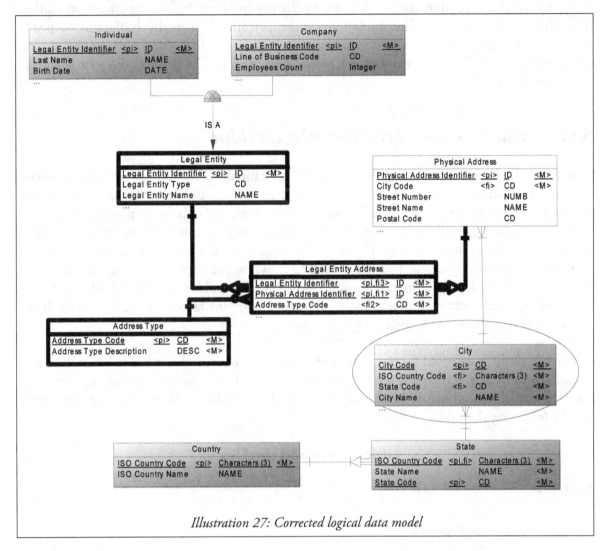

Illustration 27: Corrected logical data model

Model validation performed again resulted in two warnings (Illustration 28):

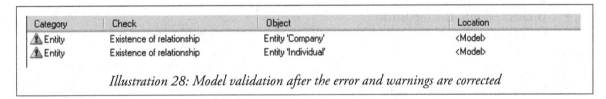

Illustration 28: Model validation after the error and warnings are corrected

These warnings inform us that entities *Company* and *Individual* do not have any relationship other than the generalization relationship to the *Legal Entity*.

By looking at the model the conclusion is that this can be allowed since both of them are sub-types within the generalization relationship in the Logical model and as such they are not currently involved in any other relationship.

Formal model validation helps to improve the quality and consistency of models by standardizing the validation criteria that the model has to satisfy before the transition to the next phase in its life cycle. The validation can be performed manually but results depend heavily on time available for validation, knowledge, experience and goals of the reviewer. For consistency reasons the recommendation is to use the CASE tool to perform the formal model validation whenever possible.

5.9. *Logical data model completeness checklist*

Over time the logical data model size can grow substantially. The number of entities, their structure and number of relationships can make a model complex even for an experienced modeler. With large data models it is becoming increasingly difficult to keep track of content modifications and overall model completeness. Large projects can have multiple modelers working on various parts of the model so the model consistency and adherence to the predefined modeling rules can become a challenge. When the models have to be integrated into the final logical model, uniformity and consistency in implementing the modeling rules, data domains and naming conventions becomes an important factor that can help (if done properly) or complicate the models integration process.

Before the model is accepted for integration into the target data model, it has to be assessed for completeness to ensure the same level of modeled details. The assessment is also applicable to the final model version before its closure. To assess the model completeness, the modeler can use the following checklist:

<u>Logical data model checklist</u>

Model

- Has the author specified
- Has the version specified
- Has a content description specified
- Is formally validated with NO ERRORS
- Is checked into the repository

Entity

- Has a unique business name
- Has two or more attributes
- Has a unique primary identifier
- Has a business definition
- Has at least one relationship with another entity
- Specification is signed off by the Business Analyst

- **Attribute**
- Has a unique business name
- Has a business definition (max length is 254 characters)
- Has a business domain assigned:
  - ☐ Data type
  - ☐ Width
  - ☐ Precision
- Has a Mandatory/optional indicator
- Specification is signed of by the Business Analyst

Relationship

- Has a 'verb phrase'
- Has cardinality defined
  - ☐ Child to parent
  - ☐ Parent to child
- Has no M:M (many-to-many) relationships defined
- If the Generalization type is present:
  - ☐ Has Covering defined (Covering/Non-covering)
  - ☐ Has partitioning defined (Exclusive/Inclusive)
  - ☐ Has a Discriminator defined
- Specification is signed of by the Business Analyst

✳ ✳ ✳ ✳

The logical data modeler will use the checklist to verify that model contains all the components required. The checklist used for model completeness introduces standardization of expected model content and ensures model completeness for the next phase. The explanation of each validation point is provided below:

Logical data model

- *Has the author specified*—it is a good practice to explicitly specify the model's author along with contact details
- *Has the version specified*—f the model repository is used, the version control is automatic. If not, then the model version has to be controlled manually
- *Has a content description specified*—description of the model content

Entity

- *Has a unique business name*—each entity must have a business name uniquely defined
- *Has two or more attributes*—it is recommended that the entity comprises of at least two attributes. Every entity that does not comply to this rule should be revisited for further analysis

- *Has a unique primary identifier*—native attribute[52] or combination of native attributes that uniquely identify an instance of an entity
- *Has a Business definition*—the entity definition will be propagated to the Physical data model creating the COMMENT database object. The COMMENT object usually has a length limitation of 254 characters, so we should try to "fit" the entity definition within this length
- *Has at least one relationship with another entity*—orphan entities should not be allowed
- *Specification is signed of by the business analyst*—by reviewing and agreeing with the logical data model we make the model available for the next modeling phase

Attribute

- *Has a unique business name*—this is the full business name as stated by the business analyst. The recommendation is to use the established logical naming conventions to properly structure the business names
- *Has a business definition*—the business definition should not be lengthy so it can be seamlessly propagated to the physical data model. Usually, the COMMENT object in the database is limited to 254 characters so we can try to limit this field to that length (if possible)
- *Has a domain assigned*—the business analyst will usually use a very broad definition of the data context (e.g. number, string, date etc.). By establishing the domains, the logical modeler will try to achieve more precision in establishing the base class of the data. Although not strictly a logical concept, the goal is to further define the data type, width and precision[53] of the domain specified
- *Has a mandatory/optional rule specified*—at the attribute level an explicit rule has to be stated specifying if the attribute is mandatory or optional. This rule will be implemented as a constraint (NOT NULL or NULL respectively) in the physical data model
- *Specification is signed off by the business analyst*—by reviewing and agreeing with the logical data model the model is made available for the next modeling phase.

Relationship

- *Has a 'verb phrase'*—each relationship, according to the logical naming conventions should incorporate a verb providing an active connotation of the relationship
- *Has cardinality defined*—explicit definition of the relationship's cardinality is required. This will drive the integrity rules in the physical data model.
- *Has no M:M (many-to-many) relationships defined*—not strictly a requirement for the logical data model[54]. Usually, the CASE tools allow relationships with M:M cardinality

---

[52] Native attribute is an attribute that is part of the entity structure comprising of business-related data. In a physical data model we sometimes define the surrogate primary key as a system-generated key that uniquely identifies a record.

[53] Where applicable.

[54] Theoretically the logical data model allows the relationship to have M:M (many to many) cardinality. However, since relationship with this cardinality is not implementable, recommendation

automatically normalizing them during the transition step from logical to physical data model.

- *If the generalization type is present*—for each generalization relationship type additional elements are required in terms of the generalization's *covering* and *partitioning*:
  - ☐ *Has Covering defined (Covering/Non-covering):*
    - o *Covering*: every instance of the supertype is related to at least one subtype instance;
    - o *Non-covering*: some instances of the supertype are not related to any subtype instances.
  - ☐ *Has partitioning defined (Exclusive/Inclusive):*
    - o *Exclusive*—an instance of a supertype is related to not more than one instance of the subtype;
    - o *Inclusive*—an instance of a supertype is related to one or more instances of the subtypes
  - ☐ *Has a Discriminator defined*—an attribute that classifies the supertype instance relationship with the corresponding subtype instance
- *Specification is signed of by the business analyst*—by reviewing and agreeing with the logical data model we make the model available for the next modeling phase

Completeness validation is the final step that effectively closes the model making it ready for the next modeling phase.

5.10. *Logical data model documentation*

CASE tools are well known for their ability to create extensive documentation. Literally, hundreds of pages can be generated with various model-related information. However printed documentation is not always a good thing when designing a system. Before pressing the button and generating few hundred pages report you should ask yourself the following questions:

- Why do we need to create the document?
- When produced, how is that document going to be maintained?

Each document is prepared for a specific target audience. Members of the business team will look for different information than members of the technical team. The business team uses the documentation to assess how the *data requirements* are implemented in the logical data model while the technical team looks for insight into the data structures and relationships that will be used in the physical data model. Compared to the documentation produced for the physical data model, the logical data model documentation is relatively less complex.

---

is to try to Normalize the model by eliminating these and replacing them with an Associative entity.

PowerDesigner can produce two types of reports:

- *List report* in a tabular format—this is an operational report that produces data in spreadsheet-like format for easy consumption
- *Report in a document format*—this is a report that is professionally formatted and it can be used as a final documentation for the model

The proposed list of logical data model reports is presented in the table 8:

Report name	Report content
Entity list report	List of entities with definitions
Entity detailed report	Entities, attributes and relationships. Detailed report including all the definitions and used attribute domains
Attribute domains report	List of the domains defined in the model
Logical data model	Entities, attributes and relationships including the pictorial presentation of the model

Table 8: Proposed list of logical data model reports

PowerDesigner provides an intuitive interface for report creation where the modeler chooses the report components. While doing the analysis and modeling, *list reports*[55] are valuable for providing a snapshot of modeled object's meta-data in a tabular format. An example of a list report creation screen is provided in the Illustration 29.

By checking the box in the left pane the modeler includes the object in the report. When creating a report, the modeler should only include information that will help the consumer of the report. This sounds obvious but in practice it is challenging when the goal is to standardize and minimize the number of reports. By minimizing the number of reports, each report might end up overloaded with information not required by the report consumer. The goal for a modeler is to find a balance between the content's complexity and number of available reports so that a report consumer can easily find the required information.

After specifying the reporting elements, PowerDesigner provides preview option allowing the user to see the sample report. The Illustration 30 shows a list of entities, with their definition specified in the previously created logical model.

---

[55] In PowerDesigner the List Report is type of report created in tabular format

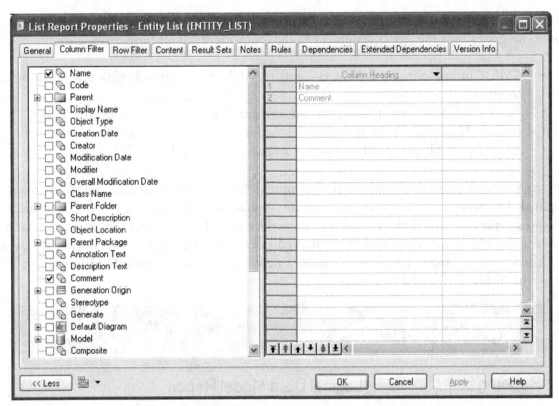

Illustration 29: Definition of a list report in PowerDesigner

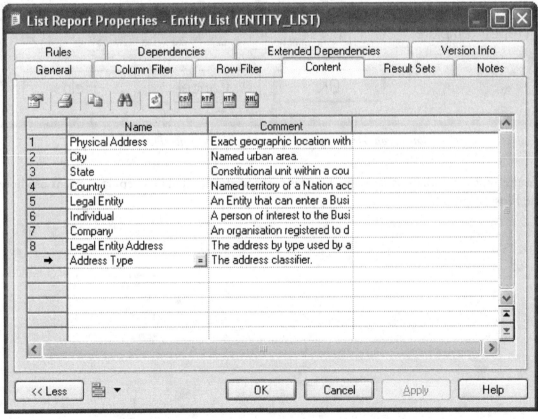

Illustration 30: List report content preview in PowerDesigner

The report preview shows the content in a tabular format. Like other CASE tools, PowerDesigner allows the report document in the following standard formats:

- *CSV* (Comma Separated Values)—a flat ASCII file with columns separated by a commas
- *RTF* (Reach Text Format)—a generic document format readable by text processors
- *HTML* (Hyper Text Markup Language)—a format readable by web browsers
- *XML* (Extensible Markup Language) is a report in standardized XML format

List reports are more operational in nature providing very useful tabular model snapshots required for various types of analysis. More sophisticated reports can be created using advanced reporting capabilities included in PowerDesigner. These reports can include pictorial presentation of the model in a nicely formatted document. The user has an option to use a predefined report from a template or create a new report from scratch. The Illustration 31 shows the dialog for the new report creation.

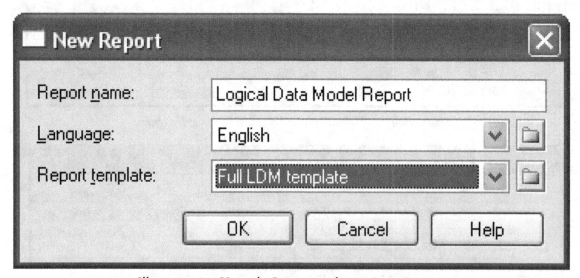

Illustration 31: Using the Report template in PowerDesigner

Once the report template is chosen, the user can specify the detailed report content as shown in the Illustration 32:

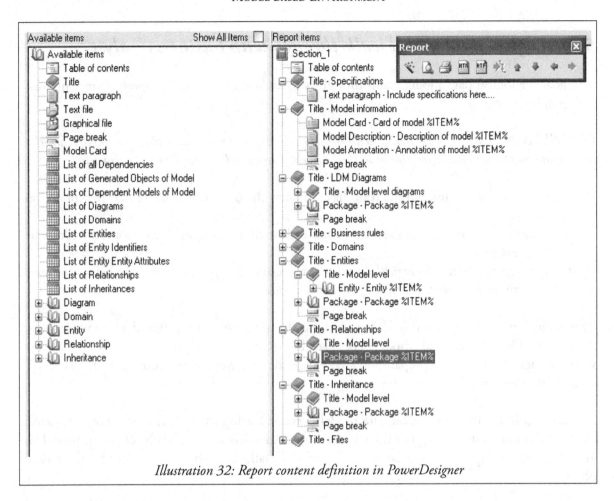

Illustration 32: Report content definition in PowerDesigner

It was already mentioned that distribution of a hard-copy report is not the best solution for the following reasons:

- report size can be massive, literally hundreds of pages
- user does not have any search capabilities to browse through the report. Finding information can be challenging
- reports get outdated quickly
- think of the trees that you will kill for the paper

Standard practice for the report distribution is to have a corporate intranet site where the data models and corresponding reports are published. The site's content is maintained by synchronizing the report content when the model is changed. Using HTML reporting capabilities of the tool, this task can be fully automated. Once the model is modified, it is simply a matter of creating and uploading the report to the corporate site where the consumers can access it.

By providing the latest report version at the corporate site the risk that users will work (and make decisions) with outdated documentation is eliminated. This is not the case when the documentation is distributed as a paper copy.

5.11. Logical data model walk-through with business analyst

The goal for logical data model walk-through is to ensure that model properly represents the data requirements.

DEFINITION: *Logical data model walk-through is a process of validating the model for the structural completeness and compliance to the business rules stated by the data requirements.*

During the model walk-through the team has to review the model and ensure that the model is:

- *complete* in terms of modeled entities and attributes required to properly store the business data
- appropriately *using the logical domains* to represent the type of the business data content
- *correctly and consistently defining the business rules*

The logical model's creation is driven by specifications stated in the data requirements document. Complexity and model size can be overwhelming for the reviewer, so the walk-through should have a preparation step where the reviewer[56] is introduced to the basics of logical data modeling.

The assumption is that the logical data model is created using the *subject-area centric approach* allowing a model walk-through in the same fashion. Knowing that each subject area is modeled as a relatively independent logical unit, the model walk-through can be completed in two phases:

- *independent review of each subject area*
- *review of the integrated logical data model focusing on entities and relationships that implement the relationships* between the subject areas defined in the conceptual data model

Using the phased review approach the business analyst can concentrate on one subject area at a time and validate completeness and compliance to the stated business rules. Review of each subject area in isolation allows focused discussion and efficient review within the allocated time frame. The model walk-through can get out of control if the discussion starts to go from one topic to another, turning into a heated debate rather than model walk-through. Involving representatives from the business sometimes brings the risk of discussing the business processes and procedures that are not directly related to the data model. It is the responsibility of the modeler to moderate the walk-through session carefully, controlling the participants' interaction.

---

[56] Model is reviewed by the business analyst but from time to time the business representatives are asked to review the model too.

Following completion of each independent subject areas walk-through, the logical data model has to be reviewed as an integral model including the implementation of the entities and relationships that represent instantiation of the major relationships in the conceptual data model.

The logical data model review by the business analyst should be the final activity completing the delivery of the logical data model. The model is frozen after the walk-through and ready for the next phase in the modeling process.

5.12. Transition from logical to the physical data model

The logical model represents the foundation for building the physical data model. Transition from the logical to the physical model is a complex step that is fully automated by the CASE tools. The modeler's role is to specify parameters relevant for the model transition and ensure that the "first cut" of the physical data model implements logical constructs in a desired way.

DEFINITION: *Transition from the logical to the physical data model is a process that ensures proper and consistent derivation of the physical constructs based on their logical counterparts.*

The model transition process:

- derives the physical objects based on the corresponding logical objects
- resolves complex logical constructs such as:
  - □ generalization relationship
  - □ relationships with M:M (many-to-many) cardinality

As mentioned before, logical constructs have corresponding physical constructs created during the model transition. The Table 9 presents a cross-reference matrix between the logical and physical data modeling constructs.

Logical modeling construct	Implemented as a corresponding physical modeling construct
Entity	Table
Attribute	Column
Domain	User defined data type (UDT)
Relationship	Reference
Comment	Comment
Business rule	Constraint: -Primary -Unique -Referential integrity -In-line validation

Table 9: Cross-reference between the logical and physical data modeling constructs

From a logical model perspective each construct has one or more corresponding physical object in the physical model. However, many objects created in the physical model do not have corresponding constructs in the logical model.

CASE tools use different approaches to store logical and physical data models. Some tools allow both models to be stored in a single file and the user simply toggles between the models, while other separate models into different physical files. In PowerDesigner the logical and physical data models are separated in two physical files. During the transition process the PowerDesigner will create meta-data with the lineage information for each derived object.

Transition from the logical to the physical data model will be demonstrated using the logical model already created in PowerDesigner. The logical model will be used as a source for the physical model produced as a result of the model transition process. The starting point for the model transition process is the logical data model shown in the Illustration 33:

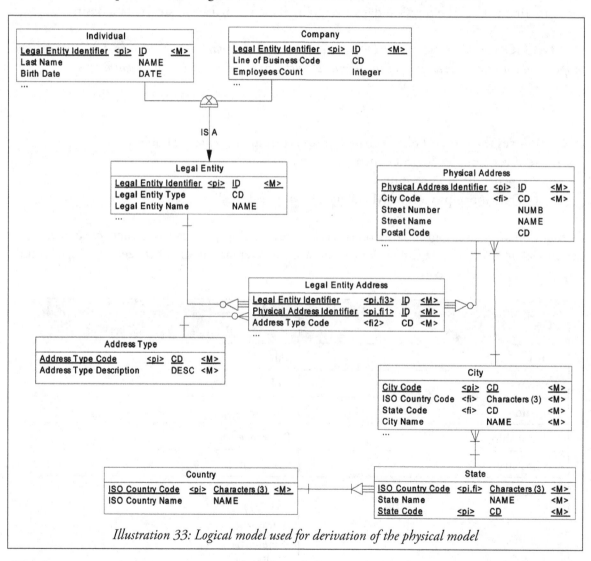

Illustration 33: Logical model used for derivation of the physical model

The first step in the transition process requires defining the target RDBMS. The modeler has to specify the *database system, version* and specific *release* information as shown below:

- RDBMS[57] (e.g. DB2, Oracle etc.) where the model is deployed
- database version (e.g. DB2 V9.5 or Oracle 10g)
- release (e.g. Oracle R1)

The modeler has to contact the DBA to obtain this information. PowerDesigner like other CASE tools stores the database-specific knowledge that is used during the model transition process to derive proper physical objects. Derived objects vary between the databases, different versions and releases.

The model transition process starts with specifying the target RDBMS details as shown in the Illustration 34:

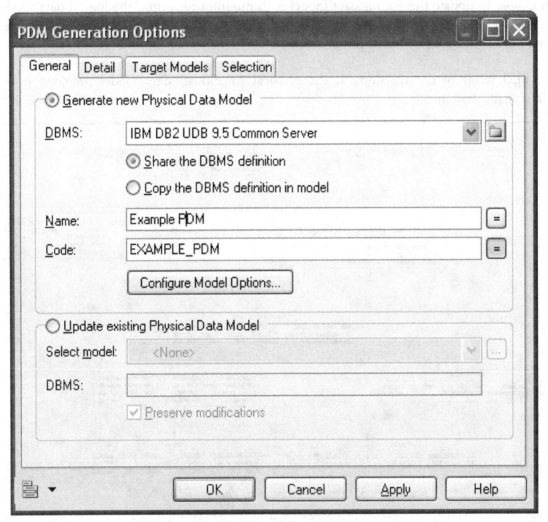

Illustration 34: RDBMS specification in PowerDesigner

PowerDesigner is certified for various relational database management systems (RDBMS) and the modeler has to choose the specific target RDBMS for physical model implementation. For

---

[57]   Relational database management system

each RDBMS, the tool supports multiple database versions and the modeler has to be specific with what database version the model is created for. If an incorrect version of the database is chosen the code generated might not work properly.

In the lower part of the dialog box the tool is providing two options:

- *new* physical model creation
- *update of an existing* physical model

If a *new* physical data model is created, PowerDesigner will create a new physical data model and store it in a file. In the case that the physical model already exists, the modeler can choose to update the *existing* data model with modifications from the logical data model. PowerDesigner keeps tracks of the physical object lineage providing the source logical object name from which the physical object is derived.

The final result of the transition is the physical (relational) data model provided in the following illustration:

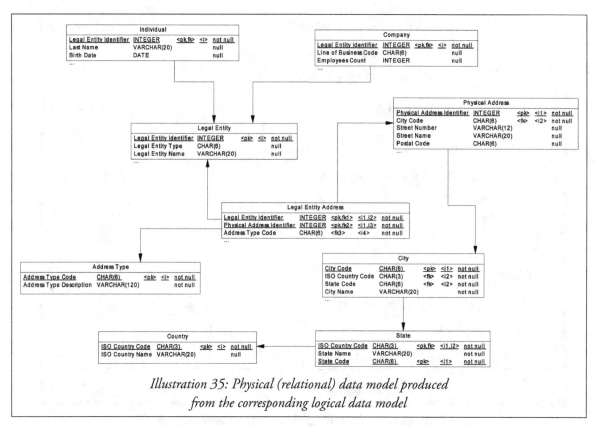

Illustration 35: Physical (relational) data model produced from the corresponding logical data model

Logical to physical model transition created the following set of physical database objects:

- tables from entities
- columns from attributes
- references from the relationships
- physical from logical data domains

The model transition process concludes the logical data modeling phase.

5.13. *Logical data domains and physical data model*

Each logical data domain in the logical data model has an underlying data type[58]. During the transition from the logical to the physical model the underlying data types are used to define the data type for each column based on the attribute's data domain defined in the logical data model. The attribute logical domain's meta-data is propagated to the physical data model.

When deriving the physical model, the modeler has two options:

- use the *base data type* (e.g. INTEGER, VARCHAR, CHAR etc.) or
- use the *data domain*. The user defined type[59] (UDT) is used to denote the data domain

Before using the UDT the modeler has to be aware of some features that might be a constraining factor if not used properly:

- user defined type (UDT) is an object-oriented feature of the RDBMS. Once defined, it can be re-used across the database
- if it is used, it cannot be modified or dropped
- when the UDT is created, the database will automatically create the following functions:
  □ constructor function
  □ destructor function
  □ comparison function
- inserting and modifying data in the column that uses the UDT requires invocation of a function that converts the data into UDT[60]
- comparing a base data type to the UDT requires the data conversion[61]

Use the UDT sparingly to avoid unnecessary complications in code development. UDTs' are very useful when data types have to be used in specific a predefined way. Take for instance a temperature. The value of 37.1 degrees Celsius and the same value in degrees Fahrenheit might be nominally the same, but they represent different temperatures. We should prevent users from comparing nominal values for the temperature to avoid confusion of having the same value representing different temperatures. In this case the UDT can be used to define two distinct data types, one for degrees Celsius and the other for degrees Fahrenheit. While the numbers are the same, user will not be able to compare them unless the conversion from one

---

[58] Depending on the RDBMS the Data Types might differ but core set of Data Types is predefined by ANSI (American National Standard Institute: www.ansi.org)

[59] If you are using DB2 the data domain is created as a DISTINCT TYPE

[60] Database uses the term casting to denote data conversion between data types

[61] Either base data type to UDT or UDT to the base data type. UDT and base data type are not directly compatible

data type to the other is performed which prevents them from drawing a conclusion that 37.1 degrees Celsius is the same as 37.1 degrees Fahrenheit.

From the modeling perspective the data domain and corresponding UDT plays an important role in standardization providing consistency, uniformity and enforcement of defined formatting and integrity rules for data elements. The modeler has to find a balance between using the UDT when required and using standard data types. Typically, overuse of UDT will result in model complexity and have a negative impact on performance.

6. Physical data modeling

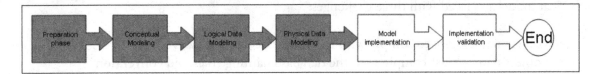

The initial, "first-cut" version of the physical model is created with elements produced during the model transition. The cross-reference between the objects of the logical and physical data models is shown in the table 10.

Logical data model component	Physical data model component
Subject area	Schema
Entity	Table
Relationship	Reference
Attribute	Column
Domain	User Defined Type (UDT)
Definition	Comment
Business rule	Constraint

Table 10: Cross-reference between the logical and physical model constructs

Before proceeding with physical modeling, preparatory work is required to standardize the modeling process. Rushing into physical modeling is not good since mistakes and inconsistencies made can have severe impact on quality as well as the model's maintainability.

6.1. Preparation phase for physical data modeling

The physical model quality depends on the model preparation and setup. The preparatory work for physical modeling is significantly more complex than the preparatory work for logical modeling. This is understandable because the model is getting closer to database implementation and requires definition of the components important for code generation. Components that have to be defined before the modeler starts with physical modeling will be explained in details.

6.1.1. Principles of physical data model naming conventions

One of the goals for the logical data model is to serve as a communication vehicle between the business and modeler. To serve this purpose, the model has to have certain level of flexibility in object naming to avoid unnecessary discussions[62] with the business representatives about imposed syntactic rules. Object names[63] defined in the logical model usually have very strong business flavour loosely complying with the guidelines for structured object names. The object names in the physical model are strongly influenced by limitations of the target RDBMS. The physical modeler is faced with three challenges:

- object names have to comply with the corporate naming rules
- object names must comply with the database naming rules and conventions
- object names should resemble the object names specified in the logical model

DEFINITION: *Physical data model naming conventions are a set of rules that define the semantic[64] and syntactic[65] definition for object names in the physical model.*

CASE tools have the ability to tightly and uniformly control the naming conventions by implementing the transformation rules for names conversion between the logical and physical models. These rules include the following:

- logical to physical object name conversion using a set of predefined rules
- implementation of database specific rules for names:
  - □ physical name length enforcement
  - □ use of database specific reserved words
  - □ use of special characters
  - □ syntactic rules for object names in database (e.g. database object name cannot start with a special character)

Although uniformity is beneficial for model quality, strict implementation of the naming conventions can sometimes cause unexpected problems. The naming rules can lead to object names with inappropriate connotations. If the decision is to implement automatic enforcement of the naming conventions review of generated names is required to avoid inappropriate names in the physical model.

The following is a set of general naming convention principles that should be followed:

- *uniform object name structuring*—object names should always be structured uniformly
- *standard abbreviation rules*—should always be used consistently
- *standard acronyms*—standardize acronyms and use them uniformly (e.g. INC for Incorporated, LTD for Limited, EOD for End-of-day etc.)

A challenge encountered during logical modeling is how to structure the object names according to the naming conventions when the business is using names that significantly deviate from the established naming rules. Blindly imposing naming conventions can cause

---

[62] And possibly confrontation

[63] Entities, attributes, relationships and data domains

[64] Semantic=Meaning

[65] Syntactic=Composition, Structure

unnecessary friction with the business forcing them to use unfamiliar terminology. Having few exceptions is normal and expected and we should not put extra effort to achieve the full compliance with naming conventions.

Implementation of naming conventions has its advantages and disadvantages summarized in the following table:

Advantages of the naming conventions	Disadvantages of the naming conventions
Increase model readability and comprehension	Strict implementation might lead to names that are sometimes inappropriate
Improve model and database maintainability	Dictionary of allowed words and their abbreviations has to be maintained
Provide efficient reporting and increased model search capabilities	

Table 11: Advantages and disadvantages of naming conventions implementation

Once again, it is important for naming conventions to be defined early in the process so the team has enough time to adopt them. Enough time should be allocated for the training on how to properly use the naming conventions.

It is also important to emphasize again that the goal is not to implement the naming conventions strictly, but wisely. When the database object name, syntactically structured using the naming conventions, does not make sense or has inappropriate connotation, consider modifying the name even if the new name deviates from established naming conventions.

When faced with a real project, the data modeler needs clear guidelines of how to formulate and use the naming conventions. As part of the database documentation, the database vendors provide clear naming rules for database objects including:

- list of reserved words
- usage rules for special characters
- maximum name lengths

Furthermore, there are many articles and white papers on the Internet that provide various approaches to object naming. A very popular standard recommended here is Oracle's *Optimal Flexible Architecture*[66] (OFA) recommended by the author. OFA provides comprehensive guidelines for naming physical database objects. If the target RDBMS is Oracle, instead of creating new naming conventions please read the OFA document[67] before trying to create new set of naming conventions. Similar documents are publicly available for DB2 too.

---

[66]   http://docs.oracle.com/cd/B28359_01/install.111/b32002/app_ofa.htm#i633068
[67]   Ibid.

6.1.2. Domains and data types in the physical data model

Logical modeling started with definition for a limited number of data domains. The list was sufficient for logical model creation but the physical modeling requires definition of very specific data types for the following reasons:

- *storage space requirements*—longer data types need more storage space which can increase the size of the database. For instance a *double precision* data type requires twice as much space as a single precision data type
- *performance impact*—longer data types will have more of a negative impact on performance
- *various technical limitations*—for instance the FLOAT data type mathematically represents the *first approximation* of a number and not the exact decimal number. A database that deals with financial data should avoid using this data type

The logical data domains have to be extended to include data domains relevant for the physical implementation. The Table 12 provides an initial list of physical data domains that can be used when the modeling starts. The list can be modified and extended as required.

Logical Domain	Physical data domain (User Defined Type)	Base Data Type[68]
Amount	LARGE AMOUNT	DECIMAL (24,2)
Amount	REGULAR AMOUNT	DECIMAL (14,2)
Amount	SMALL AMOUNT	DECIMAL (8,2)
Rate	STANDARD RATE	DECIMAL (8,4)
Rate	HIGH_PRECISION RATE	DECIMAL (20, 12)
Index	INDEX	DECIMAL (12,3)
Count	COUNT	INTEGER
Percent	PERCENT	DECIMAL (6,3)
Identifier	SMALL IDENTIFIER	SMALLINT
Identifier	REGULAR IDENTIFIER	INTEGER
Identifier	LARGE IDENTIFIER	INTEGER (BIG)
Number	FORMATTED NUMBER	VARCHAR (12)
Number	UFORMATTED NUMBER	VARCHAR (12)
String	SHORT NAME	VARCHAR (20)

---

[68] This is just an example. Particular project might have different requirements

Logical Domain	Physical data domain (User Defined Type)	Base Data Type[68]
String	LONG NAME	VARCHAR (40)
String	DESCRIPTION	VARCHAR (120)
String	FLAG	CHAR (1)
String	INDICATOR	CHAR (3)
String	SSHORT CODE	CHAR (3)
String	LONG CODE	VARCHAR (10)
Date	FORMATTED DATE	DATE
Date	TIMESTAMP	TIMESTAMP
Large Object	CHARACTER LOB	CLOB
Large Object	MULTIMEDIA LOB	BLOB
Undefined	UNDEFINED	VARCHAR (20)

Table 12: Cross-reference between the logical data domain, user defined types (UDT) and base data types (example assumes the DB2 as the target RDBMS)

Physical data domains are grouped into classes:

- *Numeric*—data types that can be used for various mathematical calculations
- *Number*—numeric-like data representing numbers that cannot be used for mathematical calculations (e.g. the street number)
- *String*—alphanumeric content
- *Date*—date or date and time[69]
- *Large object*—binary or character objects of large size
- *Undefined*—generic data type used when the data type or data domain is not explicitly defined

Each domain class is further classified into more granular data domains. Here is a brief explanation of each domain:

- *Numeric*
  - □ *Amount*—domain that represents a monetary value. This domain can be further decomposed into:
    - o *Large Amount*—large monetary values we can use this domain
    - o *Regular Amount*—generic domain for monetary values
    - o *High Precision Amount*—monetary value with extended precision (increased number of decimal places)

---

[69] Depending on internal presentation in the database.

➤ *Rate*—factor used in calculation (e.g. interest rate, fatality rate, etc.). Based on the precision, the domain is further decomposed into:
  □ *Standard rate*—rate with a standard precision
  □ *High Precision Rate*—rate with extended precision
□ *Index*—decimal number representing a ratio
□ *Count*—integer value used for counting
□ *Percent*—decimal number representing percentage
□ *Identifier*—unique value used for identification
  o *Small Identifier*—unique value that is used to identify instances in a small set of instances
  o *Regular Identifier*—unique value that is used to identify an instance
  o *Large Identifier*—unique value that is used to identify instances in a large set of instances

- *Number*—textual (alphanumeric) representation of a numeric value
  □ *Formatted number*—number that is stored using a specific format (e.g. phone number: 555-1234; numbers combined with a special character)
  □ *Unformatted number*—number stored without formatting rules (e.g. phone number stored as an integer: 5551234)
- *String*
  □ *Short Name*—short version of a name, usually used for reference purposes
  □ *Long Name*—extended name, usually the full, official name
  □ *Description*—textual explanation
  □ *Flag*—binary domain with two values: True/Yes or False/No
  □ *Indicator*—multivalued domain
  □ *Short Code*—unique symbolic identifier for a limited list of values
  □ *Long Code*—unique symbolic identifier for large set of values
- *Date*
  □ *Formatted date—Date using predefined format (for instance: North American format MM-DD-YYYY; ISO format YYYY-MM_DD)*
  □ *Timestamp—Date and time with specified precision*
- *Large Object*
  □ *Character LOB*—large object storing text
  □ *Multimedia LOB*—large object storing video, picture or sound
- *Undefined*—generic domain that needs further specification

Initially the domains are defined in the Logical model as shown in the following illustration:

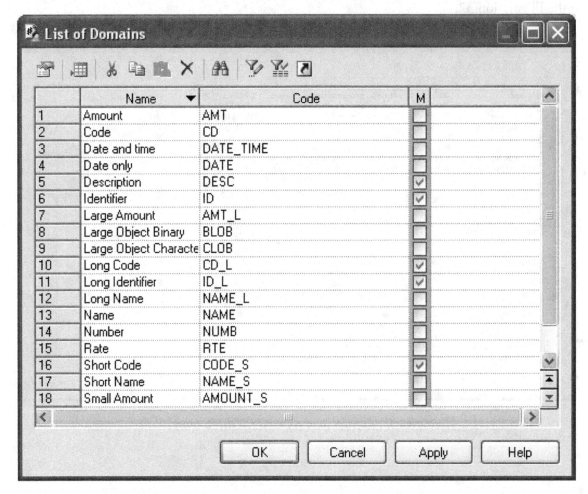

Illustration 36: List of logical data domains defined in the logical model using PowerDesigner

An enhanced list of physical data domains is created in the physical model domains as shown in the Illustration 37.

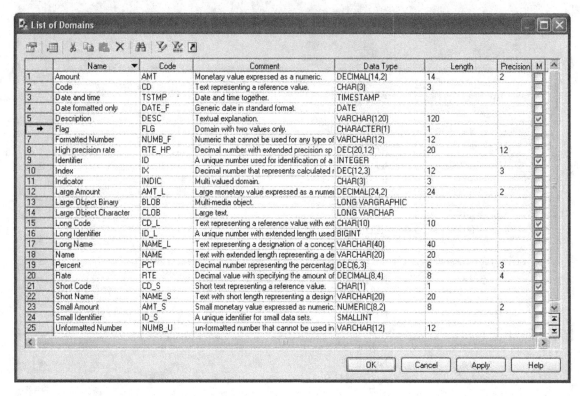

Illustration 37: Physical data domains (RDBMS DB2 V9.7)

The foundation for the physical data domains is the list of logical data domains defined in the logical model. During the model's transition the physical data domains are derived from the logical domains. Depending on the target database for which the physical model is created, the list of physical domains might differ. The previous illustration shows physical data domains derived for the model using DB2 as the target database. Transitioning the logical to the physical data model using Oracle 11g database as the target database produces the following list of physical data domains, as shown in the Illustration 38:

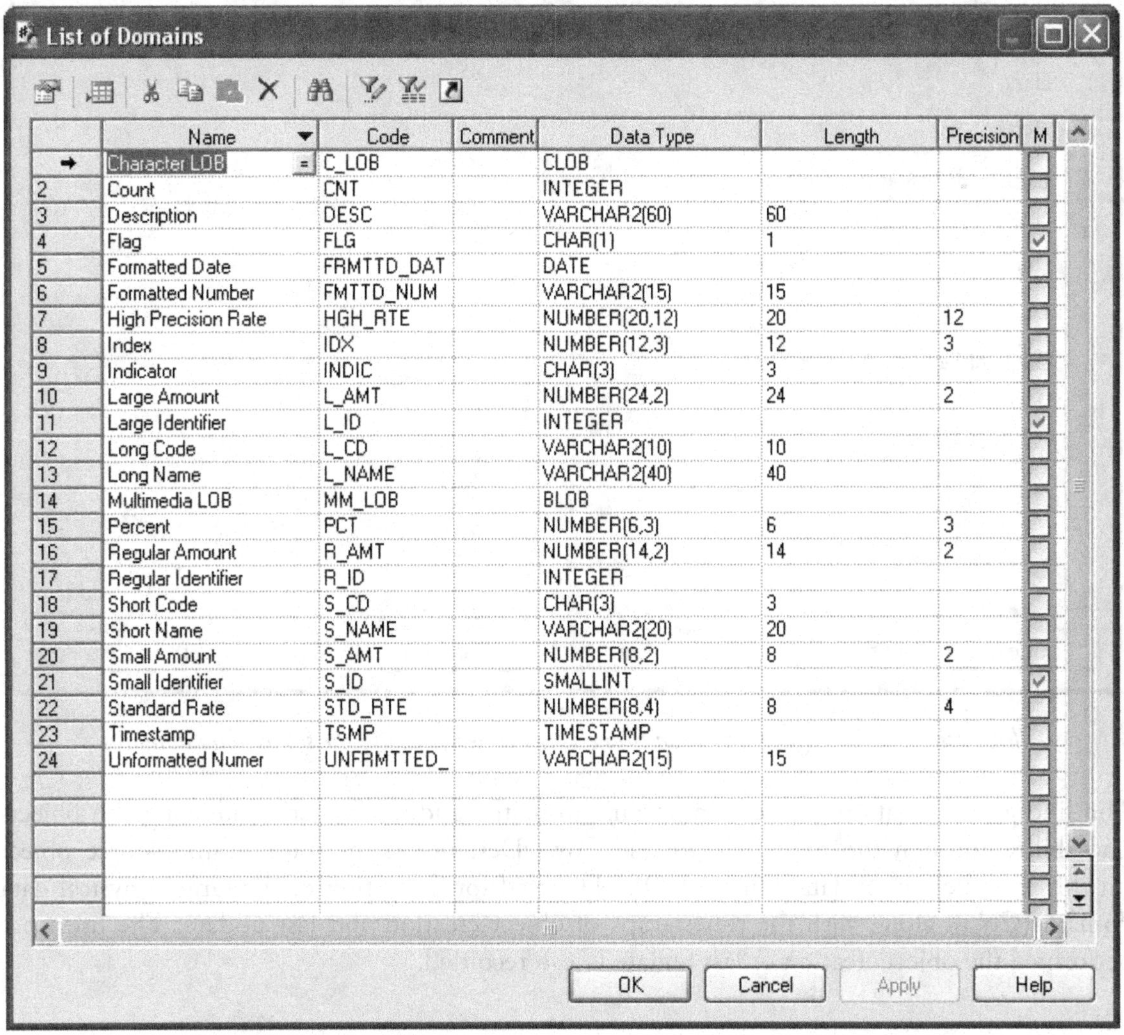

List of Domains

	Name	Code	Comment	Data Type	Length	Precision	M
→	Character LOB	C_LOB		CLOB			
2	Count	CNT		INTEGER			
3	Description	DESC		VARCHAR2(60)	60		
4	Flag	FLG		CHAR(1)	1		✓
5	Formatted Date	FRMTTD_DAT		DATE			
6	Formatted Number	FMTTD_NUM		VARCHAR2(15)	15		
7	High Precision Rate	HGH_RTE		NUMBER(20,12)	20	12	
8	Index	IDX		NUMBER(12,3)	12	3	
9	Indicator	INDIC		CHAR(3)	3		
10	Large Amount	L_AMT		NUMBER(24,2)	24	2	
11	Large Identifier	L_ID		INTEGER			✓
12	Long Code	L_CD		VARCHAR2(10)	10		
13	Long Name	L_NAME		VARCHAR2(40)	40		
14	Multimedia LOB	MM_LOB		BLOB			
15	Percent	PCT		NUMBER(6,3)	6	3	
16	Regular Amount	R_AMT		NUMBER(14,2)	14	2	
17	Regular Identifier	R_ID		INTEGER			
18	Short Code	S_CD		CHAR(3)	3		
19	Short Name	S_NAME		VARCHAR2(20)	20		
20	Small Amount	S_AMT		NUMBER(8,2)	8	2	
21	Small Identifier	S_ID		SMALLINT			✓
22	Standard Rate	STD_RTE		NUMBER(8,4)	8	4	
23	Timestamp	TSMP		TIMESTAMP			
24	Unformatted Numer	UNFRMTTED_		VARCHAR2(15)	15		

OK   Cancel   Apply   Help

Illustration 38: Physical data domains (RDBMS Oracle 11g)

Comparing these two lists with derived physical data domain we can notice some differences in the base data types that are attributed to the specific databases. For instance in DB2 a variable character is specified by the VARCHAR data type, while in Oracle PowerDesigner created VARCHAR2 as the underlying data type.

When the physical model is derived from the logical using the model transition process, PowerDesigner keeps the lineage meta-data for each physical data domain derived from the logical domain as shown in the Illustration 39:

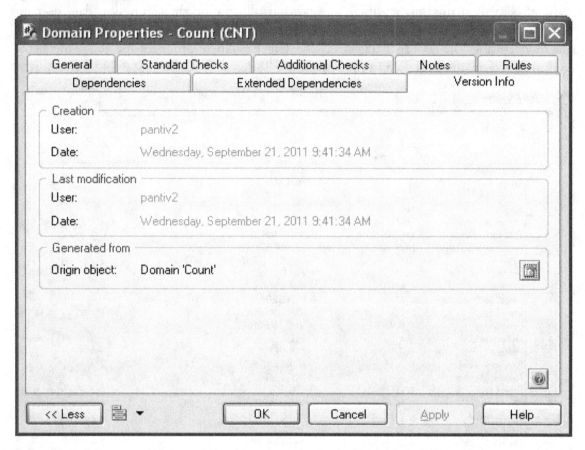

Illustration 39: Lineage information connecting the derived with the source data domains

The lineage information[70] is very important from the audit perspective allowing the objects traceability through the modeling process. PowerDesigner keeps track of the source object (in this case the logical data domain COUNT) used for derivation of the target physical data domain (CNT) along with the timestamps of object creation and last update. The user that performed the object creation or last update is also recorded.

6.1.3. Validation points in the physical data modeling process

The physical model validation process ensures the model's compliance with the data structures and business rules specified in the logical model. At the same time the data team, responsible for the physical model must satisfy the requirements for optimal database performance. The physical model validation is a complex process that has to include participants from both the business and technical community.

---

70   PowerDesigner keeps the lineage information as technical meta-data for each object in the model

DEFINITION: *Physical data model validation is a process that ensures the model complies with the following:*

- *data structures and business rules defined in the logical data model are properly propagated to the physical model*
- *performance and optimal design*—physical implementation is optimized from a storage and performance perspective[71]
- *completeness*—the model includes all components required for database implementation

Model transition is a very sensitive step and choices made during this process can negatively impact the physical model The choices made during the transition step can accidentally change the expected business behavior stated by the logical model. Further physical modeling can introduce hidden problems that are difficult to identify, so combined effects might be disastrous.

The ultimate goal of physical modeling is to create a model that will be used to generate the DDL and DCL scripts with all components properly defined. PowerDesigner, like other CASE tools, is used for physical modeling but frequently not to the full extent. The code generated from the tool is usually taken by the DBA and further enhanced[72] to achieve the fully implementable version.

The assumption is that the physical modeler is not a database expert but has sufficient knowledge to do the physical database design. The team responsible for database design and therefore the final version of the physical model must include the database administrator. The expectation is that, by having expertise in database optimization and performance tuning, the DBA can provide valuable input to optimize the physical model design.

---

[71] Performance requirements are formalized in the Service Level Agreement (SLA). This is effectively the contract between the service provider are user in terms of expected performance levels.

[72] By specifying additional database objects (tablespaces, buffer pools, partitions, relevant physical parameters etc.)

The Illustration 40 outlines the physical model validation process:

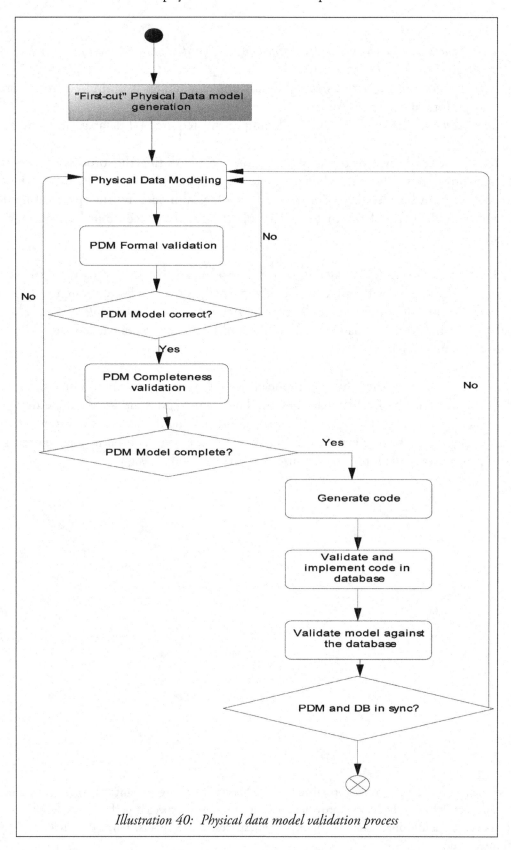

Illustration 40: Physical data model validation process

Formal physical model requires validation against the rules and best practices of physical modeling. CASE tools that provide formal physical model validation functionality differ in the types of model check they offer. Model validation performed by PowerDesigner includes the following rule checks:

- each table has at least one column
- each table has the primary key specified
- each table has at least one reference to another table
- there are no columns without data type explicitly specified
- each index has at least one column in its structure definition
- each reference has a parent and child table[73]
- primary key and foreign key columns involved in referential integrity and enforced by the database have:
  - the same data type and format
  - the appropriate column integrity rule:
    - all columns of the primary key must be mandatory (NOT NULL)
    - foreign key columns could allow optional (NULL) columns
- each column name is unique within the table
- each table name is unique within the schema
- infrastructure objects[74] are properly defined and used. For instance, PowerDesigner can discover if there is a tablespace that is not utilized by any of the structural objects[75] specified in the model. This can become very handy during the model maintenance phase when we need to clean up the database by removing obsolete objects.

---

[73] The problem is known as a "dangling" reference in some CASE tools
[74] For instance: buffer pools, tablespaces etc.
[75] Tables, indexes or materialized views

The Illustration 41 lists the physical model validation options in PowerDesigner.

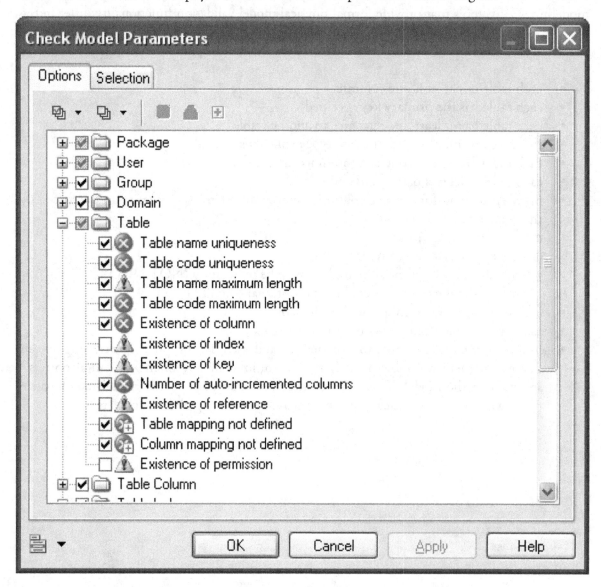

Illustration 41: Physical data model validation options in PowerDesigner

The list of choices is very lengthy and the modeler can choose to include or exclude specific types of validation. The model validation performed by the tool is a very quick process, even for large models[76] it will take just a few minutes. Model validation results in reporting the warnings and errors. When the warning is reported, the modeler can proceed with code generation but the generated script might lead to a potentially sub-optimal code. If errors are reported, the code cannot be successfully generated by the tool. All errors reported by the tool must be corrected before the modeler can proceed with code generation.

---

[76] Usually the model classification by size is defined in the following manner: small (up to 20 tables), medium (20-50 tables) and large (over 50 tables)

Validation for physical model completeness has to ensure that the generated code includes all of the required elements so that manual code change is not required. The following validation is available in PowerDesigner and should be performed before the code is generated:

- database schema is defined for each object
- all the table's physical details (e.g. compression, partitioning etc.) are defined
- for each table, every columns' physical details (e.g. compression, encryption etc.) are specified
- references are specified including the referential integrity rules[77]
- user defined data types (UDT) are defined
- naming conventions are properly and consistently implemented:
  - □ reserved words are not used in the names
  - □ object names are within the length allowed by the database
- database infrastructure objects (e.g. buffer pools, tablespaces etc.) are defined and used
- stored procedures and user defined functions (UDF) are properly created
- triggers are properly defined
- permission are defined and properly used

After the model validation is completed, the modeler can proceed with the code generation. When generating a script, the modeler can choose between two types of generated code:

- *full script*—the script to create specified objects in an empty database
- *delta script*—the script that will modify existing objects in the database

It is really impressive when you produce hundreds of pages of properly structured code with comments and explanations. Although the code generation is fully automated, the code review by the DBA is strongly recommended prior to implementation, for the following reasons:

- the DBA has detailed knowledge and experience with the latest version of the database. Sometimes the code generated by the tool has to be manually modified to be optimal
- the physical modeler may accidentally choose incorrect code generation options and the generated code might not be implementable or even dangerous[78]
- CASE tools can have a "bug" that can cause problems with the script generated

Code deployment to the database is in the domain of the DBA's responsibility. The deployment process is finalized when the modeler performs the physical model validation against the database. Although this step seems to be unnecessary if there are no errors reported, the step is required to ensure that the model is synchronized with the database. Full model deployment into an empty database is less prone to errors and omissions compared to delta script deployment, but in both cases model validation against the database is required to ensure the

---

[77] For instance: CASCADE DELETE, NO ACTION etc.

[78] For instance, when generating the delta script to implement database modifications, the assumption is that there is no data loss. If the modeler is not careful it is easy to make a mistake and implement a script that will drop and recreate the table populated with data. This can have disastrous effect on production database

completeness of the code deployment. PowerDesigner is used for comparison of the model and database. The procedure is explained below:

- the database is reverse engineered into a temporary physical model
- the existing model is compared to the temporary model created by reverse engineering the database

The following illustration depicts the model comparison with the database:

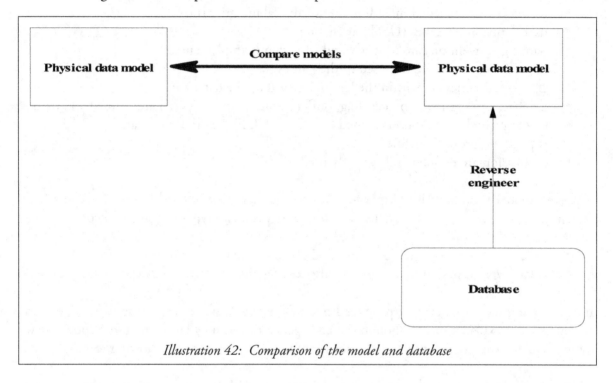

Illustration 42: Comparison of the model and database

Each model deployment has to be properly documented and the CASE tool can produce a report that outlines exact modifications implemented as part of the script. The report should be a part of the standard deployment documentation created by the data team.

The model implementation is considered successful when the model comparison with the database does not show any differences.

6.1.4. Resources involved in the physical data modeling process

Success of the physical model development phase is dependent on participation from the team members involved in the process. The initial version of the physical model is created by transitioning the logical to the physical data model. From that point onward, the model is designed by the physical modeler with help from the DBA and developers providing technical database expertise and information on database use respectively.

The Table 13 shows the direction of information flow in the modeling process:

Participant (Role)	Input provided to	Type of input provided
Logical modeler	Physical modeler	• Logical data model • Implicit/hidden business rules • Data access path
Developer	Physical modeler	• Data access patterns • SQL statements • Stored procedures • User Defined Functions
DBA	Physical modeler	• Information on the database infrastructure objects used • Code modifications required • Performance/storage related guidelines for physical design[79]

Table 13: Information flow in the physical data modeling process

Interactions among participants in the physical modeling process are shown in the diagram 43.

After the model transition from the logical to physical model, the model is reviewed by both modelers and additional clarifications, if required, are provided to the physical modeler. Physical model design is the responsibility of the physical data modeler and DBA.

Ideally, both the DBA and physical modeler should work and communicate using the model, but typically the DBA prefers reviewing the scripts to perform the analysis. The script can be generated on demand from the model and submitted for review to the DBA. The modeler should expect the DBA to provide input relevant for model optimization. The model will be modified accordingly based on the input from the DBA. From time to time, minor script modifications are required to make the generated script optimal from a performance and implementation perspective. This has to be done manually since the tool is not that sophisticated to be able to produce code that will optimally execute in any situation. Manual script modifications are in the DBA's domain of responsibility.

---

[79] For instance: table partitioning, indexing etc.

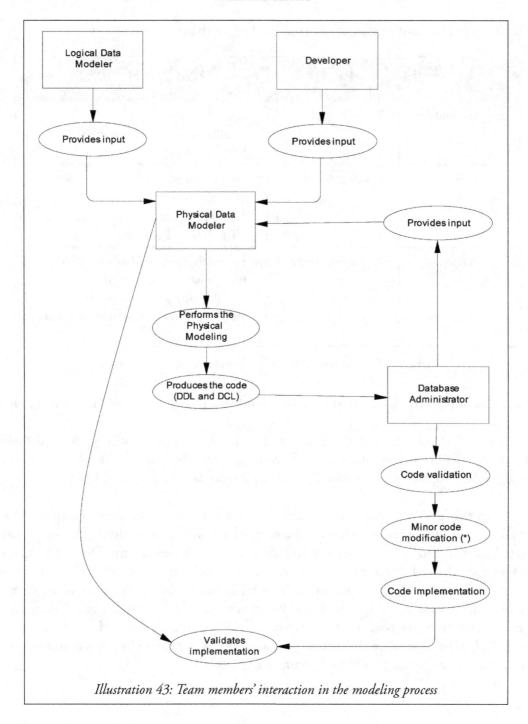

Illustration 43: Team members' interaction in the modeling process

Physical database design recorded in the model is also dependent on the way data is accessed in the database[80]. For this information the development team has to provide the SQL code used in application. Analysis of the stored procedures and user defined functions will provide insight into data access pattern providing further information for performance optimization by adding or removing indexes.

---

[80]   The data access pattern

6.2. Overview of the physical modeling process

The model transition step is performed by both logical and physical modelers working together. Once the initial version of the physical model is ready, the logical data modeling phase can be closed. The detailed overview of the physical data modeling process is shown in the Illustration 44. Each step in the physical data modeling process will be explained in details.

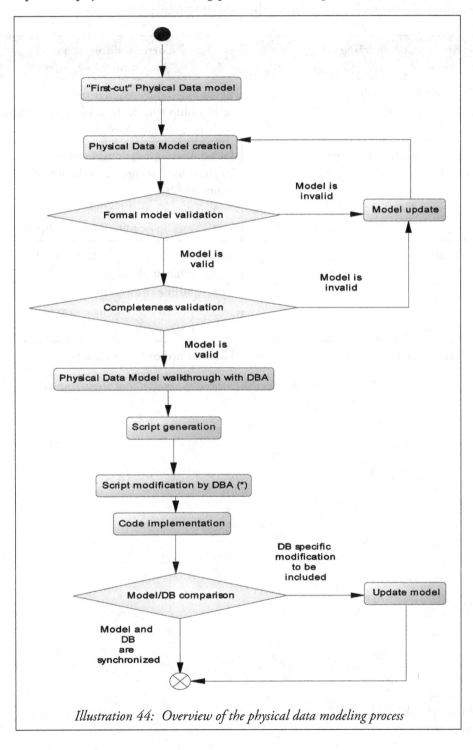

Illustration 44: Overview of the physical data modeling process

6.3. Logical to physical data model transition

The complexity of the model transition process is partially hidden from the modeler when using the tool to perform the model transition. Both, logical and physical data modelers are responsible for the model transition and will create the initial version of the physical model together. Constructs of the logical model are transitioned into corresponding physical modeling constructs. A cross-reference is provided in the following table:

Logical data modeling construct	Corresponding physical data model construct
LDM[81] allows relationship with M:M (many-to-many) cardinality	Relational model requires that each relationship with M:M cardinality be replaced with an associative table
Generalization relationship type	Generalization relationship type is implemented using one of the following approaches[82]: • direct transition • roll-up or roll-down transition
Business rules	Business rules are implemented using: • referential integrity • in-line constraints • primary or unique constraints • triggers
Logical data domain	User-defined or base data types

Table 14: Logical to physical data modeling concepts transition

---

[81]   Logical data model
[82]   Discussed later

Below is a table with a cross-reference between the database objects (defined in DB2 and Oracle databases) with their corresponding logical data modeling concept.

Logical concept	DB2 object	Oracle object	Object type
Subject area	Schema	Schema	Structural
Entity	Table	Table	Structural
		Nested Table	Structural
Entity	Table clusters	Clustered tables	Structural
Entity	Object	Object	Structural
	View	View	Structural
	Table Partitions	Table Partitions	Structural
	Materialized Query Table	Materialized view	Structural
		Dimension	Structural
Attribute	Column	Column	Structural
Domain	Distinct Type	Type	Structural
Comment	Comment	Comment	Structural
Business rule	Primary Key	Primary Key	Structural
Bus. rule	Foreign Key	Foreign Key	Structural
Bus. rule	In-line constraint	In-line constraint	Structural
	Index	Index	Structural
	Sequence	Sequence	Structural
	Alias	Synonym	Structural
	Nick name	Dblink	Structural
	Wrapper		Structural
	Stored Procedure	Stored Procedure	Behavioral
	User Defined Function	User Defined Function	Behavioral
	Trigger	Trigger	Behavioral
	Method	Method	Behavioral
	Buffer pool	Buffer pool	Infrastructure
	Tablespace	Tablespace	Infrastructure
	Storage	Storage	Infrastructure
	Event Monitor		Infrastructure
	Security Label	Security Label	Infrastructure
	Security Label component		Infrastructure

Table 15: Cross-reference between the logical and physical objects (DB2 and Oracle)

When creating the physical model, the modeler and DBA have to decide which objects should be part of the model and which should be excluded and controlled directly by the DBA. For instance the DBA usually directly controls the infrastructure database objects such as tablespaces. These are reverse engineered into the model after they are created in the database.

The logical to physical model transition step will be explained in more details in the following section.

6.3.1. Transitioning the relationship with M:M cardinality

The logical data model allows creation of the relationships with multiple instances cardinality at each end (denoted as M:M relationship cardinality). Here is a very simple example using the logical model stating the following rule:

A client owns many accounts and an account is owned by many clients

The logical data model that implements the stated business rule is shown in the following illustration:

Illustration 45: Relationship with M:M cardinality between the Customer and the Account

Relationships with many-to-many cardinality are allowed for simplicity but it cannot be implemented as such in the physical model. When the CASE tool encounters the relationship with M:M cardinality the following actions are performed:

- a table is created to replace the relationship with M:M cardinality
- primary keys from the tables involved in M:M relationship are propagated as foreign keys into the newly created table
- both new references are declared as identifying

The transition of the relationship with M:M cardinality is depicted in the Illustration 46.

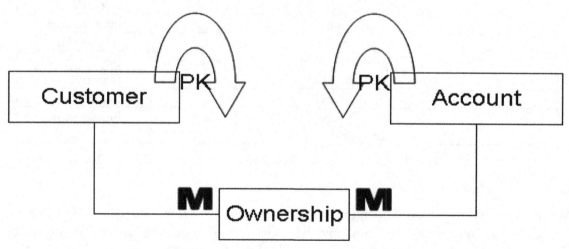

Illustration 46: Transition of the logical M:M relationship into the physical model

PowerDesigner will perform the transition automatically when the physical model is generated from the logical by creating the associative (intersection) table that replaces the M:M relationship. In the example above, the table named *OWNERSHIP*[83] replaces the relationship with M:M cardinality specified in the logical model.

6.3.1.1. Transition rules for relationships

Based on the relationship's cardinality the physical model defines the referential integrity rules to preserve the business rules stated in the logical model. Referential integrity rules are defined for both sides of the reference[84] stating the actions triggered by data modifications in the tables. Actions sensitive to the referential integrity enforcement are the insert, update and delete.

Referential integrity rules implemented in the database are explained in the following table 16:

Referential integrity rule	Description
RESTRICT or NO ACTION	If the rule is violated an exception is reported
CASCADE	When parent record is modified, modification of a child records occurs

Table 16: Referential integrity rules

Each reference has the enforcement state defined as:

- *enforced*—database actively enforces the reference
- *not enforced*—the reference is implemented in the database but not actively enforced

Depending on the database additional options might be available. For instance in Oracle validation of the referential integrity rules can be further specified by the VALIDATE option[85] as:

- not deferrable
- initially deferred
- deferrable initially deferred
- initially immediate deferrable
- deferrable

---

[83] During the transition process the table will not be named as such. The modeler will have to manually change the name to reflect the business nature of the table in the model

[84] The logical data model operates with relationships between two entities while in the Physical model each relationship is replaced with a reference

[85] For detailed explanation please refer to the database manual

An example will demonstrate specifics of the transition from logical to the physical data model. As part of the model transition process in PowerDesigner the reference generation option has to be specified as shown in the Illustration 47:

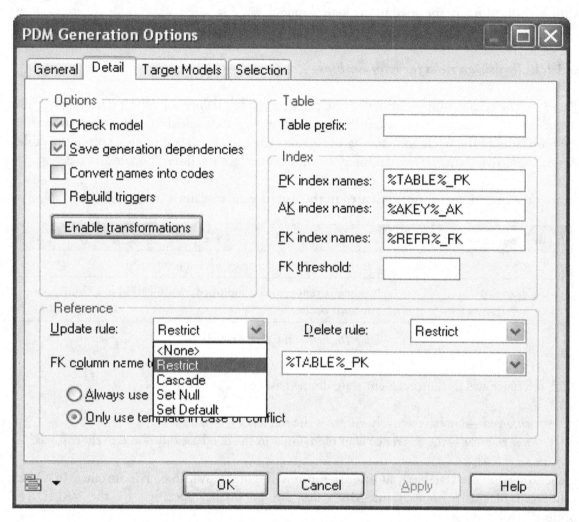

Illustration 47: Specification of the referential integrity rule for the model transition

Referential integrity rules are derived from the relationships using a uniform strategy for both DELETE and UPDATE rules. PowerDesigner also requires a specification of the naming convention rules for foreign keys when performing the transition from the logical to physical model.

After the model transition some of the references might need the referential integrity rule modified manually as part of the physical modeling process.

6.3.1.2. Generalization relationship transition

The complexity of a generalization relationship requires special attention during the model transition. The important generalization relationship parameters are the following:

- the type of covering:
  - □ *complete*—each instance of the supertype is related to at least one subtype instance
  - □ *incomplete*—some instances of the supertype are not related to any of the subtype instances
- the type of partitioning:
  - □ *exclusive*—an instance of the supertype is related to no more than one subtype instance
  - □ *inclusive*—an instance of the supertype is related to one or more subtype instances

The Illustration 48 shows the details of a generalization relationship defined in the logical model. The *mutually exclusive children* option (Illustration 48) refers to the type of supertype partitioning stating the rule that children are mutually exclusive. The type of covering is defined as *complete* if every supertype instance is related to at least on subtype instance.

The model transition process requires a specification of how to implement the generalization relationship type in the physical model. The following alternatives are available:

- implement the generalization relationship type 'as-is', using the direct transition of the entities from the logical data model to the tables
- roll-up the sub types into the supertype
- roll-down supertype into the subtypes

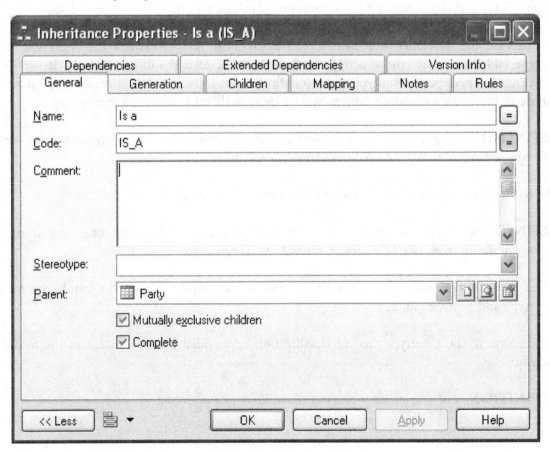

Illustration 48: The generalization relationship definition in PowerDesigner

The generalization relationship is implemented in the logical model using the concept of the supertype entity that is a parent of the entities defines as subtypes. At the supertype level, there is a classifier attribute called the *discriminator* that classifies an instance of the supertype as one (or more, depending on the partitioning) of the subordinated subtypes. To perform the model transition the following has to be specified:

- covering type
- partitioning type
- supertype discriminator
- attribute inheritance strategy

The specification of the generalization relationship transition parameters will have an impact on the business rules implemented in the physical model. We will discuss each point separately.

DEFINITION: *Generalization relationship with the full covering type defines the rule that each instance of the supertype is related to at least one related instance in the subtype.*

When extracting the data from the relational tables involved in the covering relationship type the developer will use the INNER JOIN between the supertype and the subtype tables.

DEFINITION: *A generalization relationship with a partial covering type states that a supertype instance is not required to have a related instance of a subtype.*

In that case the developer will use the LEFT OUTER JOIN between the supertype and subtype tables to extract the supertype with or without related subtype records. If the join between the supertype and subtype tables is defined as an INNER JOIN, the supertype records that do not have corresponding subtype will be incorrectly omitted from the resulting set.

DEFINITION: *A generalization relationship with an exclusive partitioning states that each supertype instance have at most one subtype instance related to it.*

The resulting set is assembled of supertype/subtype record pairs.

DEFINITION: *A generalization relationship with inclusive partitioning states that a single instance of the supertype can be related to multiple subtype instances.*

When partitioning is defined as inclusive the resulting set requires a complex join between the supertype and subtype tables.

Information of the supertype's record classification is provided by the concept of the record's *discriminator*.

DEFINITION: *The discriminator classifies the instance of a supertype.*

By defining the *discriminator* we are implementing a classifier that segregates the records relating it to a corresponding subtype (exclusive partitioning) or multiple subtype records (inclusive partitioning).

PowerDesigner allows the modeler to define the *attribute inheritance strategy* by specifying one of the following alternatives:

- all supertype attributes are inherited in the subtype entities
- attribute inheritance is limited to the supertype's primary key only

The impact of various transition alternatives for the generalization relationship type will be best explained using an example. The starting point is the logical model presented in the Illustration 49:

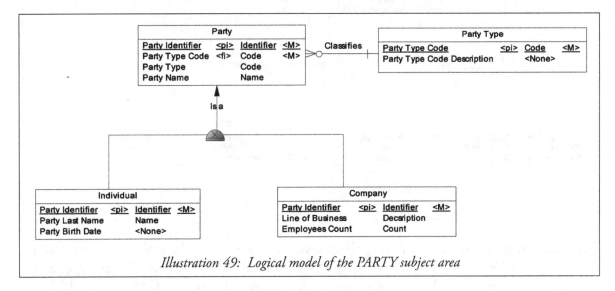

Illustration 49: Logical model of the PARTY subject area

The model defines the following business rules:

- PARTY is classified using the PARTY TYPE CODE discriminator. The subtypes of a PARTY are defined as:
  - □ an INDIVIDUAL or
  - □ a COMPANY
- An instance of a PARTY must be related (classified as) either an INDIVIDUAL or COMPANY making it an exclusive generalization type

Using the tool the model transition is defined with following options:

- propagate only the primary keys
- implement the following referential integrity rules:
  - □ DELETE with CASCADE option
  - □ UPDATE with RESTRICT option

The result of the model's transition is the physical model shown in the Illustration 50:

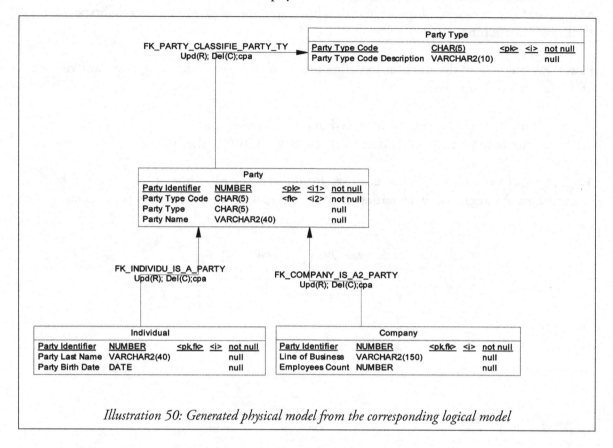

Illustration 50: Generated physical model from the corresponding logical model

The physical model generated during the transition process kept the table structures intact. The attributes local to the supertype entity remained localized in the derived supertype table. The references from the subtype tables were implemented with enforced CASCADE DELETE and UPDATE RESTRICT rules.

Alternatively a generalization relationship can be transitioned to the physical model using the *roll-down* approach. This strategy will distribute all attributes and relationships inherited from the supertype, to every subtype table. The created physical model will not have the supertype table as shown in the Illustration 51:

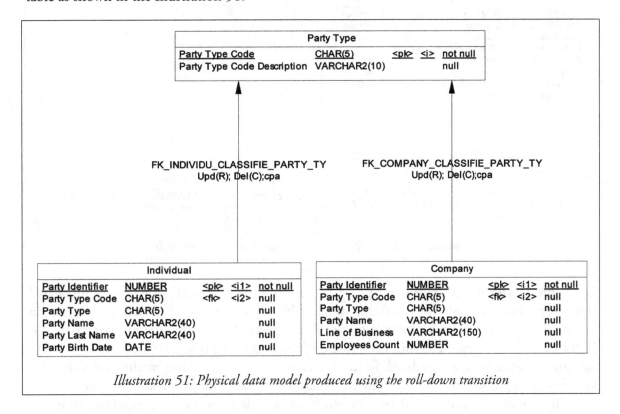

Illustration 51: Physical data model produced using the roll-down transition

The following rules will be used for the *roll-down* transition:

- all attributes from the supertype are propagated to all subtype tables
- primary keys in both subtypes are the same, inherited from the supertype
- all relationships are inherited from the supertype

Further model optimization is possible. Rolling-down the supertype into two subtype tables does not need a reference to the PARTY TYPE table used originally as a discriminator. The table PARTY TYPE can be safely removed from the model as shown in the following illustration:

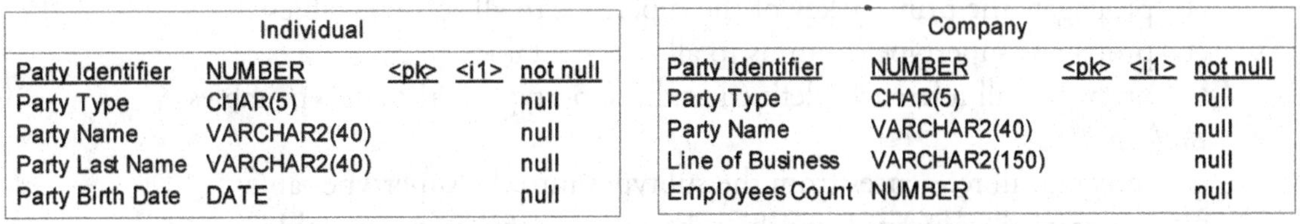

Illustration 52: Final model version after removing the PARTY TYPE classifier

The third model transition approach is based on having subtypes *roll-up* into the supertype table. The resulting physical model is shown in the Illustration 53:

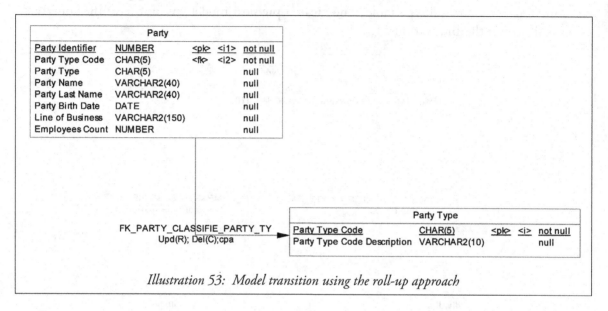

Illustration 53: Model transition using the roll-up approach

Using the *roll-up* model transition approach, the attributes from all subtypes are integrated (rolled-up) into the supertype, creating a single table. However, this approach might result in potential integrity problems. If attributes, local to a particular subtype, are mandatory then it is not possible to integrate them into a single table considering that the values are not always present when the table is populated. In this case, a single integrated table might have a complex set of rules applicable to specific scenarios when data is being populated. This is not a good modeling practice and it should be avoided, however this option is very attractive from the performance optimization perspective considering that data access does not involve any tables join.

The summary of the model transition strategies implemented in PowerDesigner are provided below:

- *Propagate the primary keys only*
    - □ propagate the primary key of the supertype to all subtype tables
    - □ do not propagate supertype to subtype table columns
    - □ do not propagate references defined at the supertype to the subtype tables
- *Roll-down*
    - □ propagate the primary key of the supertype to all subtype tables
    - □ propagate supertype columns to all subtype tables
    - □ propagate all references defined at the supertype to the subtype tables
- *Roll-up*
    - □ integrate all references from the subtypes into the supertype table
    - □ integrate all columns from the subtypes into the supertype table

The rules are implemented automatically by PowerDesigner when you specify the desired model transition option.

6.3.1.3. Transition of the constraints

The transition from the logical to the physical data model has to ensure that business rules stated in the logical model are not accidentally relaxed or completely modified during the transition process. By default the business rules defined in the logical model are transitioned into constraints. Constraints can be enforced by the database or using the application.

The following table shows the constraints created in the physical model during the model transition:

LDM to PDM	Primary Key	Alternate Key	Reference	In-line constraint
Primary identifier	x			
Alternate identifier		x		
Relationship			x	
Attribute constraint				x

Table 17: Cross-reference between the logical and physical data model constraints

DEFINITION: *Primary identifier defined in the logical data model represents an attribute or set of attributes that uniquely identify an instance of an entity.*

DEFINITION: *Primary key defined in the physical data model represents a column or set of columns that uniquely identify a record in a table.*

The model transition creates a corresponding primary key constraint based on the primary identifier defined in the logical model. It is important to state that the primary key constraint implementation in the database will automatically trigger creation of a unique index unless the unique index already exists (in which case the index will be used as an underlying index to enforce the primary key constraint), so it is not required to explicitly create an index to support the primary key constraint.

DEFINITION: *The alternate identifier is a unique constraint enforced by the database. An alternate key must have at least one column mandatory.*

By specifying an alternate identifier in the logical data model we can choose to propagate it as a unique constraint or a unique index. The difference is subtle: an alternate key is a constraint supported (enforced) by unique index while unique index is a stand-alone index. The functionality is effectively the same.

DEFINITION: *A reference is a type of constraint defined and enforced by the database, trigger or programmatically. Each reference is physical implementation of a relationship from the logical model.*

Each relationship is defined as:

- *identifying*—states that a dependent (child) entity cannot be fully identified by its attributes requiring that the primary identifier from the parent entity is to be *entirely* included in the child's primary identifier. The existence of the child entity instance is dependent on the existence of the parent entity instance
- *non-identifying (dependent)*—states that dependent entity can be fully identified by its own attributes. Each entity, the parent and the child, related via the non-identifying relationship type have their own, independent primary identifiers. Additionally the non-identifying relationship type has two options:
  - □ mandatory parent
  - □ optional parent

Based on the type of relationship, the model transition rules differ:

- **identifying relationship:**
  - □ the primary identifier of the child entity will have the parent's primary identifier entirely included in its structure. The model transition step will perform the following:
    - o create a child table's with its primary key comprising of combined columns of the primary keys of parent and child tables
    - o establish[86] the *CASCADE DELETE* referential integrity rule between the parent and child tables
- **non-identifying relationship with mandatory parent entity:**
  - □ primary identifier of the child table will be independent of the primary key of the parent table
  - □ CASCADE DELETE referential integrity rule will be specified between the parent and child tables
- **non-identifying relationship with optional parent entity:**
  - □ primary identifier of the child table will be independent of the primary key of the parent table
  - □ *SET NULL* referential integrity rule will be specified between the parent and child tables

Classification of the relationship types provided here is to describe the nature of the relationships and impact on the implementation in the physical model.

Constraints defined at the attribute level will result in the creation of in-line column-level constraints in the physical model.

---

[86] If the CASCADE rule is defined as required in the model transition.

6.3.1.4. Transition from logical to physical data domains

Logical data domains standardization is one of the requirements for efficient modeling process. In the preparation step, logical data domains were defined and the model transition process creates the corresponding physical data domains. The definition of each logical data domain includes the database-specific data types that are used as the target data types during the model transition.

Logical data modeling concentrates on business analysis trying to document the business rules and data structures. Initially chosen data types for each logical domain might not be appropriate for the following reasons:

- *performance*—some data types perform better than the other. For instance it is known that the INTEGER is slightly faster than the DECIMAL data type due to physical implementation specifics
- *available range*—sometimes the range applicable to the underlying data type is not sufficient. For instance the range for the data type INTEGER might not be sufficient so we have to use the data type with extended length[87]
- *storage*—storing the data might be challenging due to a records count so the modeler has to choose appropriate data type. For instance the CHARACTER data type uses the fixed while the VARCHAR uses the variable length thus optimizing the storage

The physical modeler has to work with the DBA to specify the data types for each physical data domain. Before performing model transition, the physical modeler must familiarize himself with the data types that will be used for the physical domains. Most of the base data types are defined in ANSI/ISO standard but there is also a variety of platform-specific types that can be used when physical domains are created. For instance, to solve the problem with floating point arithmetic and optimize the speed of calculation in financial applications, IBM's DB2 V9.7 recommends using the DECFLOAT data type instead of FLOAT. The FLOAT[88] data type might introduce accidental imprecision not acceptable for financial applications.

When performing the model transition the following has to be considered:

- for each logical domain, the physical modeler has to specify appropriate data type based on:
  - □ performance considerations
  - □ required range of allowed values
  - □ storage characteristics
- decision has to be made if the physical data domain will be implemented as:
  - □ User Defined Data type (UDT) or
  - □ the base data type

---

[87] The INTEGER data type is commonly used for the table's primary key's data type. For large tables the range for the INTEGER data type might not be sufficient so the compatible data type with extended length is used (e.g. in DB2 the BIGINT is used instead)

[88] Mathematically defined as a first approximation of the number

The best way to demonstrate the effects of the model transition is to provide a simple example starting with the logical model (Illustration 54):

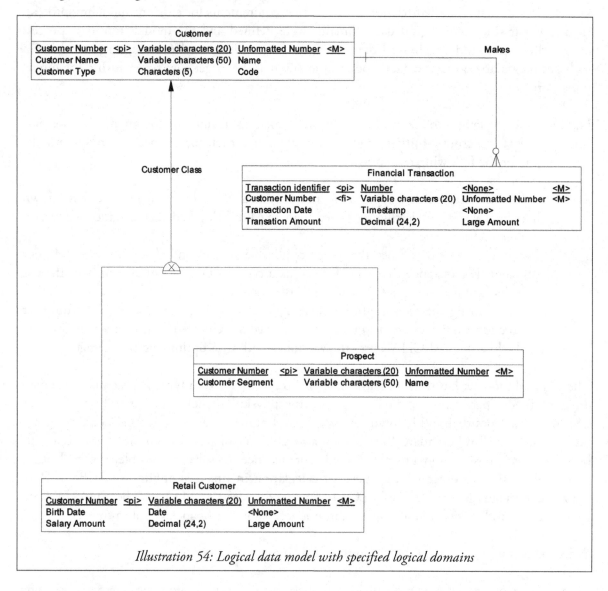

Illustration 54: Logical data model with specified logical domains

The data type for each logical data domain is already specified as shown in the Illustration 55:

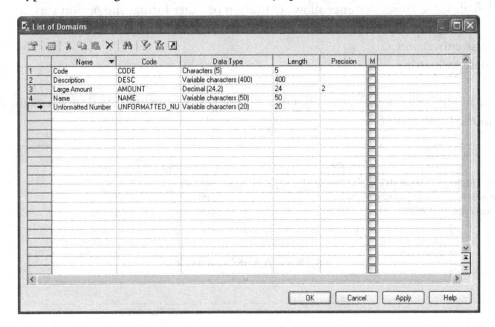

Illustration 55: List of logical and corresponding physical data domains

Along with the underlying data type the modeler can define a constraint that disallows NULL values making the content mandatory by simply checking the box in the M (mandatory) column. Additional data validation for the AMOUNT data domain can be defined to validate the business rule that the AMOUNT has to be in the range between 0 and 100,000 as shown in the Illustration 56:

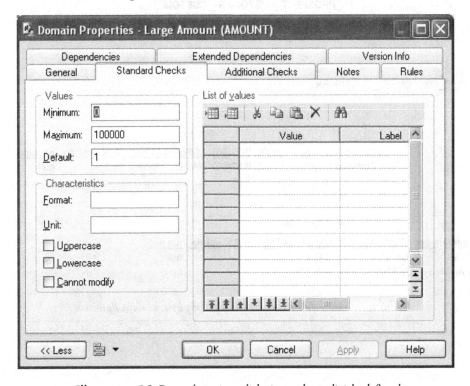

Illustration 56: Data domain validation rule explicitly defined

The AMOUNT logical domain has also a *default* value of *one* defined in the model. In addition to the default value PowerDesigner allows definition of other formatting option such as:

- case conversion
- date formatting

After the model transition, logical domains are converted into the physical data domains as shown in the Illustration 57:

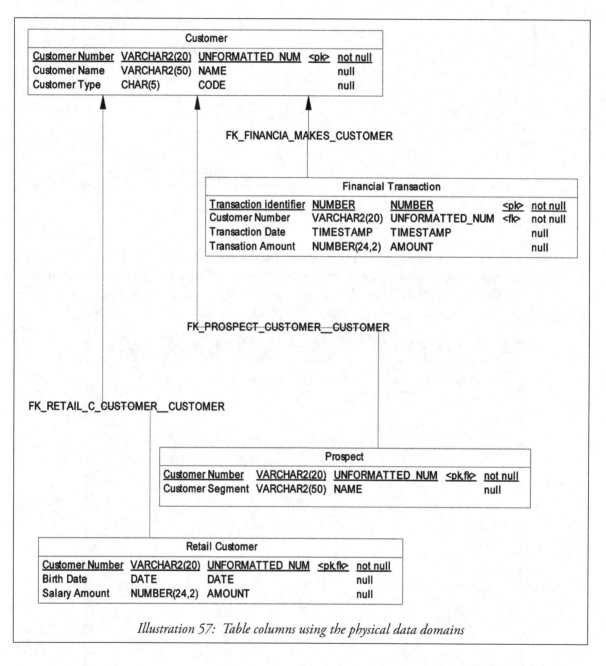

Illustration 57: Table columns using the physical data domains

Even when the physical data domains are used in the model, when generating the DDL code the modeler has options:

- to use the physical data domains or
- implement the underlying (base) data types that are used by the domains

The physical data domains implementation, although attractive from the modeling point of view, might cause some challenges for the developers. When the UDT[89] is used, the developer must specify a conversion function to cast the data between the UDT and the base data type. This is a performance hit as well as additional code complexity, for those reasons the implementation of the UDT is not very popular among the developers.

6.3.1.5. Implementation of the physical naming conventions

Each RDBMS imposes certain rules for object naming:

- object name has a predefined maximum length
- not all characters are allowed in the name. For instance, the name cannot contain *blank space* character
- reserved words should not be used for object names (e.g. try to avoid naming the table a *TABLE* or view a *VIEW*)

PowerDesigner must enforce the physical data model compliance with the naming conventions specific for each database. The conventions are not standardized across different databases and for each database the modeler has to be aware of applicable rules. As part of preparation for the physical data modeling, the modeler has to familiarize himself with the naming conventions for the target database. Failing to follow the database naming conventions will cause problems if the object names have to be changed when the application code is developed.

---

[89] User defined data type

Each database vendor publishes the database naming conventions. Provided here is the naming conventions used in IBM's DB2 and Oracle Corporation's Oracle databases:

Identifier for a data source user (remote-authorization-name)	128
Identifier in an SQL procedure (condition name, for loop identifier, label, result set locator, statement name, variable name)	128
Index name	128
Index extension name	18
Index specification name	128
Label name	128
Namespace uniform resource identifier (URI)	1000
Nickname	128
Package name	128
Package version ID	64
Parameter name	128
Password to access a data source	32
Procedure name	128
Role name	128
Savepoint name	128
Schema name[2]	128
Security label component name	128
Security label name	128
Security policy name	128
Sequence name	128
Server (database alias) name	8
Specific name	128
SQL condition name	128
SQL variable name	128
Statement name	128
Table name	128
Table space name	18

Illustration 58: Object name lengths in IBM's DB2

The list provided here specifies the length of a name for each database object defined in DB2. Exceeding the predefined name length is not allowed and will cause an error when the code is executed. Along with specification of the maximum name lengths for each object type in the database, there is a published list of reserved words that should be avoided when database objects are named. Below is a sample of the reserved words list in IBM's DB2:

---

however, it is recommended that these words not be used as ordinary identifiers, because it reduces pc

For portability across the DB2 database products, the following should be considered reserved words:

ACTIVATE	DOUBLE	LOCATORS	ROLLBACK
ADD	DROP	LOCK	ROUND_CEILING
AFTER	DSSIZE	LOCKMAX	ROUND_DOWN
ALIAS	DYNAMIC	LOCKSIZE	ROUND_FLOOR
ALL	EACH	LONG	ROUND_HALF_DOWN
ALLOCATE	EDITPROC	LOOP	ROUND_HALF_EVEN
ALLOW	ELSE	MAINTAINED	ROUND_HALF_UP
ALTER	ELSEIF	MATERIALIZED	ROUND_UP
AND	ENABLE	MAXVALUE	ROUTINE
ANY	ENCODING	MICROSECOND	ROW
AS	ENCRYPTION	MICROSECONDS	ROWNUMBER
ASENSITIVE	END	MINUTE	ROWS
ASSOCIATE	END-EXEC	MINUTES	ROWSET
ASUTIME	ENDING	MINVALUE	ROW_NUMBER
AT	ERASE	MODE	RRN
ATTRIBUTES	ESCAPE	MODIFIES	RUN
AUDIT	EVERY	MONTH	SAVEPOINT
AUTHORIZATION	EXCEPT	MONTHS	SCHEMA
AUX	EXCEPTION	NAN	SCRATCHPAD
AUXILIARY	EXCLUDING	NEW	SCROLL

Illustration 59: Snapshot of reserved words in IBM's DB2

Similarly Oracle's documentation provides the list of reserved words that should be avoided when database objects are named. The sample list is shown in the Illustration 60:

E Oracle SQL Reserved Words

This appendix lists Oracle SQL reserved words. Words followed by an asterisk (*) are also ANSI reserved words.

Note:
In addition to the following reserved words, Oracle uses system- generated names beginning w subobjects. Oracle discourages you from using this prefix in the names you explicitly provide to conflict in name resolution.

The `V$RESERVED_WORDS` data dictionary view provides additional information on all keywords, including whether *Oracle Database Reference* for more information.

```
ACCESS
ADD *
ALL *
ALTER *
AND *
ANY *
AS *
ASC *
AUDIT
BETWEEN *
BY *
CHAR *
CHECK *
CLUSTER
COLUMN
COMMENT
COMPRESS
CONNECT *
```

Illustration 60: Sample list of reserved words in Oracle 11g

Even for an experienced modeler, keeping track of all reserved words in the database is challenging so the model validation should ensure that the reserved words are not used to name the database objects.

PowerDesigner helps in enforcing the naming conventions in the model by defining the following:

- uniform name derivation rules implemented via the *naming templates*[90]
- maximum object's name length
- characters that should not to be used in the object's name
- character case formatting[91]

The example in the Illustration 61 shows implementation of the naming convention in PowerDesigner using IBM's DB2 as the target database.

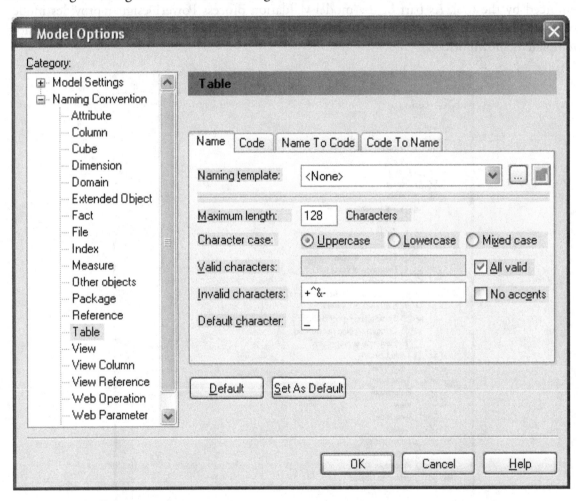

Illustration 61: Enforcement of naming convention options in PowerDesigner

The left pane provides the list of database objects for which the modeler can explicitly specify the naming conventions. In case when specific rules for names conversion are required, the modeler can use the *naming template*. Example shows the definition of the naming conventions

---

[90] Naming template can be defined to perform the logical to physical object name conversion automatically using predefined conversion rules

[91] Important for case sensitive databases

for the database table. Using the default *table naming template* provided in the model options, the tool will apply the following rules[92]:

- the name cannot exceed 128 characters
- the name will be converted to upper characters
- all characters are valid except explicitly specified special characters
- the following special characters are explicitly not allowed: * ^ & -
- default concatenation character is an underscore (_)

Once the naming convention rules for all database objects are defined they will be automatically enforced by the tool. As part of the model validation process PowerDesigner provides model object name checking for compliance with the naming conventions. The model validation template is shown below:

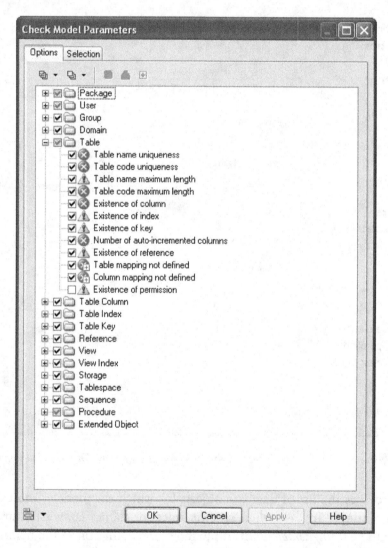

Illustration 62: Model validation template

---

92   As specified

As shown, violation of the *table code maximum length* is reported as an error that has to be fixed before the code is generated. All offending database objects for which the name validation check is specified are reported.

The physical model object names standardization leads to improved model quality and standardized database design, however it is not always a good idea to follow the naming conventions blindly. Strict implementation of the naming convention can sometimes result in inappropriate names derived through automatic object names generation. To be safe, always perform manual validation of the names when the automatic enforcement of naming conventions is used, and modify the object names if required.

6.4. Physical model design

The physical modeling process starts with performing the transition from logical to the physical model. Initially, a limited set of details is defined when the "first-cut" physical model is produced. Although derived physical model is implementable, it is far from being completed. Through the modeling process, the modeler and DBA will gradually model the database objects required for model completion and code generation. However there is always a gray area in defining what needs to be included and what should be out of scope for the physical model.

It is impossible to have a generic specification of elements included in the model considering that the database architectures are not standardized and each database has slightly different set of objects required. The modeler and DBA have to discuss specific objects that should be included in the model. The DBA might retain control of some infrastructure objects that will be included in the model for reference purposes only.

6.4.1. Physical data modeling process

The goal for the physical model is to define a sufficient set of database objects grouped into the following classes:

- *structural objects* (e.g. tables, indexes, views etc)
- *behavioral objects* (e.g. stored procedures, user defined functions, sequences)
- *infrastructure objects* (e.g. tablespaces, buffer pools)
- *permissions*

From the Model Based Environment perspective, the model is used to generate a comprehensive script ready for implementation in the database. Manual code modification should not be needed except in rare situations where the PowerDesigner does not provide required functionality. Advantages of this approach are listed below:

- *repeatability*—script generation is "on-demand"
- *uniformity*—the script generation is consistent because it is automatically generated by PowerDesigner

- *validation*—after implementation model can be compared against the database so the deployment can be validated
- *efficiency*—code generation and model vs. database validation is quick and fully automated

The modeling process assumes that the CASE tool will be used to design and implement model in the database. This book will provide more details on how to efficiently use PowerDesigner to design the implementation-ready physical model.

6.4.2. Target database definition in the physical data model

CASE tools support a variety of RDBMS and different database versions. One of the challenges the CASE tools faces is to keep up with the current version of the supported database. Each tool vendor has a certification process in which they are validating and certifying the CASE tool's functionality for a specific RDBMS version. Behind the scenes, the tool has a knowledge-base relevant to each supported database. Specific technical details are incorporated within the tool itself and they are readily available when you specify the target database.

To understand the complexity of the challenge that tool vendors are faced with, provided here is a short list of database platforms supported in PowerDesigner:

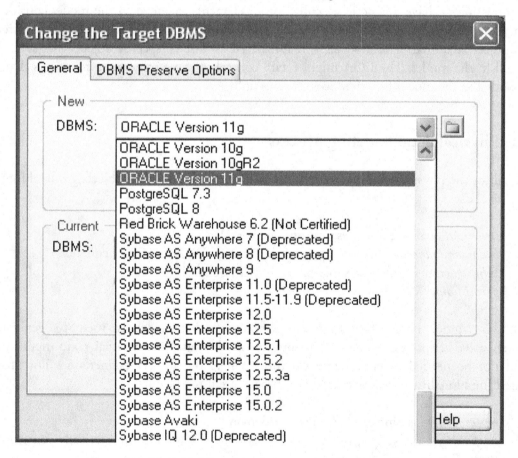

Illustration 63: Partial list of databases supported by PowerDesigner

By looking at the list we can see that some of the database versions are depreciated but still available. The CASE tool has to be able to handle situations in which outdated versions of the database are used. Situations where the reverse-engineered model is needed, the modeler can take advantage of this functionality offered by the tool. When a specific database version is chosen the tool will help by including the options that are specific for the version of the database chosen.

Sometimes, PowerDesigner provides support for a database without completed certification for a specific release. When this is the case the tool can still be used but with caution.

Unfortunately even though significant efforts are invested to provide rich functionality, there are inconsistencies in terms of database support. Generally, the modeling tool can support most options but on occasion, a feature or option may not be available. In such cases we have to find a work-around to include these in the model and subsequently in the code generated by the tool. The problem with work-around solution is that there is no specific meta-data included in the model and it is impossible to validate implementation in the database by comparing the model to the database.

6.4.3. Modeling database objects

The modeling process starts by segregating classes of database objects included in the model into:

- *structural* (e.g. tables, indexes, views)
- *behavioral* (e.g. stored procedures)
- *infrastructure* (e.g. buffer pools, tablespaces)

Although included in the model, not all objects are in the domain of the modeler's responsibility. The modeler has to integrate input from various participants and structure the components creating a model that can ultimately be used to generate the code for database implementation. The Illustration 64 shows the interaction between the participants in the physical modeling process:

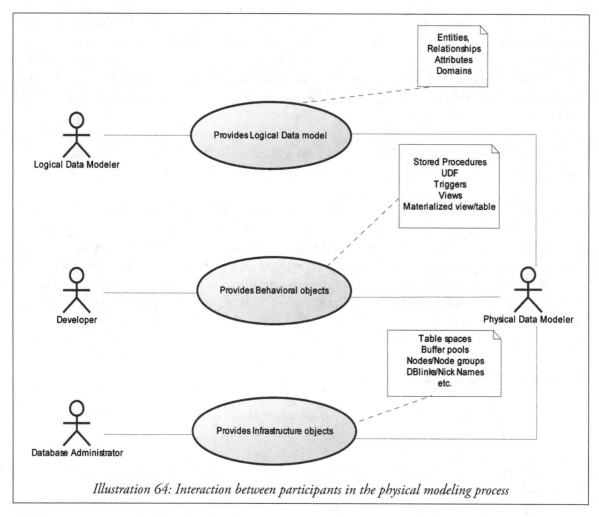

Illustration 64: Interaction between participants in the physical modeling process

The starting point for the physical model is a completed logical model provided by the logical modeler. The fist-cut physical model is created during the model transition process.

From the application development perspective, the development team provides the code for various behavioral components. The challenge with the application code is that applications use various technologies making it difficult to store the code in the model. For instance, in Oracle and DB2, stored procedures defined in Java, C can be included along with the regular stored procedures and functions defined in the standard database scripting language (PL/SQL for Oracle or SQL PL for DB2), but the design might include components defined in unsupported programming languages causing administration problems for code management. The decision should be made if the behavioral code should be included in the model or not. If the decision is to include the behavioral components in the model, the following advantages are expected:

- the model becomes the *central code repository* providing a centralized solution for all components
- model validation against the database includes also the *code validation*. Each deployment can be quickly validated by comparing the model and database
- *code deployment* can be performed from the model

The decision to include behavioral objects in the model certainly has some disadvantages too:

- CASE tools that support data modeling are usually not cheap so extensive number of users equipped with PowerDesigner might not be justifiable from the cost perspective
- PowerDesigner is an excellent data modeling tool but including the stored procedures, functions and other behavioral objects might encounter some problems if the deployment requires very specific compiling or binding options[93]
- corporate standard might require that a centralized code repository already in place is used instead of the model repository offered by PowerDesigner

When deciding on storing the behavioral system components in the model, the team has to take into consideration all advantages and disadvantages that PowerDesigner offers. Rushed or uninformed decision might have a heavy impact on the overall project progress and team efficiency.

6.4.4. Working with your DBA

The modeling process is a collaborative effort between the physical modeler and the DBA. Creating a physical model requires that a modeler has knowledge and solid understanding of database technology. However we cannot expect that modeler has the same level of expertise as the DBA. Therefore the team responsible for data modeling has to include the DBA who will provide more specialized technical expertise during the model design. Failing to include the DBA will potentially result in the following:

- *high risk of sub-optimal model design*—the physical data model is not limited to the tables and indexes only. Many other performance-improving techniques can be used to optimize the database performance and space utilization. Expertise, provided by the DBA plays a crucial role in optimized model design and collaboration is required on an ongoing basis
- *omissions of component required for complete model*—complexity of the physical model can be overwhelming and it is a good idea to work with the DBA to create a list of object classes that will be included in the model. The list of modeled components will help the modeler to avoid any omissions that will be discovered later during the model review

---

[93] For instance: isolation level, optimization level etc.

Before the modeler and DBA start working together certain expectations should be set. Setting the expectations within the modeling team is important to avoid potential misunderstandings and confusion in terms of responsibilities. The following illustration defines expectations that the physical modeler has from the DBA:

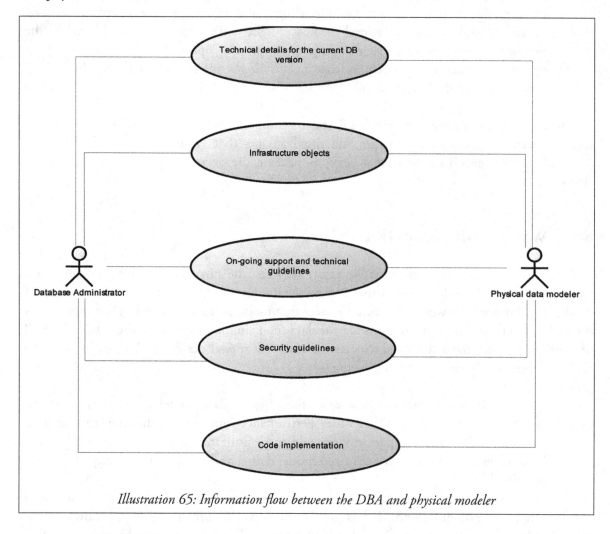

Illustration 65: Information flow between the DBA and physical modeler

The database administrator (DBA) has to provide technical information about the database and environment where the database resides:

- database version and release number (e.g. Oracle 11g R1)
- database server. Usually the URL or the IP address is provided
- port (e.g. 1521)
- user identification and password to access the database
- required permissions to perform the work[94]
- storage information

---

[94] As the project progresses moving the database from the development closer to the production environment, more and more access restrictions are put in place. This is normal and expected, so the modeler can expect very wide authorizations (e.g. to directly deploy the code) only in the

- tablespaces name and type
- buffer pools

The modeler has to be aware of the infrastructure objects included in the model. Usually these are under the DBA's control and physical model is synchronized with the database by reverse engineering infrastructure objects into the model.

On-going support by providing information on various optimization techniques, instructions on the security requirements and specifics about the code structuring and implementation is in the DBA's domain of responsibilities. Once included in the model, these components can be further modeled by the modeler.

Parallel with the physical model development, the DBA will start with creating the development database. The development database is usually created with low maintenance in mind. To minimize the administration effort the development database can be created using automated storage maintenance. For instance, in Oracle database it is a good idea to use OMF[95]. Both Oracle and DB2 supports the ASM[96] providing an automated alternative for minimal database administration.

Although the database administration costs might make the simplified infrastructure implementation attractive, it is a good idea to mimic the final production environment in all environments-at least structurally. Having the set of models that are very similar will help the model promotion explained later in this book.

6.4.5. Modeling structural database objects

Structural database objects are the objects that store data (e.g. tables, indexes etc.) or other static objects (e.g. schemas). These objects do not have components that are executable in nature.

6.4.5.1. Schemas

The logical model will contain groups of entities known as *subject areas*. The goal is to create a cohesive logical unit comprising of entities and corresponding relationships, useful for analysis. Although beneficial for understanding the business rules and data structures during the discussion with business analysts, subject areas are usually not directly transferred to the database schemes. Comparing to the subject areas defined in the logical model, grouping tables

---

development environment. Every other environment will have restrictions allowing the modeler to have read-only access to the database.

[95] Oracle Managed Files (OMF) is database implementation that requires minimal database administration making it very cost-efficient

[96] Automated Storage Management

and corresponding references into schemes has a goal to improve manageability of the logically related physical model components.

When the database structural objects[97] are created, object name implicitly includes the schema. The database object[98] can be referenced by the name using the partial or full reference. Object referenced by the full name includes the schema name. Very quickly it becomes obvious that having plenty of schema names creates confusion with the developers requiring them to use the schema name, explicitly when referencing the object name.

To simplify the referencing, synonyms[99] can be used allowing transparent access to the database object. Creating synonyms does not create a performance problem but it definitely complicates the database administration by increasing the number of objects to be administered.

When modeling the schema consider the following guidelines:

- mark structural objects[100] in each schema with the same color. Colors can be used effective at distinguishing tables in different schemas
- distinguish between the schema from the implementation perspective and physical diagram created to show logically related objects:
  - physical diagram should include related tables in a specific schema to help better understand the concept modeled in the schema
  - implementation schema should include objects that reside in the same physical schema
  - avoid putting excessive number of tables in the schema
- *group tables* into schemas based on the same or similar:
  - *backup strategy*. A schema can group tables that have the same backup strategy. One solution is to design the storage landscape aligning the schemas with the tablespaces so that backup can incorporate logically consistent set of objects stored in the schema
  - *volatility*. Tables can be segregated into different schemes based on the frequency of modifications
  - *access profile*. For instance a schema can be created for the read-only tables

Physical schema design should include the DBA who is well aware of existing corporate backup strategy and all pertinent details. The modeler should understand that failing to consider the backup strategy when designing the model, can severely impact the database performance and availability.

---

[97] Tables, references, views and materialized views
[98] For instance a table or view
[99] For the concept of Alternate Name Oracle is using SYNONYM and DB2 is using ALIAS. DB2
[100] Tables, views and materialized views/query tables

6.4.5.2. Schema creation procedure

The physical modeler together with the DBA is responsible for the schema creation. Understanding the relationship between the schema and user is important for their implementation. Generally CASE tools are taking the approach that the schema and user are synonymous as modeling objects. However the relationship between the schema and the user is a bit more complex.

Both Oracle and DB2 databases define the schema as logical grouping of objects. There is a subtle difference between the treatments of user-schema relationship between the two databases:

- in Oracle the user is created along with the schema
- DB2 is using authentication performed by the operating system (external authentication) so the concept of a user is completely independent of the schema object

In both databases the user that creates the schema is authorized as the schema owner.

While performing the transition from the logical to physical model, the modeler can define a default schema ownership effectively defining the default user. The physical modeling process will continue with refining the derived schemes. An overview of the schema management procedure is provided in the Illustration 66.

The process starts with the physical modeler implementing the schemes in the model. The logical model defined the initial set of subject areas that are the foundation for diagrams in the physical model. These are not the schemas to be created in the database.

The physical modeler and DBA's responsibility is to define schemes for physical database implementation. These will be defined as users in the model and used for object ownership when the database objects are modeled.

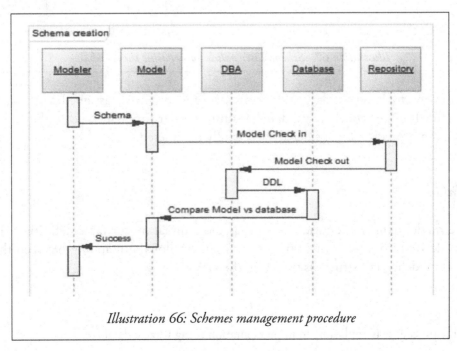

Illustration 66: Schemes management procedure

127

After checking-out the model, the DBA will create schema by specifying the schema name and authorization (ownership). After the implementation, the physical model is compared with the database to ensure that the list of schemes corresponds to what was defined in the model. The Illustration 67 demonstrates the model comparison against the database in IBM's DB2[101].

The list of users is shown and modeler has to choose the users that will be included in the model. Each user will correspond to the schema defined in the model. However, it is not required that all users have a corresponding schema.

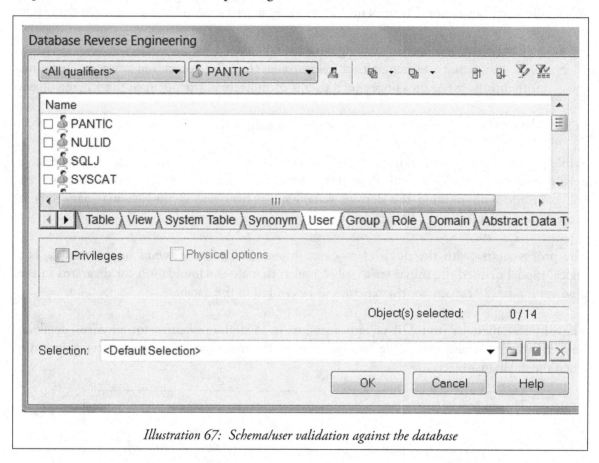

Illustration 67: Schema/user validation against the database

For each user the tool can validate the permissions and privileges assigned to the user. Once the users defined in the model are validated against the users implemented in the database, the implementation procedure is considered successfully completed.

6.4.5.3. Tables

During the model transition entities are used as the foundation for table definition. The table structure is derived from an entity structure using the following mapping between the logical and physical modeling constructs as shown in the table 18.

---

[101] The same procedure is applicable to implementation using Oracle database.

Logical construct	Derived physical construct
Entity	Table
Attribute	Column
Business rule	Constraint[102]

Table 18: Cross-reference between the logical and physical constructs

Table definition in the physical model requires the following:

- *table ownership*—the schema where table resides
- *table physical name*—the name of the table. It must comply with the naming conventions enforced in the database
- *table definition*—business definition of the table content. Both Oracle and DB2 implement the definition as a *comment*
- *table physical details*—additional details important for implementation such as: compression, logging etc.
- *table columns*—by creating the columns, the modeler defines the table's structure
- *column definition*—business definition of the column's content. The definition is implemented as a *comment*
- *column physical details*—detailed column definition including: data type, default value, in-line constraints etc.
- *table and column-level constraints*—primary, alternate, foreign and in-line constraints

For instance, the Illustration 68 shows an example of the table properties definition in PowerDesigner.

Some of the components defined in the table definition screen will result in code generation and some of them won't. As a minimum for each table is the name and table's structure (columns). If the owner[103] is not defined, the schema name default for the user that deploys the code will be used.

The number of rows, if defined, will provide information to the PowerDesigner to estimate the database size. In case that data model is using the Dimensional modeling technique, the table can be classified as a fact or dimension table by specifying the *dimension type*. The *object type* allows the PowerDesigner to work with *relational* and *object oriented* modeling techniques by defining the *relational* table or an *object*.

---

[102] Implementation of the business rule in the physical model can take different forms. For instance the rule can be implemented as a constraint, trigger or procedure or a server expression.

[103] Database schema

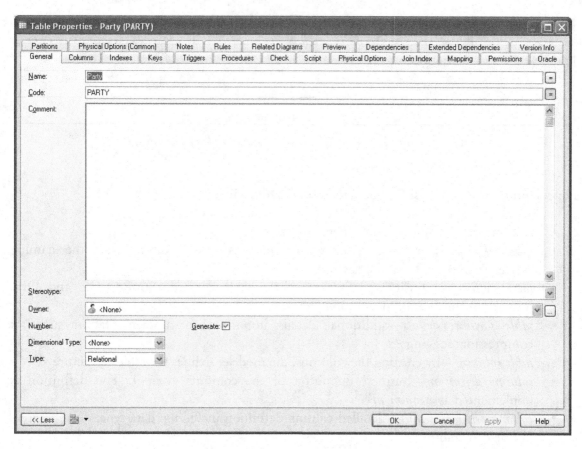

Illustration 68: Example of the table definition in PowerDesigner

The table design requires specification of the physical details. If the table organization is not specified, the table is considered to be the heap (regular) table. List of the table's physical details is provided in the table 19:

Physical characteristic	Required[104]	Default value
Table type (database dependent; e.g. heap, index-organized clustered etc.)	No	heap
Tablespace	No	predefined
Partitioning strategy	No	no partitions
Partitions	No	no partitions
Parallelism	No	no parallelism
Compression	No	no compression

Table 19: Table-level physical options

---

[104] If the parameter is not defined, the default value is used.

The table physical options are dependent on the database platform and version for which the model is created.

Although the CASE tools offers comprehensive tables design capabilities surprisingly low number of modelers are fully utilizing it for various reasons:

- lack of knowledge or understanding of the table and column related options
- lack of DBA cooperation

Instead of providing a full table design, frequent approach taken by the physical modelers is to create the DDL script that will have the basic tables CREATE statements including the referential integrity and let the DBA finish the work by adding all the physical options required for the full implementation-ready code. This approach causes the following problems:

- implementation cycle duration is prolonged because the DBA has to work on the code provided by the modeler
- physical modeler is usually not aware of the implementation details until the code is actually by the DBA. The DBA is usually performing code modifications in complete isolation from the physical modeler. Furthermore, before the code modifications are implemented, the modeler is rarely informed about the modifications

The approach promoted in this book requires that the physical design is implemented as a joint effort of the modeling team. The physical modeler and DBA should work on producing the final version of the model. By positioning the database design as a team effort rather than a responsibility of the modeler, joint ownership of the final deliverable (the model) is built.

It is important to mention that modelers will encounter strong opposition when trying to introduce the Model Based Environment. Developers and DBA who were not exposed to physical modeling will perceive the model creation as unnecessary task that is slowing down the progress of the development effort. Initially, the modeling will require more time giving impression that the development is negatively impacted by the progress in data modeling. However, once the model is in place and database is synchronized with the model, making any modification to the model and the database is much faster and error-free if done through the model than manually by the DBA.

From the table physical design perspective the following benefits are expected when the modeling tool is used:

- tables are always uniformly and consistently created with the same structure and physical characteristics
- tables structure with their physical characteristics can be compared against the physical implementation in the database allowing us to validate the deployment

The following example demonstrates the table design process.

Table design starts with defining the basic table meta-data: table name, schema and comment as shown in the Illustration 69:

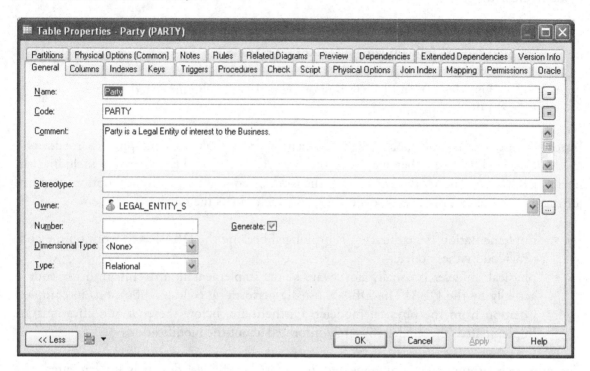

Illustration 69: Definition of the basic table meta-data: name, schema and comment

The table name is the only mandatory element. Other table properties are optional and default values are used as explained previously.

By providing the number of records per table, the modeler can use the PowerDesigner to calculate the database size taking into consideration:

- table column with specific data types and their physical lengths in bytes
- indexes

Each table must have at least one column defined, so the next task is to create the table structure by defining the columns[105]:

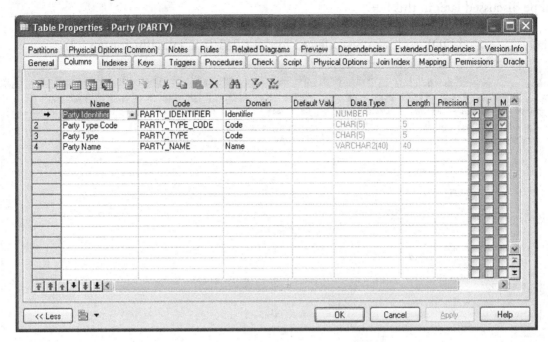

Illustration 70: Table structure definition

After defining the table's structure, the table's physical details are specified as shown in the Illustration 71:

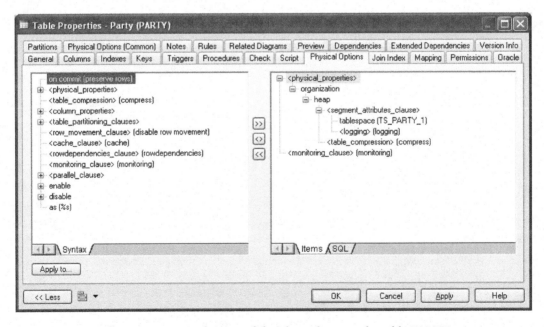

Illustration 71: Definition of the Physical options for table PARTY

---

[105]   If the physical model is derived from the logical, the initial table structure is already created

Additionally, to optimize the data access, indexes should be created. Index creation requires the involvement of a DBA who will provide technical guidelines for index creation. Index creation will be discussed later in this book.

Finally, generated DDL code can be reviewed in the *PREVIEW* tab (Illustration 72):

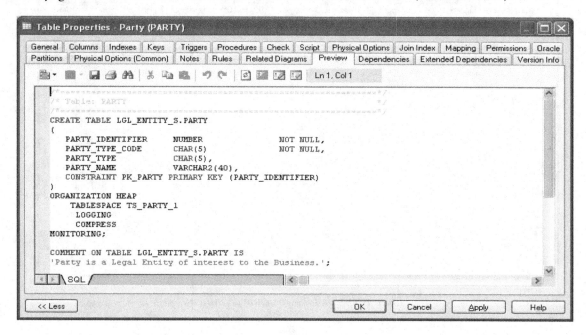

Illustration 72: DDL code generated based on table details specification

The *preview* option in PowerDesigner offers opportunity to review the code that will be generated for specific database object. To efficiently utilize the *preview* option it is important to understand how it works. Code generation from PowerDesigner requires creation of a profile to specify how the code will be generated as shown below:

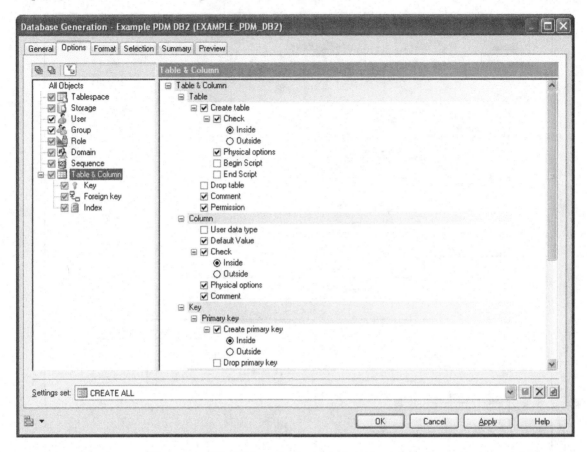

Illustration 73: Table and column code generation options

The database generation options are object type-sensitive. The example shows options that are available for the table code generation. Chosen options per object type are active when the code is previewed in the object preview pane. Therefore, the modeler has to be sure that appropriate options are active while the generated code is previewed.

6.4.5.4. Table creation procedure

The procedure for table creation is described in the following sequence diagram shown in the Illustration 74:

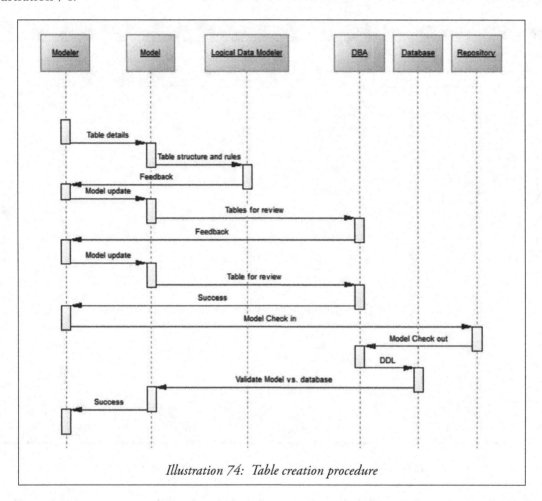

Illustration 74: Table creation procedure

After the transition from the logical to physical model, the modeler starts with the table design. The tool is used to store the table details including the structure, constraints and physical parameters. Following completion of the design, the model is reviewed by the logical modeler. The review includes the following:

- assessment of the table's structure completeness
- format and data types validation
- assessment of the business rules implementation (e.g. in-line constraints, mandatory/ optional constraints)

The review has to ensure that the business rules and corresponding data structures defined in the logical model are properly implemented in the physical model. Based on the review's feedback, the physical model is modified and submitted to the DBA for review. The physical model review by the DBA is significantly different from the review performed in the previous step. The DBA will assess the technical aspects of the model's design including:

136

- naming conventions implementation
- referential integrity implementation
- existence and appropriate use of indexes
- applicable table physical options (e.g. various storage-related parameters etc.)
- partitioning strategy (if partitioning is used)
- column physical options (e.g. GENERATED columns)
- appropriate use of data types and UDT

The DBA provides feedback to the physical modeler who is responsible for model modification as per DBA's input. The challenge that the physical modeler faces is that model modifications proposed by the DBA might not take into account complex data integrity rules. The emphasis of the DBA's recommendations is mostly on the database performance and storage. The version that is ready for implementation is checked into the repository.

The DBA checks-out model from the repository and generates the DDL. The DDL implementation in the database is followed by comparison of the physical model against the database. Successful comparison completes the procedure.

In the development environment the procedure can be relaxed by allowing the physical modeler to implement the model directly to the database.

6.4.5.5. Synonyms

Database objects can be referenced by alternate names providing locational transparency to the user.

DEFINITION: *Synonym represents an alternate name that is used to reference a database object.*

Although the concept of a *synonym* is the same in both Oracle and DB2, the syntax differs. Instead of synonym the reserved word *alias* is used in DB2. The synonym's visibility can be classified as a *public* or *private*. The *public* visibility allows the synonym access to all authenticated database users while a *private* visibility limits the access to the user that defined the synonym. Synonyms with *public* visibility should be used with caution because of potential security problems.

A synonym requires definition of the following elements:

- schema where the synonym resides
- synonym name
- synonym scope[106]
- base object[107] for which the synonym is defined

---

[106] Private synonym, visible by a particular user or Public synonym visible by all users.
[107] Synonym can be defined for various objects, not just tables.

The following illustration demonstrates the synonym creation for a table:

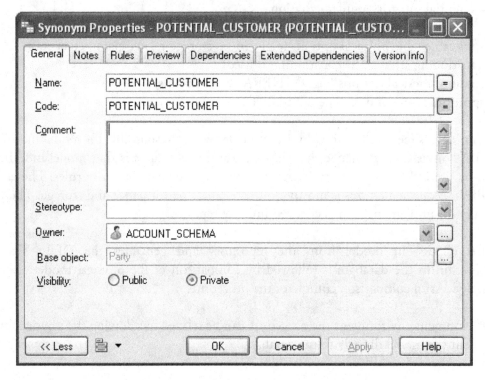

Illustration 75: Table's synonym definition

The DDL code preview is shown in the Illustration 76:

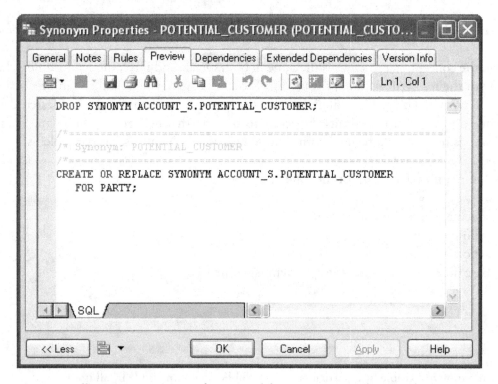

Illustration 76: DDL code generated for synonym (RDBMS Oracle)

The synonym's implementation requires slightly different syntax in DB2:

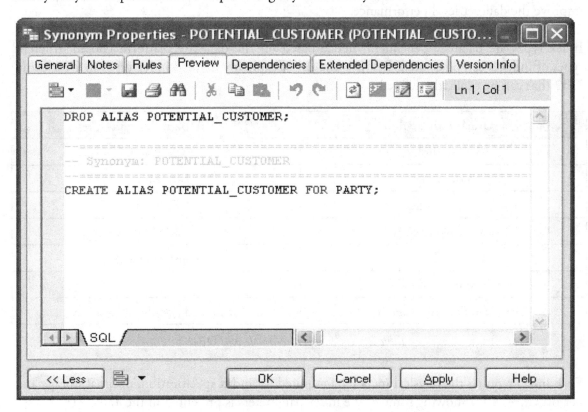

Illustration 77: DDL generated for synonym (RDBMS DB2)

Synonyms are used to simplify the reference to a database object. User must have access to the base object for which the synonym is defined. When the base object is dropped the synonym is invalidated (orphan) and it has to be dropped explicitly.

6.4.5.6. Indexes

Index design is perceived by modelers more as a "black magic" rather than exact science because of limited understanding of the functionality provided by an index. The general perception is that whenever there is a performance problem, solution is to create more and more indexes hoping that the problem will disappear. This is not always true. Sometimes it is actually faster to do a dreaded full table scan rather than scanning an index and then retrieving the data based on the index scan. Data is never retrieved record by record! The database always retrieves blocks of data so if the data distribution is not favorable (in-line with the corresponding index) we might end-up hurting the database performance. Performance is also impacted when the data is inserted, modified or deleted because the index maintenance has to be performed at the same time.

This book will not get into detail index design. The modelers should understand the basics of indexing while working with the DBA to come up with optimal indexing strategy. Each index has potentially positive performance benefits on data retrieval but definitely negative impact on insert, update and data delete. Therefore indexes should not be blindly created hoping to improve the data retrieval performance.

Index types are database-dependent, hence based on the database platform chosen different types of indexes can be created. Below is the list of explicitly defined index types in Oracle and DB2 that can be explicitly defined:

Oracle index type	DB2 index type
Unique index	Unique index
B-tree index	B-tree index
Bit map index	
Bit-map join index	
Clustered index	Clustered index
Function based index	
Partitioned (locally and globally)	Partitioned (locally and globally)

Table 20: Index types in Oracle and DB2

Each index requires the physical meta-data required for index specification, optimal storage and performance. A list showing some of the index parameters is presented in the Table 21:

Index component	Required	Default value
Schema where index is created	No	Table's schema for which the index is defined
Index name[108]	Yes	
Index type	No	B-tree index
Columns included in index	Yes	
Columns order	No	Ascending
Inactive columns[109]	No	
Uniqueness	Yes	Non-unique
Clustered	No	Not clustered

Table 21: Index parameters

---

[108] Index name is not always required. If the index is built to support a unique or primary constraint the index name is automatically specified by the database

[109] DB2 only

Each database has some specific set of parameters related to the index storage characteristics and performance optimization. For instance the table 22 lists such parameters in DB2 and Oracle databases:

Physical options for Oracle index	Required	Default value
Tablespace	No	Tablespace of the Table for which index is defined
Index Partitioning	No	Not partitioned
Specification only[110]	No	
Page split[111]	No	
Percent free	No	Database specific default value
Percent used	No	Database specific default value
Reverse[112] scan index	No	
Parallelism	No	No parallelism
Visibility[113]	No	Visible

Table 22: Physical options available for indexes (Oracle and DB2)

Index creation does not always solve the problem with the database performance. Existence of an index is always detrimental for the data maintenance performance slowing down the data insert, update and delete. Despite this, many still seem to believe that another index will speed up access.

---

[110] DB2 only

[111] DB2 only

[112] Oracle only

[113] Oracle only

Below is an example demonstrating the creation of an index in Oracle using PowerDesigner. We start with defining the basic elements of an index such as the index name and schema where the index resides:

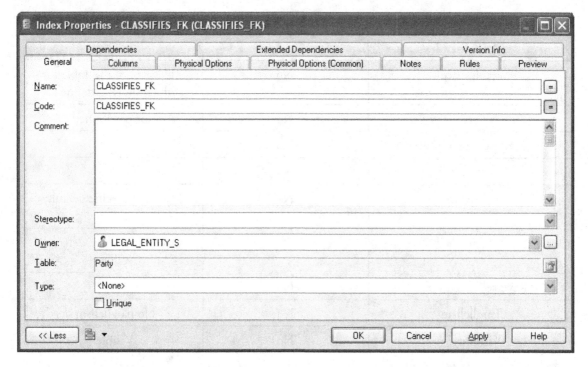

Illustration 78: Definition of basic index components: name, schema and type

The index type is specific to Oracle:

- regular (B-tree) index—optimized for data with high cardinality
- bit-map index—typical for fast data retrieval of data with low data cardinality

When defining the index structure pay attention to the following:

- *column order*—order the columns so that the resulting set returns the least number of records
- *column length*—having a column or columns with excessive length can negatively impact the index performance and required storage space
- *sort order*—data can be ordered in ascending (default) or descending order. This is important when the index is used for sorting

The index in our example has to support the foreign key. The following is the definition of the index structure in PowerDesigner (Illustration 79):

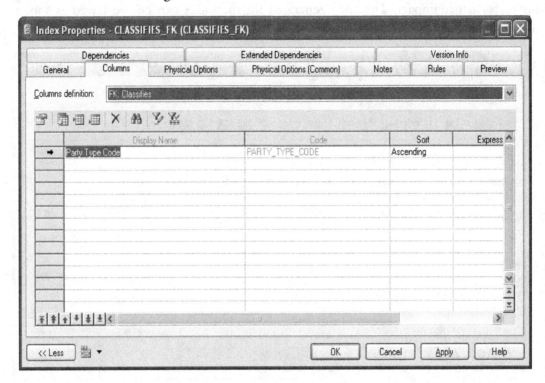

Illustration 79: Definition of the index structure

For demonstration purposes we defined just a few physical options as show in the Illustration 80:

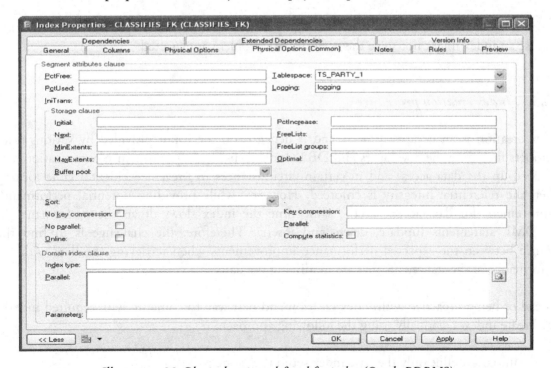

Illustration 80: Physical options defined for index (Oracle RDBMS)

Complexity and number of parameters require careful index design. The DBA should be involved in index design and parameters specification considering that each parameter can have serious performance impact. The code generated for the index can be previewed as shown in the Illustration 81:

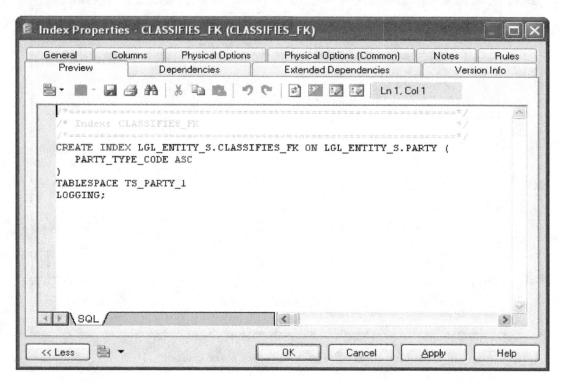

Illustration 81: Generated code for an index creation (Oracle RDBMS)

Again, it should be emphasized that thorough problem analysis should precede index creation because an index might not solve the performance problem as expected.

6.4.5.7. Index creation procedure

Index creation is an iterative process and it depends on the input provided by various team members including the developers and DBA. Index is used as a performance optimization tool to speed-up the data access and in certain circumstances to prevent accidental table locking when the referential integrity is enforced. However, while providing potential performance improvement for data access, at the same time the index slows down the performance of the DML statements (update, delete and insert). Therefore, the challenge is to find the balance between the expected performance improvements when retrieving the data with the performance of the statements that are modifying the data.

Instead of being proactive with index creation and best way to come up with required indexes is to create indexes gradually using the following approach:

- initially, define only the base index set in the model:

- ☐ *primary key* indexes[114]
- ☐ *unique* indexes[115]
- ☐ indexes that *support the foreign keys*
- define additional indexes when you understand the following:
  - ☐ *access pattern*—the database optimizer plan for the SQL statements
  - ☐ *frequency of data access* for:
    - o data retrieval
    - o data modifications
  - ☐ *data distributions*—index performance heavily depends on the data distributions
  - ☐ *join strategy*—statements that are performing table joins can usually benefit from indexes. However, column cardinality compared to the table size (record count in the table) has to be assessed to use the appropriate index type[116]
  - ☐ *frequency of DML*[117] (insert, update, delete and merge) and query operations—creating indexes that will speed-up the statements that are issued infrequently is usually not a good idea considering that the index requires space to be stored and processing cycles to be maintained

Index design is a task where heavy involvement from the DBA and developers is expected. The DBA has to provide technical knowledge about the index while the developers are responsible for providing the SQL statements used to access and manipulate the data (insert, update and delete).

Assuming that the initial index set is created as recommended, when performance problems with data access is identified, the procedure outlined in the Illustration 82 can be used to assess if an index can improve the performance.

When performance problem is identified the DBA has to assess the optimizer access plan to understand the source of the problem. Adding index without doing a root-cause analysis is not an optimal solution for the following reasons:

- index might not rectify the problem, actually it can make it even worst
- even if index fixes the problem, it might have a negative lateral effect on other queries not taken into consideration during the problem analysis
- there might be an existing index that can be used[118]

---

[114] When you create a primary key constraint, the index is automatically created for you by the database. In the case when the unique index exists before the creation of the primary key constraint, the constraint will re-use the index already in place

[115] Behavior is similar to the indexes created to support the primary key constraint. The difference between the primary and unique Constraint is that some columns in the unique constraint might be optional while the primary key constraint requires all the columns in its structure to be mandatory.

[116] For instance, in Oracle an index that supports column with high cardinality can be created as a B-tree index while an index on the column with low cardinality can use a Bit-map index type

[117] Stands for Data Manipulation Language

[118] Oracle provides an index skip scan feature allowing index to be used even if leading index columns are excluded from the search

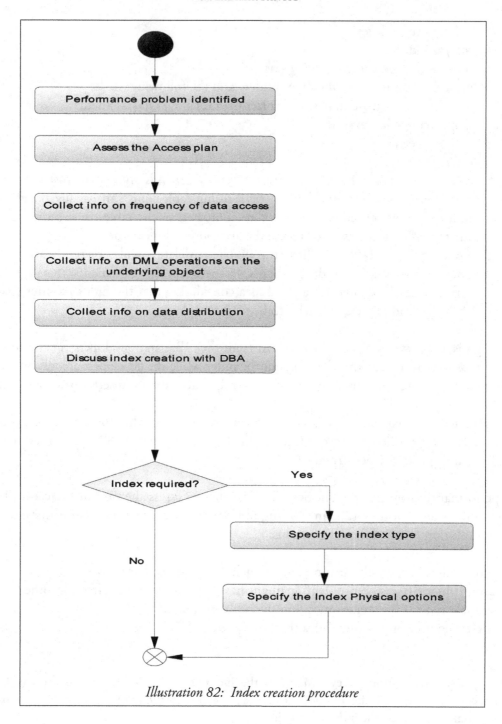

Illustration 82: Index creation procedure

The modeler and DBA have to discuss the index design and impact it will have. If index is required then index type and physical options have to be specified before the index is recorded in the model.

6.4.5.8. References

Relationships are converted to references during the transition from logical into the physical data model. The transition process will establish the default referential integrity rules in the physical model. To further explain the details the following physical model will be used:

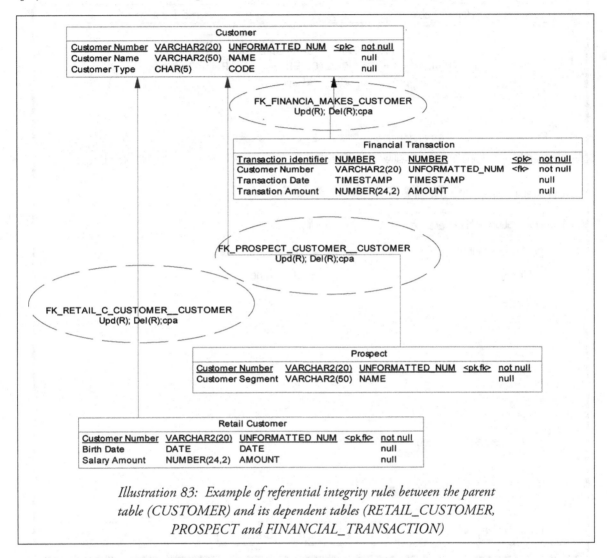

Illustration 83: Example of referential integrity rules between the parent table (CUSTOMER) and its dependent tables (RETAIL_CUSTOMER, PROSPECT and FINANCIAL_TRANSACTION)

Each reference implemented in the database enforces the integrity rules for the *insert, delete* and *update* database actions. Each reference that defines an integrity rule between two tables can have two states:

- *enabled*—the reference is enforced by the database
- *disabled*—the reference is not enforced by the database

The actions, enforced by the referential integrity rules, can be further specified in the tool (Illustration 84):

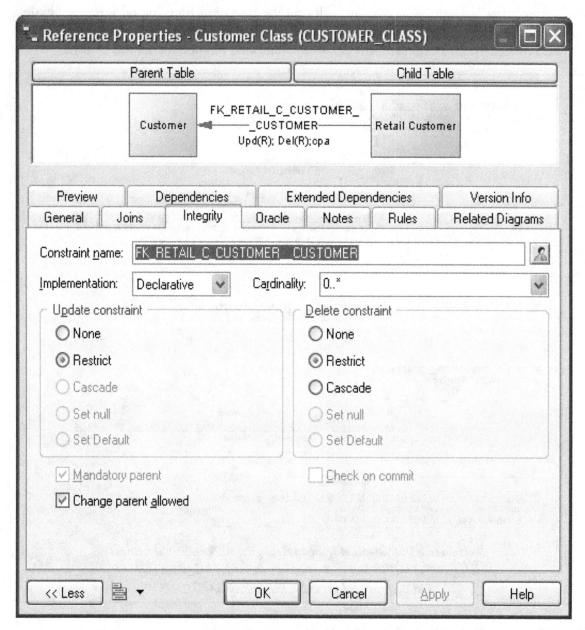

Illustration 84: Definition of the referential integrity rule in PowerDesigner

The specification for the referential integrity rules is strictly dependent on the database platform for which the physical model is designed. PowerDesigner allows implementation of the referential integrity rules in both directions: from dependent to the parent table and vice versa. The referential integrity rules can be implemented and enforced in various ways:

- using the database engine
- using triggers
- using the application code

In PowerDesigner the referential integrity rule can be implemented by either the declaration[119] or using the trigger. Declarative implementation of the referential integrity rule will create a reference as an object with explicit enforcement by the database. If a trigger is used, referential integrity is enforced via the code embedded in the trigger allowing for more complex rules comparing to the database enforced referential integrity. The following illustration shows the reference specification using PowerDesigner:

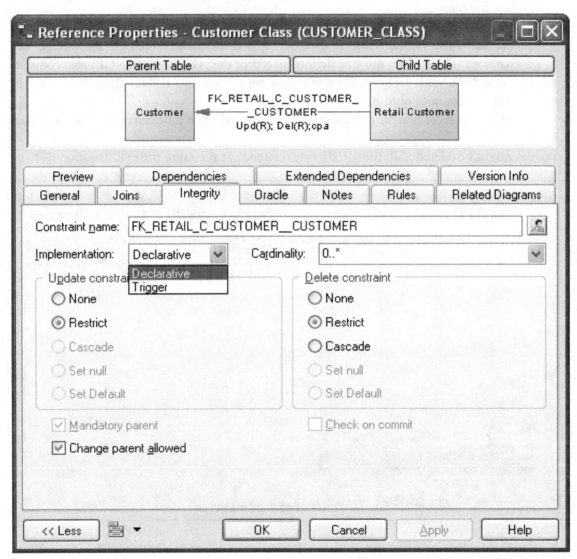

Illustration 85: Referential integrity implementation in PowerDesigner

---

[119] Database enforced

Data integrity controlled by the referential integrity rules defines actions performed on *insert*, *update* and *delete* activities to the related tables. The following rules can be explicitly defined and implemented either declaratively or using the database triggers is:

- *none*—no referential integrity action is performed
- *restrict*—the rule restricts the action if there is a record in the child table that would violate the rule
- *cascade*:
  - □ *set null*—the NULL value is used to replace the value stored in the foreign key column. The column must be defined to accept the NULL value (NULLable column)
  - □ *set default*—the default value for the column is used to replace the value stored in the foreign key column
  - □ *delete*[120]—records in the dependent table are deleted when the referenced record is deleted

Two tables might be related with more than one reference at the same time (Illustration 86):

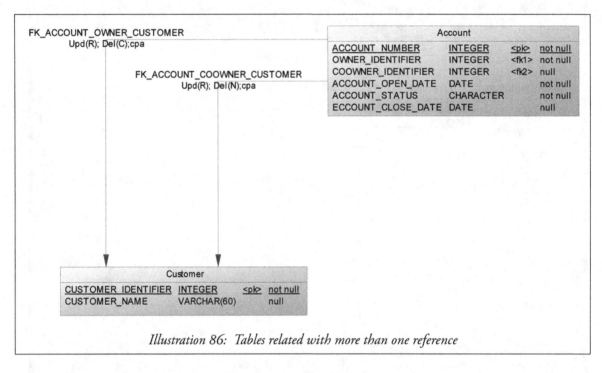

Illustration 86: Tables related with more than one reference

Each relationship between the two entities is transitioned into a separate reference. When creating multiple references between two tables the modeler has to be careful to establish the referential integrity properly. Each created reference propagates the parent's table primary key to the child table. In our example the CUSTOMER_IDENTIFIER column (the primary key in the CUSTOMER table) is propagated twice to the ACCOUNT table:

- owner identifiers
- co-owner identifier

---

[120] Not shown

Each column that holds the foreign key (and therefore supports the established reference) must be uniquely named and PowerDesigner will perform the column naming automatically. Subsequently the modeler has to manually adjust the column names for the automatically generated columns. The DDL code generated based on our model is shown in the Illustration 87:

```
/*==============================================================*/
/* Table: ACCOUNT                                               */
/*==============================================================*/
CREATE TABLE ACCOUNT
(
   ACCOUNT_NUM           INTEGER            NOT NULL,
   OWNER_IDENTIFIER      INTEGER            NOT NULL,
   COOWNER_IDENTIFIER    INTEGER,
   ACCOUNT_OPEN_DATE     DATE               NOT NULL,
   ACCOUNT_STATUS        CHARACTER          NOT NULL,
   ECCOUNT_CLOSE_DATE    DATE,
   CONSTRAINT PK_ACCOUNT PRIMARY KEY (ACCOUNT_NUM)
);


/*==============================================================*/
/* Table: CUSTOMER                                              */
/*==============================================================*/
CREATE TABLE CUSTOMER
(
   CUSTOMER_ID           INTEGER            NOT NULL,
   CUSTOMER_NAME         VARCHAR(60),
   CONSTRAINT PK_CUSTOMER PRIMARY KEY (CUSTOMER_ID)
);

ALTER TABLE ACCOUNT
   ADD CONSTRAINT FK_ACCOUNT_COOWNER_CUSTOMER FOREIGN KEY (COOWNER_IDENTIFIER)
      REFERENCES CUSTOMER (CUSTOMER_ID)
      ON DELETE SET NULL;

ALTER TABLE ACCOUNT
   ADD CONSTRAINT FK_ACCOUNT_OWNER_CUSTOMER FOREIGN KEY (OWNER_IDENTIFIER)
      REFERENCES CUSTOMER (CUSTOMER_ID)
      ON DELETE CASCADE;
```

Illustration 87: DDL code showing implementation of two references between the tables CUSTOMER and ACCOUNT

The generated code provides the following functionality:

- table structure includes two columns OWNER_IDENTIFIER and COOWNER_IDENTIFIER
- referential integrity constraints are using these two columns for the foreign key constraint to the primary key of the CUSTOMER table

If implementation of the referential integrity is done via the triggers, the tool will generate the trigger SQL code to implement the referential integrity rule. Declaratively, databases can implement very limited referential integrity rules using references while with triggers these rules can be far more complex. Here is a sample code produced by PowerDesigner that implements the referential integrity rules via the triggers[121]:

```
CREATE TRIGGER TIB_ACCOUNT NO CASCADE BEFORE INSERT
ON ACCOUNT REFERENCING NEW AS NEW_INS FOR EACH ROW MODE DB2SQL
WHEN (
    -- PARENT "CUSTOMER" MUST EXIST WHEN INSERTING A CHILD IN "ACCOUNT"
    (NEW_INS.OWNER_IDENTIFIER IS NOT NULL AND
    NOT EXISTS (SELECT 1
        FROM CUSTOMER
        WHERE CUSTOMER.CUSTOMER_ID = NEW_INS.OWNER_IDENTIFIER)) OR
    -- PARENT "CUSTOMER" MUST EXIST WHEN INSERTING A CHILD IN "ACCOUNT"
    (NEW_INS.COOWNER_IDENTIFIER IS NOT NULL AND
    NOT EXISTS (SELECT 1
        FROM CUSTOMER
        WHERE CUSTOMER.CUSTOMER_ID = NEW_INS.COOWNER_IDENTIFIER)) OR
    (0=1)
    )
BEGIN ATOMIC
    SIGNAL SQLSTATE '70001' ('Cannot create child in ACCOUNT.');
END;


CREATE TRIGGER TSQ_ACCOUNT NO CASCADE BEFORE INSERT
ON ACCOUNT REFERENCING NEW AS NEW_INS FOR EACH ROW MODE DB2SQL;


CREATE TRIGGER TUB_ACCOUNT NO CASCADE BEFORE UPDATE
OF ACCOUNT_ID,
    OWNER_IDENTIFIER,
    COOWNER_IDENTIFIER
ON ACCOUNT
REFERENCING NEW AS NEW_UPD OLD AS OLD_UPD FOR EACH ROW MODE DB2SQL
WHEN (
    -- PARENT "CUSTOMER" MUST EXIST WHEN UPDATING A CHILD IN "ACCOUNT"
    (NEW_UPD.OWNER_IDENTIFIER IS NOT NULL AND
    NOT EXISTS (SELECT 1
        FROM CUSTOMER
        WHERE CUSTOMER.CUSTOMER_ID = NEW_UPD.OWNER_IDENTIFIER)) OR
    -- PARENT "CUSTOMER" MUST EXIST WHEN UPDATING A CHILD IN "ACCOUNT"
    (NEW_UPD.COOWNER_IDENTIFIER IS NOT NULL AND
    NOT EXISTS (SELECT 1
```

---

[121] Generated DDL code is for Oracle 11g database

```
            FROM CUSTOMER
            WHERE CUSTOMER.CUSTOMER_ID = NEW_UPD.COOWNER_IDENTIFIER)) OR
    (0=1)
        )
BEGIN ATOMIC
    SIGNAL SQLSTATE '70002' ('Unexisting parent or non updatable child. Cannot update ACCOUNT');
END;
```

Sample script showing implementation of the referential integrity using the triggers in Oracle 11g database

A quick preview of the trigger's functionality shows that, along with the referential integrity rules enforcement, the trigger also defines standardized exception handling. Although very useful for the integrity rules enforcement in the database, triggers can cause many problems if not used properly. The modeler has to fully understand the trigger's functionality and behavior if the choice is to use the triggers. List below shows some of challenges encountered when triggers are used:

- during the *direct data load*[122] triggers are not fired, potentially causing the data integrity problems
- triggers might be involved in cascading actions where a trigger "fires" triggers in other tables causing an avalanche effect. This can put significant pressure on the log space in the database
- to understand the rule, the modeler must analyze the trigger's code. Having simple triggers is not a problem but sometimes triggers are enhanced with additional functionality that makes the trigger's logic complex

Referential integrity implemented on a single table is the type of reference known as a *self-reference*. Establishing the referential integrity between two tables requires the primary key to be propagated from the parent to the dependent[123] table and the reference will establish the rules for keeping the data integrity between the tables. In case of a single table the primary key will be propagated too but it will end up in the same table. The tool will automatically rename propagated primary key columns keeping the model consistent with the rules of referential integrity as shown in the Illustration 88.

---

[122]   In Oracle using SQL loader or load command in DB2
[123]   Child table will be used as a synonym

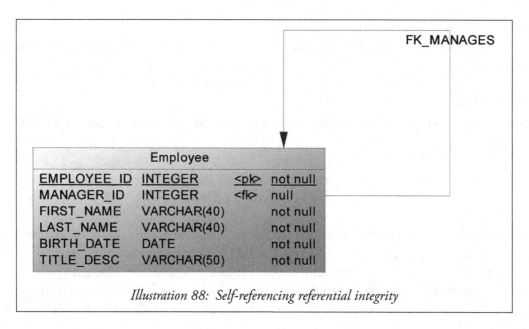

Illustration 88: Self-referencing referential integrity

When the self-referencing referential integrity rule is specified, the foreign key column's name should be modified so it complies with the established naming conventions. According to the SQL standard, columns that compose the foreign key do not have to have the same name allowing us to create a "role" for the foreign key implementation.

References are the physical instantiation of the relationships defined in the logical data model. Each reference has a set of physical options that have to be defined. Here is an example that will demonstrate detailed definition of a reference using PowerDesigner.

The reference's name is the design's starting point as shown in the Illustration 89.

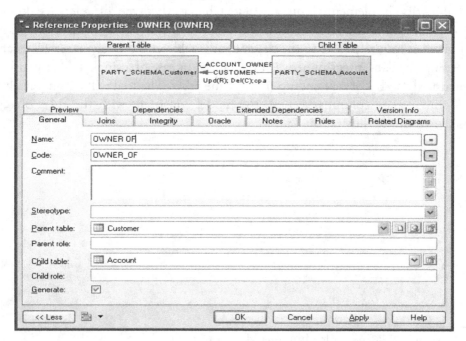

Illustration 89: Reference name definition

Each reference states the business rule implemented by the referential integrity as shown in the Illustration 90.

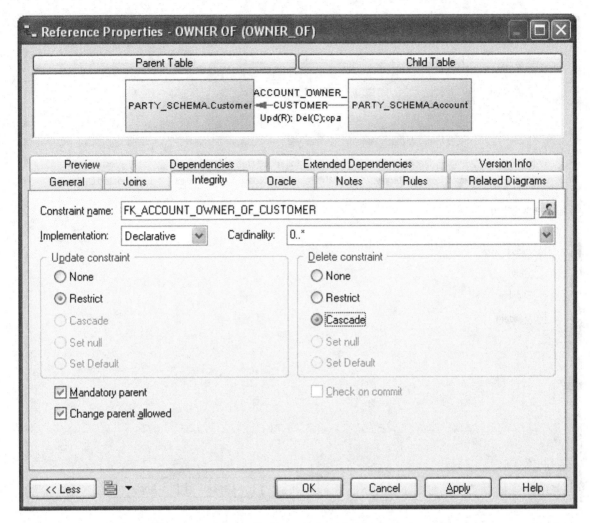

Illustration 90: Specification of the referential integrity rules

Implementation of the referential integrity rules does not necessarily require enforcement by the database (known as a declarative enforcement). Application code or triggers can be used instead. The implementation approach[124] specified by the physical modeler and has to be reviewed by the DBA for assessment of potential performance impact. If triggers are used for referential integrity enforcement, the development team should be familiarized with specifics of trigger's functionality.

---

[124] Declarative (database enforced) or via the triggers.

In this example the target RDBMS is Oracle and database enforced referential integrity provides some additional options that can be specified as shown in the Illustration 91:

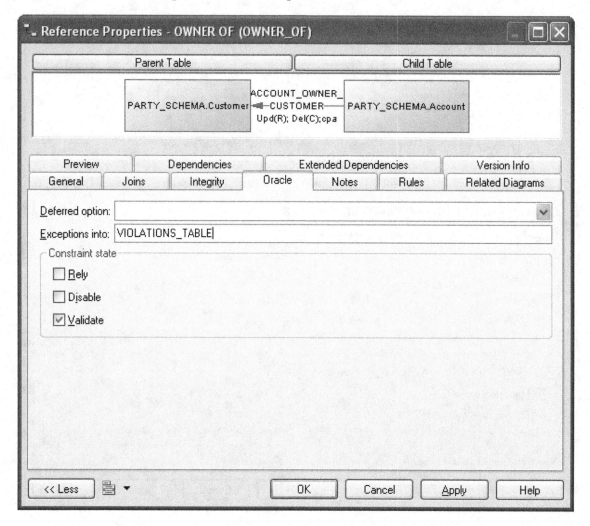

Illustration 91: Specification of additional reference-related parameters

If there is a violation of the referential integrity rule, the offending record will be relocated to the explicitly specified exception table called VIOLATIONS_TABLE.

Referential integrity enforcement can be enabled or disabled. In both Oracle and DB2 the references are used to ensure data integrity and help the optimizer perform the query optimization. If the referential integrity constraint is not enforced it can still be used for query optimization. The *RELY* option in ORACLE is used to instruct the database to keep the reference not enforced. The reference will be used for query optimization only. In DB2 the reference is automatically used for query optimization unless the clause *DISABLE QUERY OPTIMIZATION* is explicitly specified.

When the reference is established, the database will automatically check the rules established between the parent and child tables. This activity can take a long time to complete; instead the modeler can specify that data should not be validated when the reference is created. In our example the data validation is enforced automatically.

The physical modeler and DBA have to make the following decisions regarding the referential integrity implementation:

- reference implementation strategy:
  - ☐ database enforced
  - ☐ triggers enforced
  - ☐ application controlled
  - ☐ not enforced but used for query optimization
  - ☐ not enforced and used for documentation only
- strategy for handling the exceptions produced by the reference constraint violation:
  - ☐ with exception table
  - ☐ without the exception table
- type of referential constraint implementation:
  - ☐ none
  - ☐ restrict
  - ☐ cascade delete or update
- are the references required for query optimization?
- what additional referential integrity options will be implemented[125]

Referential integrity is perceived as a database feature that has a negative impact on performance however modern databases require the references for data access plan optimization. Therefore the referential integrity should be in place.

6.4.5.9. Creation procedure for references

Reference specification requires special attention because of potentially serious impact to the performance as well as concurrent database access[126]. The starting point for decision on the referential integrity should be considered when defining of relationships in the logical data model. The transition step from the logical to the physical data model produces basic set of the referential integrity rules that the physical modeler together with DBA have to review and adjust to finalize the model design.

---

[125] For instance: in Oracle we have option to define the timing of the referential integrity rule check (e.g. INITIALLY DEFERRED etc.).

[126] Concurrency is defined as ability of the database to allow access specific database object by multiple users at the same time performing various activities on the database object.

The procedure for the references creation is shown in the Illustration 92.

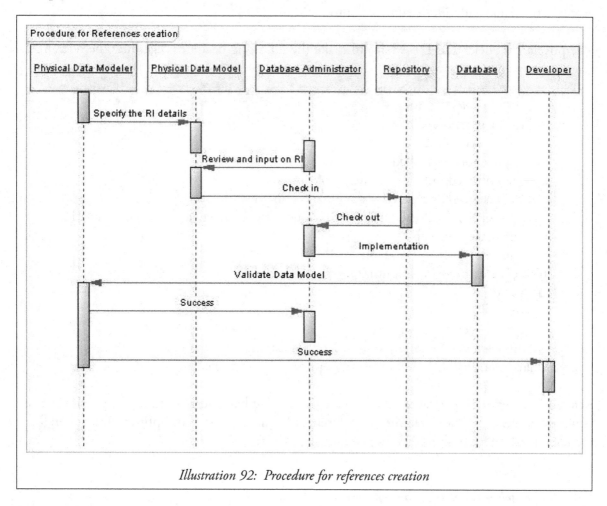

Illustration 92: Procedure for references creation

After implementing the referential integrity in the model, the DBA will perform the model review assessing the potential impact of the defined constraints to the performance. In order to improve performance, the DBA might suggest modification of some rules or a different approach in their implementation.

For instance, having referential integrity rules enforced by the database in a system classified as a DSS[127] is not recommended due to a frequent massive data load[128]. Data validation via the database enforced referential integrity will have significant impact on performance and, in some cases, database availability. On the other hand, the database optimizer[129] requires references to optimize the query execution. A solution might be to implement the *references without enforcement*[130] when large tables are involved. Implementing the reference without

---

[127] Stands for Decision Support Systems also known as Data Warehouse Systems. These are systems that supports analytical rather than transactional processing.

[128] Also known and Extract, Transform and Load (ETL) operation.

[129] Optimizer is a part of the database responsible for finding the best solution for SQL execution.

[130] In Oracle this is the RELY and DB2 uses NOT ENFORCED option.

enforcement is not impacting the data load performance while helping the optimizer to do the query optimization relying on the existing references.

After DBA completes the model review, the model is checked into the repository. Model implementation is performed by the DBA who checks the model out of the repository generates the DDL code and implements it into the database.

The model validation against the database is the final step performed by the physical modeler who confirms that the model has been successfully implemented in the database. Informing the team members that the database is synchronized with the model completes the implementation.

6.4.5.10. Views

DEFINITION: *View is a database structural object comprised of a SQL statement that is issued dynamically against the base table or set of tables involved in a join.*

From the user perspective the view looks like a regular table. Views are used for various purposes but mostly to simplify data access by hiding complex table joins from the end user. Views are also used to control the data access by limiting what the user can access to.

View creation is relatively simple and involves defining the SQL statement used to access the underlying tables. For the view, there is a limited set of data that the modeler has to define:

- schema name where the view resides
- SQL statement that is used within the view
- view classification: updatable or read only
- the view's data validation rule to be checked when performing the DML[131] operation

---

[131] Data Manipulation Language (DML) operation refers to inserting, updating or deleting data from the table

In the following example a view will be created based on the table join between the CUSTOMER and ACCOUNT tables. The view defined in PowerDesigner is shown in the Illustration 93:

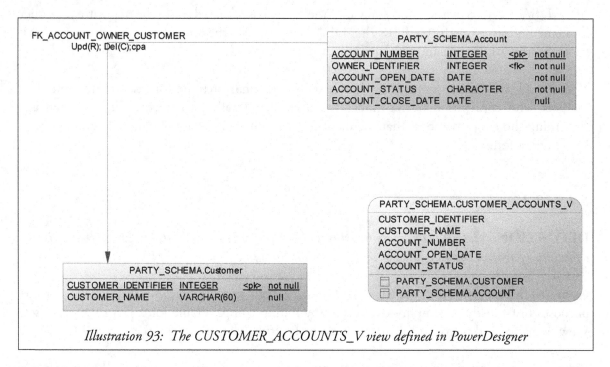

Illustration 93: The CUSTOMER_ACCOUNTS_V view defined in PowerDesigner

To distinguish between a table and a view, PowerDesigner is using a symbol of a square with rounded corners. By opening the view's properties we can see details of the view:

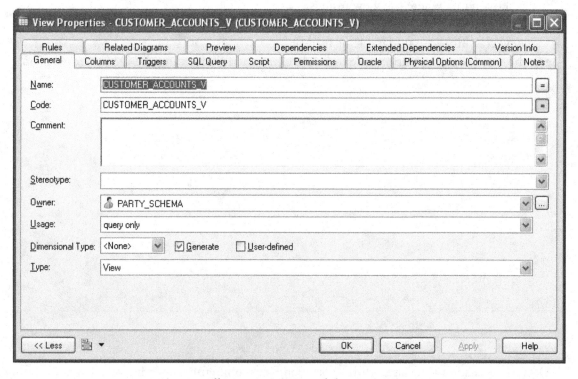

Illustration 94: View definition

The schema where the view resides and the physical name are required along with an explicit definition of the view's usage:

- *query only*—this is option will create a regular view
- *materialized view*—this option will create a *materialized view (MV)* in Oracle or *materialized query table (MQT)* in DB2

Each view or materialized view requires an explicit definition of the underlying SQL query that is used to access the data (Illustration 95):

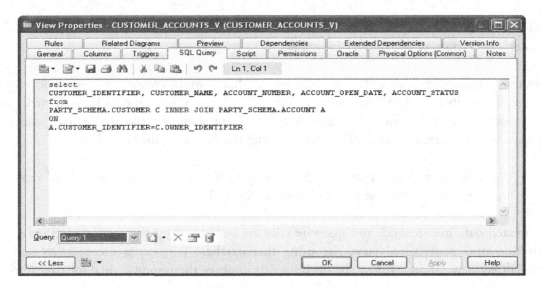

Illustration 95: SQL query used for the view or MV/MQT definition (Oracle and DB2)

Once the view is defined, the DDL code that creates the object in the database can be reviewed (Illustration 96):

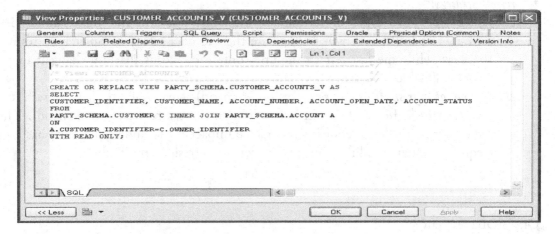

Illustration 96: View creation script preview

The code shown above will be generated when the view is deployed to the database.

6.4.5.11. Materialized View/Materialized Query Table[132]

Data processing always requires some form of aggregate data. This is typical for databases that support the DSS[133]. Retrieving millions to produce few hundreds of resulting records is a common request in a data warehousing environment. Frequent request to perform a massive data retrieval to produce relatively small resulting data set might put lots of pressure on the system potentially causing performance problems. To optimize the response time modern RDBMS provide the concept of aggregate tables that are known as *materialized query tables* (MQT) in DB2 or *materialized views* (MV) in Oracle databases.

DEFINITION: *MV/MQT is a table with its content automatically maintained by the database based on data extraction from underlying tables.*

Creating a materialized view[134] is more complex than simply creating a view. The view is nothing more than a data dictionary object that "fires" a dynamic SQL statement after invocation. Materialized view on the other hand represents a table in the database with sophisticated maintenance mechanism that provides the following functionality:

- *the data synchronization* between the underlying (base) tables and materialized view
- *query rewrite* for the query performance optimization

Automated data maintenance and query rewrite are controlled by parameters specified in the definition of a materialized view. Assuming that database parameters are properly set[135], a materialized view can be used by the optimizer to improve the response time for data retrieval by automatically rewriting the original SQL query, pointing to the materialized view instead of a base table or set of tables involved in a join.

The following is a list of elements important for building the materialized view:

- *refresh strategy*:
    □ *refresh type*—two types of refresh are available: fast and full materialized view refresh. The full refresh will re-populate the full data set by completely refreshing the view, while the fast refresh modifies only the records that are changed in the underlying tables
    □ *timing of refresh* (on commit, or on demand)—materialized view refresh can be performed after each commit or on explicit user request (on demand). This parameter might have serious performance impact if the underlying table has high frequency of data modifications and *on commit* refresh is specified

---

[132] Oracle/DB2 respectively
[133] Decision support system
[134] The term materialized view will be used to reference both concepts: materialized query table in DB2 or materialized view in Oracle
[135] Both Oracle and DB2 require special parameter settings to enable the query rewrite. Please refer to the manuals for further details

- *materialized view population* with data (immediate or deferred)—the materialized view can be populated with data immediately after it is created or on user demand
- specification of the *query rewrite* strategy—automatic query rewrite requires database parameter settings and explicit specification if the stale data in the materialized view can be used for query rewrite
- the *table-level physical details* (e.g. partitioning, tablespace etc.)—considering that materialized view is implemented as a table, all the table-related physical parameters are applicable to the view
- *indexes*—in case of large materialized views additional indexes might be able to improve the data access performance. Indexes can be explicitly specified for a materialized view

Here is an example of a materialized view in Oracle 11g as shown in the Illustration 97:

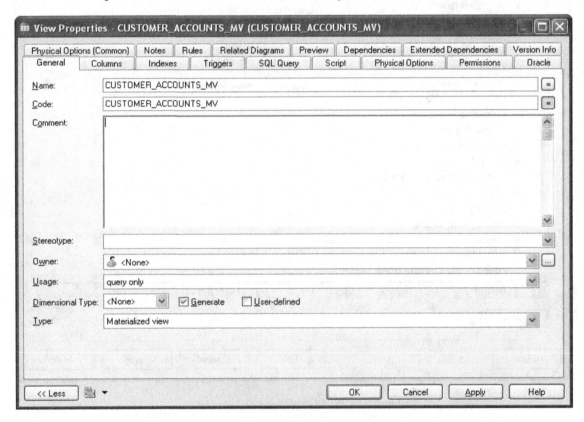

Illustration 97: Materialized view meta-data defined in Oracle 11g

By specifying the *usage* a *view* can be created as a *regular view* or *materialized view*. Materialized view is implemented as a database table hence variety of table-related physical details can be defined as shown in the Illustration 98:

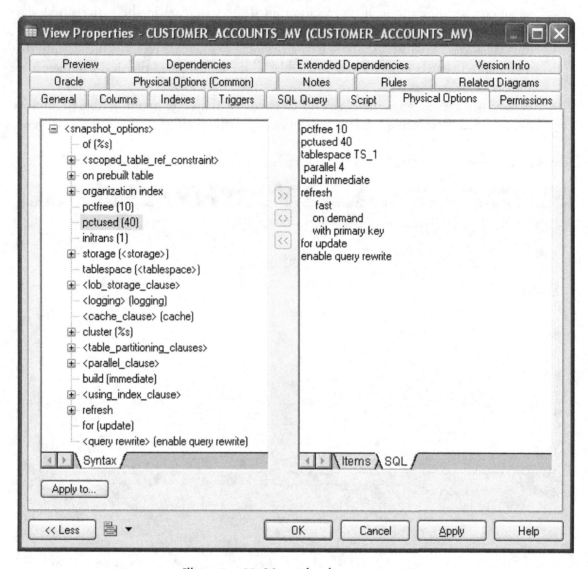

Illustration 98: Materialized view properties

Performance and data availability are impacted by the data synchronization with the underlying tables. When designing the materialized view, the modeler and DBA have to discuss the following topics:

- the timing of when the data is initially populated (e.g. immediate)
- type of refresh (e.g. fast, full)
- refresh time (e.g. on commit or on demand)
- query rewrite implementation (e.g. used for query rewrite)
- schedule when the materialized view is refreshed (e.g. start with time)

Definition of these parameters is shown in the Illustration 99.

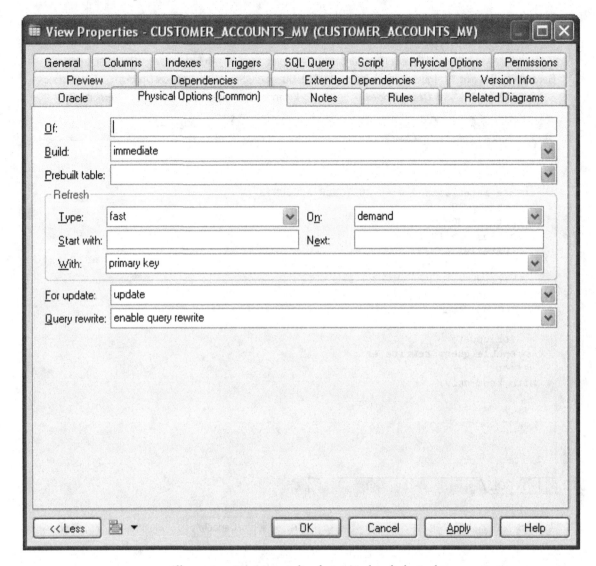

Illustration 99: Materialized view's related physical
parameters relevant for data synchronization

After completing the specification, the DDL created by the tool can be previewed (Illustration 100):

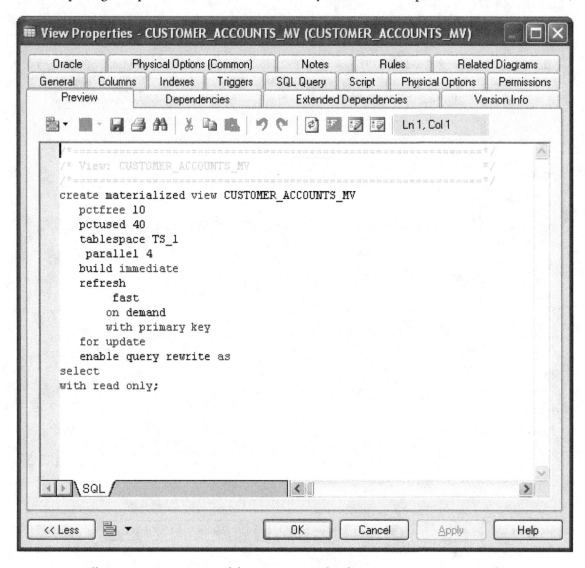

Illustration 100: Preview of the create materialized view DDL (RDBMS Oracle)

Performance optimization of data content synchronization between the base table and materialized view might require definition of the *materialized view log*[136] that will help tracking records that have been modified in the underlying tables. Instead of traversing the table for the records modified, the log is used to pinpoint modified records and update the materialized view accordingly. Conceptually, materialized views implemented with materialized view logs are shown in the Illustration 101:

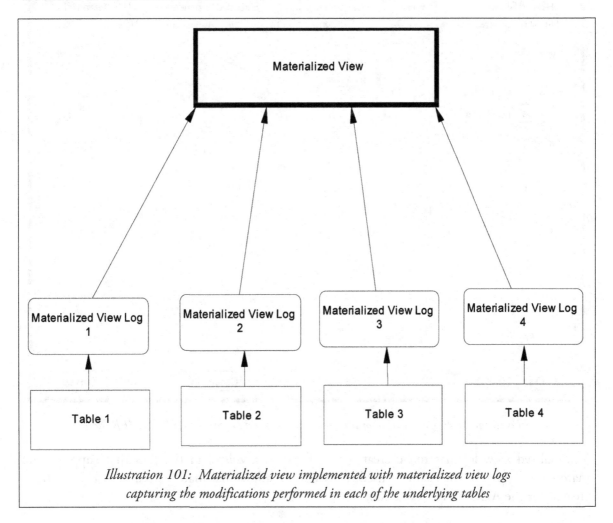

Illustration 101: Materialized view implemented with materialized view logs capturing the modifications performed in each of the underlying tables

A *materialized view log* is created for each table included in the materialized view data refresh request. The log keeps track of modified records:

- new record *inserted* in the table
- records *removed* from the table
- records *updated* in the table

---

[136] Specific to Oracle

The materialized view logs can be included in the model. The following is the illustration of the log creation in the model (Illustration 102):

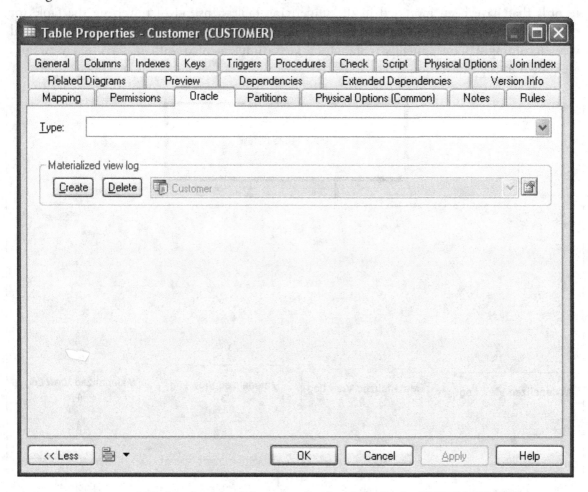

Illustration 102: Specification of the materialized view log for the CUSTOMER table

Materialized view log has to be created for all tables involved in the join that supports the materialized view. In the example used in this book, additional materialized view log has been created for the ACCOUNT table too.

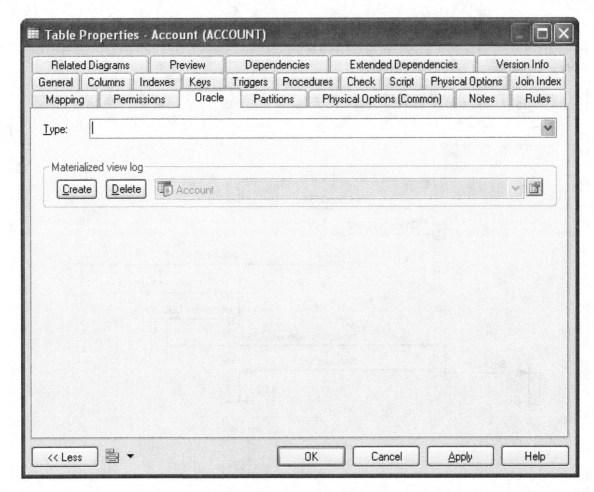

Illustration 103: Illustration Specification of the materialized view log for the Account table

Materialized views in Oracle or Materialized Query Tables in DB2 provide significant performance improvements for data retrieval. Query optimization technique based on the query rewrite is a very sophisticated technique to optimize the queries. The DBA has to provide guidance to the modeler in terms of reaching a balance between the data access and performance of the materialized view maintenance activities. The time required to maintain the materialized view should not be overlooked when tight SLA is in place.

6.4.5.12. Views and materialized views creation procedure

Similarity of objects allows us to define a uniform creation procedure. The difference is that *materialized view* represents a special type of physical table with predefined refresh strategy while the *view* represents a data dictionary object that creates the resulting set dynamically.

The creation procedure for views (including the materialized views) is provided below:

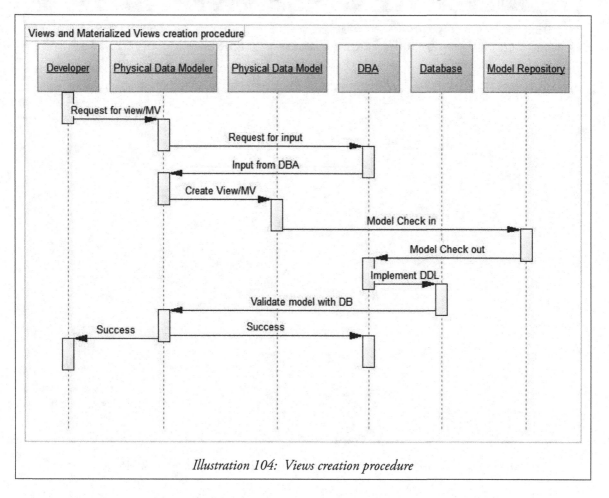

Illustration 104: Views creation procedure

Requests for views are usually received from the developers that are trying to simplify the complexity of data access through the table joins. It is a responsibility of a modeler to assess the request for view or materialized view creation. The following are the criteria that impact the decision making process:

- decide on the object type required: view or materialized view/query table
- if materialized view is requested then:
  □ assess the size of the newly created object
  □ assess the time required to synchronize the data between the base tables and materialized view
  □ potential locking issues
  □ acceptable tolerance for stale data[137]

---

[137] Maintenance of large materialized views can take prolonged period of time and, sometimes, the business can tolerate stale data. The modeler has to asses if there is a room for stale data tolerance so that additional time (if required) can be allocated for the materialized view refresh

- if the view is requested then assess the impact on performance of the queries that are accessing the view[138]

The modeler and DBA are responsible for the design of views or materialized views. After the model is updated with a new object, it has to be checked into the repository. The DBA generates the DDL from the model checked out from the repository and implements it in the database.

Final step is the implementation validation by the physical modeler who compares the model with the database. After the model has been successfully validated, confirmation message is sent to the DBA and Developers. This will conclude the implementation of the view or materialized view in the database.

6.4.6. Behavioral database objects

Application development requires development of a business logic layer that comprises of the following behavioral objects:

- stored procedures and packages[139]
- user-defined functions
- triggers
- sequences
- objects

This list is typical for most relational databases including both Oracle and DB2. We will discuss each behavior object class separately.

6.4.6.1. Stored procedures and user defined functions

The CASE tool provides functionality to maintain both stored procedures (SP) and user-defined functions (UDF) in the model. However, practical CASE tool implementation in the model life-cycle traditionally does not include these for pragmatic reasons. Dynamic paste of modifications and responsibility for objects by the team that is not organizationally part of the data team, historically prevented centralized maintenance of these objects in the model.

---

[138] By hiding the complexity of underlined table joins the view presents the data as a table. User is not aware of the SQL that retrieves the data within the view and if some options (e.g. sorting in particular order) are used, the calling query might accidentally reverse the option effectively forcing the query to perform mutually opposite operations

[139] Oracle and DB2 are using the term PACKAGE in different ways. In DB2, the PACKAGE refers to a code with locked-in plan while Oracle uses the same term to reference the object that comprises of multiple stored procedures and/or User-defined Functions

Although the generated code can be recorded and maintained in the model, the development and maintenance is more efficient using specialized development tools and code repositories. For the stored procedures and UDF both Oracle and DB2 have appropriate development tools highly integrated with the database. Oracle has its *Oracle SQL Developer*[140] while IBM's DB2 has the *Data Studio*[141]. Both provide variety of specific functionality useful for code development, testing and deployment including the version control.

The approach that taken here is that the code development should reside with the developers and a toolset they are using. The data team should not try to force them to use the modeling tool for code development. However, once developed, both the SP and UDF should be stored in the model using the reverse engineering capabilities of the PowerDesigner. The team will benefit from the PowerDesigner's model validation and model/database comparison facilities providing a high quality and uniform certainty in model implementations.

The diagram in the following page is the SP and UDF development and maintenance procedure.

From a development perspective it is assumed that the stored procedures (SP) and UDF are under the developer's responsibility. Once the SP and UDF are created there are two alternative reverse engineering options to bring them to the model:

- *reverse engineer* already implemented code *from the database* or
- *reverse engineer* the code *from the text file containing the code*

Traditionally each environment is faced with maintenance of the software documentation. Having multiple repositories, development tools and different approaches when developing code can be challenging during the deployment. Once the code is implemented in the database the physical modeler can reverse-engineer the code into the model. The goal of including the SP and UDF in the model is twofold:

- keep the snapshot of the code in the model. Later we can actually compare the code stored in the model against the code implemented in the database
- uniformity in specifying additional details (e.g. permissions) that are critical for the deployment

The development environment is very fluid and each project usually has multiple developers that are developing code in parallel. Instead of keeping up with frequent code modifications, the synchronization points should be where the model is synchronized with the database specifically for the SP and UDF. The model is then checked into the model repository making it available to all users.

The procedure is completed by informing the team of successful model validation.

---

[140] http://www.oracle.com/technetwork/developer-tools/sql-developer/overview/index.html
[141] http://www-01.ibm.com/software/data/optim/data-studio/

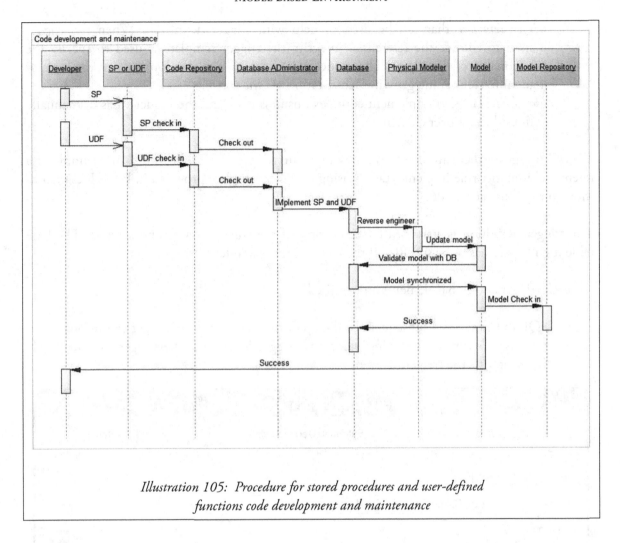

Illustration 105: Procedure for stored procedures and user-defined functions code development and maintenance

6.4.6.2. Triggers

From time to time, automatic actions are required when specific events occur in the database. For this purpose, both Oracle and DB2 provide automated behavioral objects that implement the code executed before or after an event.

DEFINITION: *A trigger is a database mechanism that automatically performs actions defined for a triggering event.*

Depending on database, a triggering event can be defined for the following database events:

- *data modifications* (such as insert, update or delete statements)
- *DDL events* (such as drop table)
- *system events* (such as the database start-up or shutdown)
- *triggers that modify behavior of DML operations*, so called "instead-of triggers"

Based on the database platform chosen an appropriate options for trigger definition is provided. To help the modeler, PowerDesigner offers two alternatives for a trigger design:

- *trigger template* that can be used to help with trigger definition. When the trigger is used to enforce the referential integrity the trigger template is used to specify the functionality of the trigger. The modeler does not have to develop and test the logic of manual referential integrity implementation via the trigger
- *user defined triggers* implement complex business rules and the modeler has to manually define all the trigger elements

We will not go further into details on how to create triggers. The following is an example of a referential integrity rule implementation using a trigger template provided in PowerDesigner as show in the Illustration 106.

The trigger definition is starts with specification of the trigger's name and schema. The base table for a trigger has to be specified if the trigger is the table-level trigger.

For each trigger additional elements are required:

- SQL to be executed subsequent to the event that invokes[142] the trigger execution
- the trigger's timing specifying when the trigger is "fired". The trigger can be "fired" *before* or *after* the triggering event

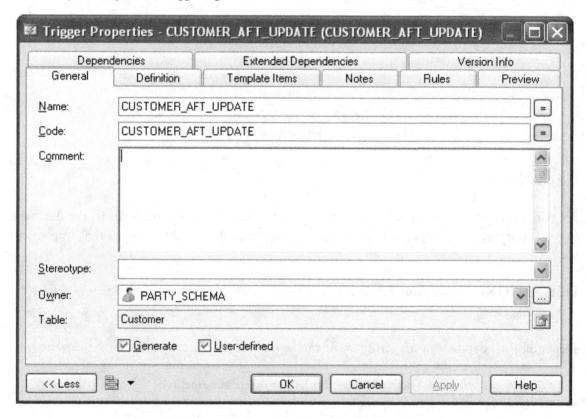

Illustration 106: Basic trigger's meta-data (target RDBMS is IBM's DB2)

---

[142] Term "firing" a trigger is usually used to denote a trigger invocation

The following is an example of a code generated for the trigger defined for a table in the previous example shown in the Illustration 107.

This trigger will be invoked[143] after the update activity on the table CUSTOMER in schema PARTY_SCHEMA. After the CUSTOMER table update, the SQL specified in the trigger's body will insert a record into the CUSTOMER_HISTORY table.

Oracle database allows for more sophisticated triggers invoked on events not always related to a table. The following is an example of a trigger defined for a database event, as defined in the *scope* section of the screen (Illustration 108).

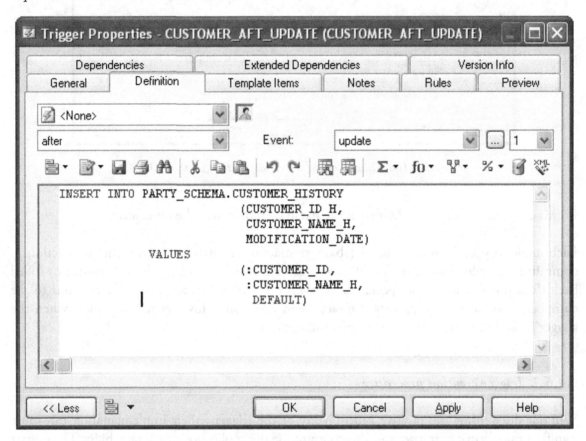

Illustration 107: Trigger's DDL code generated by PowerDesigner

---

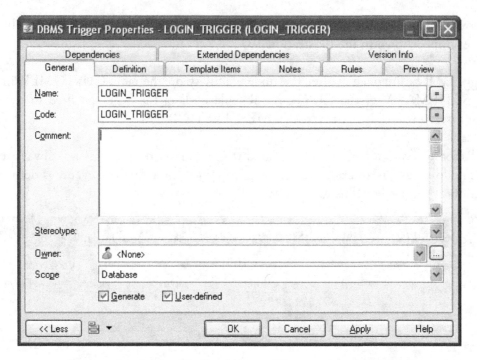

Illustration 108: Database level trigger definition (Oracle RDBMS)

In this example the trigger is defined at the database rather than the table level.

Each table trigger is under the database transaction control so when the transaction is committed or rolled back, data modifications caused by the trigger are also committed or rolled back. It is possible to define special *autonomous transaction* issuing special instructions to the compiler[144] to treat the triggering transaction in isolation. This scenario is typical when the trigger is used to audit unsuccessful login attempts by the user.

6.4.6.3. Trigger creation procedure

Without discounting the positive functionality of the triggers, their implementation can cause significant performance impact and also compromise the application's maintainability. The impact of triggers implementation should not be discounted especially if the decision is to use triggers to implement referential integrity. When deciding on using the triggers consider the following:

- triggers are behavioral objects invoked using an automated mechanism controlled by the database. The user cannot invoke them manually
- each trigger is almost "invisible". The user is not aware of its existence
- some database activity that performs data modifications at the table level will not invoke the trigger[145] execution

---

[144] Pragma—specialized instruction to the compiler
[145] Typical for the data load using direct method

Use the following procedure for trigger creation (Illustration 109):

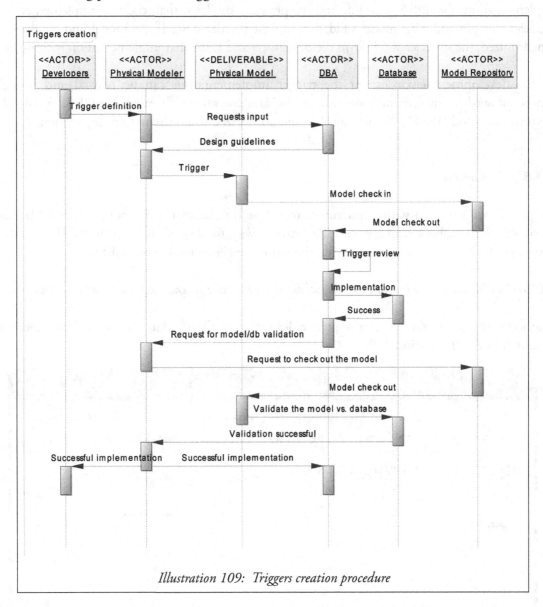

Illustration 109: Triggers creation procedure

The developer submits the request to the modeler for a trigger by specifying the trigger type, triggering action and the SQL statement that has to be executed. It is the developer's responsibility to define triggers that will implement complex business rules but the modeler can decide to use the tool generated triggers if the referential integrity is to be implemented by the triggers.

The modeler should always work with the DBA who will provide technical guidance to help optimize the trigger's functionality and impact it can have on the database performance. The trigger is defined in the CASE tool and model is checked in the model repository. The DBA will check out the model and review the trigger specification. If the trigger definition needs modification, the DBA will discuss his recommendations with the modeler and after a consensus is reached, the modeler will implement the modifications in the model. The validation step is not explicitly shown in the diagram but it is assumed that every modification has to go through the review before the implementation.

The trigger implementation is in the domain of the DBA's responsibility. After the code implementation the DBA will inform the physical modeler that code is implemented and modeler can proceed with model validation against the database. If the model and database are synchronized, the modeler will inform the developers and DBA that implementation is completed.

In the development environment the trigger implementation can be relaxed and modeler can be allowed to implement it directly in the database after informing the DBA. In all other environments only the DBA is responsible and authorized to do the trigger deployment.

6.4.6.4. Sequences

Frequently we are faced with requirement to define unique sequential values that will be used to populate the table's primary key. The easiest way to do this is to generate the database *sequences*. Both DB2 and Oracle provide the sequence generator functionality.

DEFINITION: *Sequence is defined as a database object that can generate sequential values automatically.*

The following is an example of a sequence definition in Oracle database using PowerDesigner as shown in the Illustration 110.

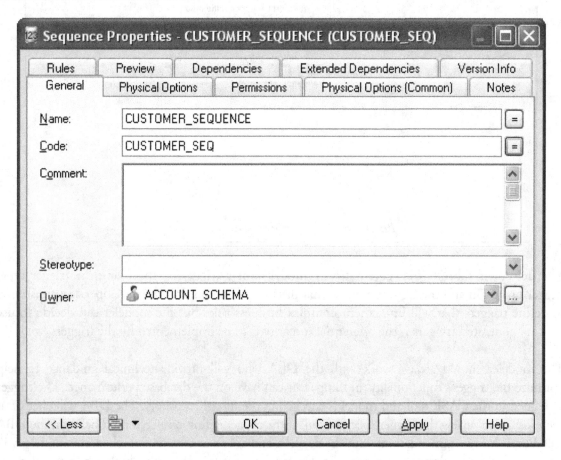

Illustration 110: Sequence definition (RDBMS Oracle and DB2)

Mandatory sequence components are the sequence name and schema where it resides. The modeler can provide a comment specifying the description of the sequence usage.

All other sequence-related parameters are optional and, if not explicitly defined, the value is specified by the database. The modeler can choose to explicitly specify the sequence-related parameter values using the following PowerDesigner screen as shown in the Illustration 111.

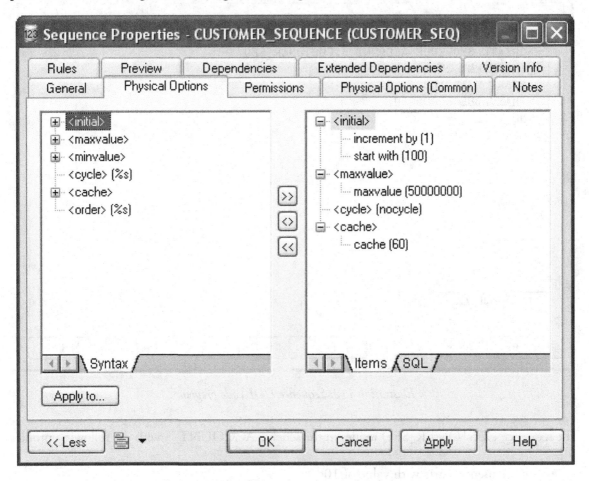

Illustration 111: Physical, sequence-related parameters

This sequence is defined to start with value of 100 with the increment of 1. Maximum number that can be generated is 50,000,000 and the database will cache 60 values. Values will be generated in order and there is no re-start (cycle) once the maximum value is reached.

An important performance factor to be discussed between the DBA and modeler is the sequence caching factor. Frequent sequence generator invocation can have negative impact on database performance sequence values caching positively affects the database performance.

The DDL code that will be generated by the tool can be previewed as shown in the Illustration 112:

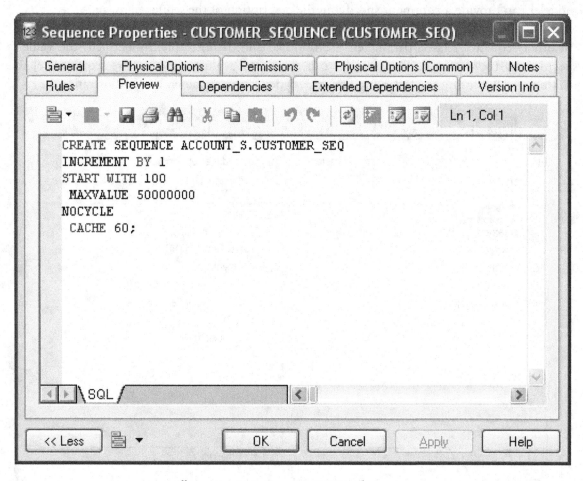

Illustration 112: Sequence DDL code preview

The sequence CUSTOMER_SEQ resides in the schema ACCOUNT_S with the following profile:

- the sequence starts with value of 100
- every invocation increases the value by 1
- the maximum sequence value is limited to 50,000,000
- the sequence will not be recycled
- 60 values are cached before the sequence is refreshed

When dealing with database maintenance, the modeler has to be careful not to accidentally re-create sequences with the starting values stored in the model. Considering that the sequences are already used and their current value is not equal to the starting value defined in the sequence DDL, there is a risk that the delta script generated by the tool simply drops and re-creates the sequence using the initial starting value as defined in the model.

Before implementing the sequence, the modeler has to find out the value that must be used as the sequence's starting value when it is re-created. Otherwise, the application that works with the target database will not function properly.

6.4.6.5. Creation procedure for sequences

The sequence creation is a relatively straight forward process. Developers usually request a sequence and a request is communicated to the physical modeler. Depending on the operational requirements for the sequence[146] the DBA might recommend specific parameter settings.

After receiving the input from the DBA, the modeler will create required sequence in the model and define all the required physical parameters. The model is checked into the repository and modeling process is completed. The DBA will check out the model and generate the DDL for implementation in the database. After implementation, the physical modeler will validate the implementation by comparing the model and the database. If the model and database are synchronized, the implementation is deemed successful. The process is finalized by the physical modeler sending the informing to the developer and DBA that the implementation is completed successfully.

The sequence creation procedure described is shown in the following sequence diagram (Illustration 113).

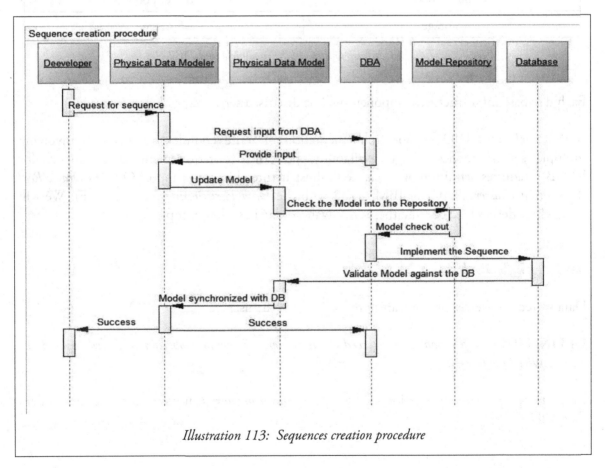

Illustration 113: Sequences creation procedure

---

[146] For instance: frequency of the sequence invocation

There are various options for generating sequential numbers. For instance DB2 supports definition of a column as an *identity* providing the same functionality as the sequence. The difference is that the sequence is an external object that can be optionally invoked, while the sequence is an internal table object with automatic invocation.

6.4.7. Infrastructure database objects

Database design is not limited only to the structural and behavioral objects. These objects reside in the database using various infrastructure concepts. The following is the list of these objects in Oracle and DB2 (Table 23):

Oracle	DB2
Tablespace	Tablespace
Data file	Container
Buffer pool	Buffer pool
Storage	Storage

Table 23: Infrastructure objects in Oracle and DB2

Each database infrastructure component will be discussed separately.

Both Oracle and DB2 support implementation of more complex architectures involving multiple servers (nodes). High availability, performance requirements and support for VLDB[147] requires definition of specialized infrastructure objects to support Oracle's *Oracle Real Application Clusters* (RAC) or IBM's DB2 with the *Data Partitioning Feature* (DPF). We will not go into details here because these are advanced database design topics.

6.4.7.1. Buffer Pool

Data stored on the disk is not transferred directly to the user[148].

DEFINITION: *Buffer pool is a reserved database server's memory portion intended to keep the data required for processing.*

Buffer pool represents the portion of the *server's central memory*[149] used to store the cached data that will be:

---

[147] Very large databases.
[148] This statement is not absolutely correct considering that databases provide direct data read bypassing the buffer pool. However, this is rather an exception than the norm.
[149] Further in this text we will use the word Memory.

- written into the table[150] or
- retrieved from the table

An important parameter for the buffer pool definition is the page size[151]. Buffer pool directly works with the tablespace (or multiple tablespaces) buffering the data for optimized throughput. The tablespace must correspond in page size to the buffer pool's page size.

One page size is always used as a database default. The buffer pool and corresponding *system tablespace* is using this default page size automatically, however both Oracle and DB2 database have a concept of alternative page sizes for the buffer pools and correspondingly allocated tablespaces. Buffer pools with different page sizes are defined for various performance optimization purposes. It is important that the DBA and modeler discuss the details related to the buffer pool definition so that the modeler clearly understands the reasons for specific buffer pool design.

The following is the illustration that depicts the relationship between the buffer pools and associated tablespaces.

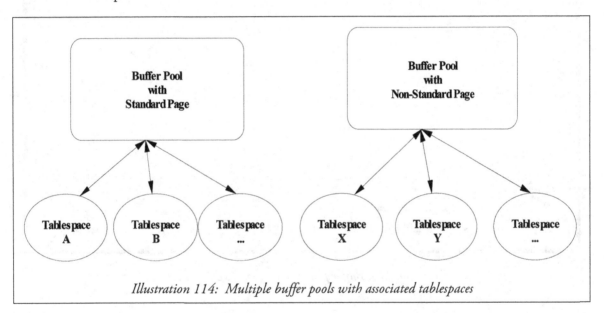

Illustration 114: Multiple buffer pools with associated tablespaces

Each buffer pool can serve many tablespaces. A buffer pool with predefined default page size is automatically used for the system schema in the database. Once the default page size is defined it cannot be modified in either DB2 or Oracle databases.

Buffer pools design is in the DBA's domain of responsibility. Information about buffer pools will be stored in PowerDesigner after the DBA creates the buffer pools in the database. By reverse engineering the database into the model, the modeler brings them into the model.

---

[150] So called "dirty" data blocks.

[151] DB2 and Oracle are using different terminology to refer to the minimum unit of allocated space. While DB2 is using the term page, Oracle is using the term block. The terms will be used as synonyms in this book.

For demonstration purposes we will present the details of the storage definition in DB2 database using PowerDesigner (Illustration 115):

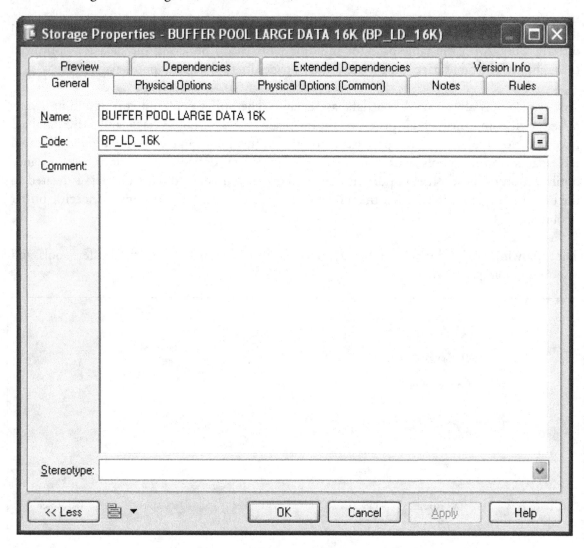

Illustration 115: Buffer pool specification (RDBMS DB2)

The buffer pool name followed by physical parameters has to be defined (Illustration 116):

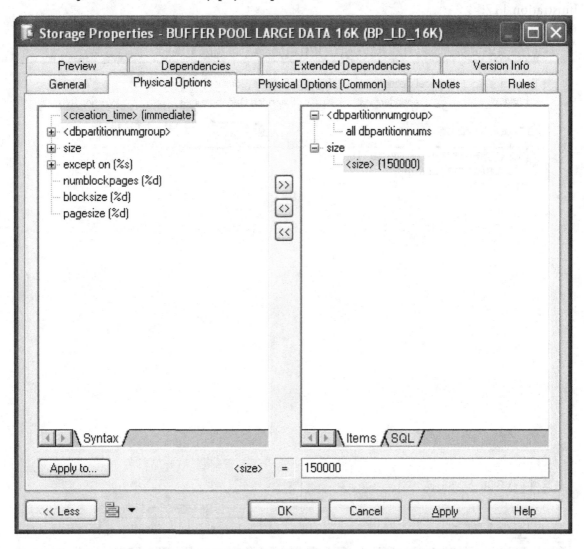

Illustration 116: Buffer pool physical parameters (RDBMS DB2)

Based on the buffer pool definition PowerDesigner can generate the DDL code shown in the Illustration 117:

Illustration 117: Code for buffer pool creation (RDBMS DB2)

In Oracle the buffer pool specification procedure is slightly different than in DB2. Buffer pools are defined using the parameter settings at the database level. After buffer pools implementation, the DBA will provide a list of buffer pools to the modeler so that these can be used when tablespaces are designed[152].

---

[152] Irrespective of RDBMS, each tablespace must be associated to a buffer pool

6.4.7.2. Tablespaces

Database administration is challenged with administering a large number of structural objects. Without proper organization of the underlying infrastructure objects, it would be increasingly difficult to efficiently manage the database.

Data and indexes are stored in physical files organized into tablespaces. The concept of a tablespace is the same for DB2 and Oracle databases.

DEFINITION: *A tablespace is a named logical grouping of files.*

The DBA can define multiple tablespaces within the database, but large number of tablespaces will increase administration efforts and cost. New trend in storage administration is to employ the *Automatic Storage Management* (ASM) database feature bringing the following benefits:

- easier tablespace maintenance due to a small number of tablespaces to be administered
- alignment with modern storage solutions based on SAN[153] and NAS[154]

Storage design is a complex topic and requires involvement of various technical teams that directly or indirectly support the database:

- architecture team
- database administration team (DBA)
- infrastructure team (operating system administrators, network administrators etc.)
- physical modeler

Database architecture implements the tablespaces as logical groupings of the physical storage, hiding the complexity of underlying storage components. The tablespace design is in the DBA's domain of responsibility. However the sizing information is provided by the physical modeler. The concept of a tablespace is tightly coupled with the following components:

- *database files* where the objects are stored
- *buffer pool* where the objects are temporarily stored

---

153 Storage area network
154 Network-attached storage

Relationship between the tablespace, buffer pool and storage components is shown in the Illustration 118.

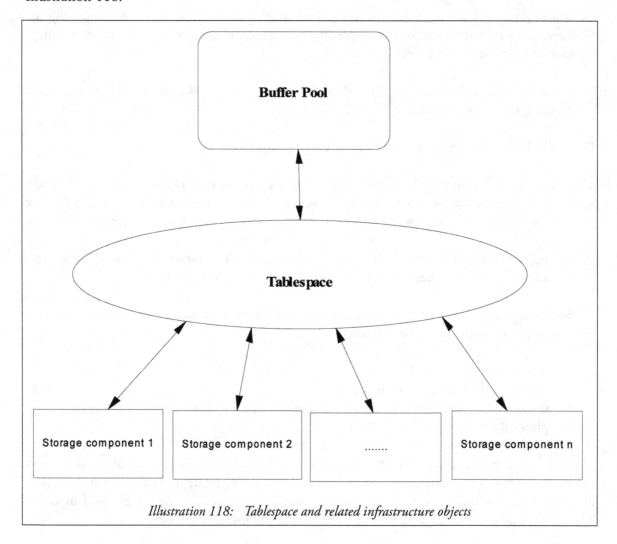

Illustration 118: Tablespace and related infrastructure objects

Both Oracle and DB2 can use the ASM[155] simplifying tablespace maintenance and administration. When the ASM is used, underlying storage details do not need to be explicitly specified because the storage-related components are managed automatically by the database. The modeler has to have the information if ASM is used in the database. When performing the database reverse engineering, underlying storage (Oracle files or DB2 containers) should not be specified for processing since they are under the database engine control. Furthermore including the storage-related components in the model might cause problems when moving the model from one database to another. Database is using specific naming conventions to maintain the file name ensuring the uniqueness of created objects at the database level. Trying to replicate files with their names in another database will cause problems.

---

[155] Automatic Storage Management (ASM)

Although tablespaces can be modeled in PowerDesigner, by including them in the model and specifying all the applicable physical details, recommended approach is to let the DBA handle this task for the following reasons:

- tablespace creation requires special permissions at the O/S[156] level. There is usually reluctance to provide permissions of this kind to the modeler
- DBA might need to involve other infrastructure personnel to complete this task. Given the nature of their work, the DBA has very close connections to the other technical team so the tasks can be done quickly
- physical options pertinent to the tablespaces require intimate knowledge of performance related issues so that the design can take these into consideration as early as possible. The DBA is ultimately responsible for the overall database health including the performance and they have access to specialized tools that help them optimize the tablespace design

The following is an example of a *temporary tablespace* definition in DB2 using PowerDesigner:

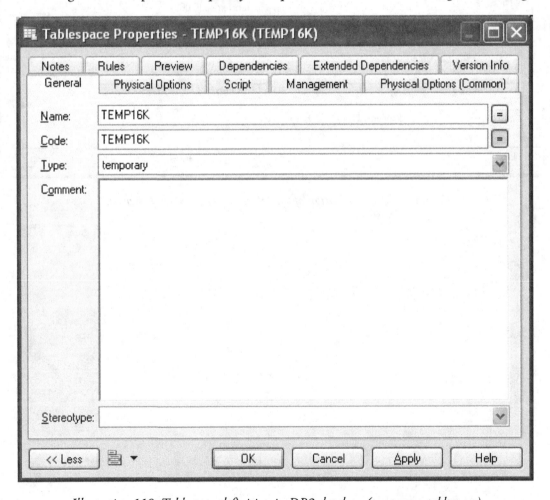

Illustration 119: Tablespace definition in DB2 database (temporary tablespace)

---

[156] Operating system.

In this example the modeler defines a *temporary* tablespace named TEMP16K. For each tablespace physical characteristics have to be specified[157]:

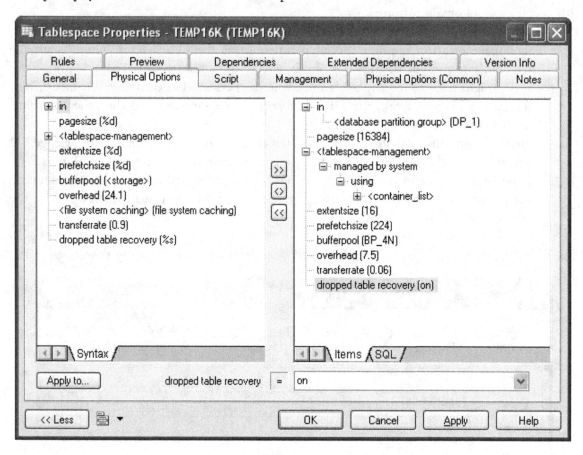

Illustration 120: Definition of the tablespace physical characteristics

---

[157] Specific physical options will not be explained. For explanation see the database documentation

Many of the tablespace parameters are taking default values if not explicitly specified. In case of the *manual storage management* the modeler has to define the tablespace containers (files) where the data is actually stored. After the tablespace has been defined the DDL code can be reviewed as shown in the Illustration 121:

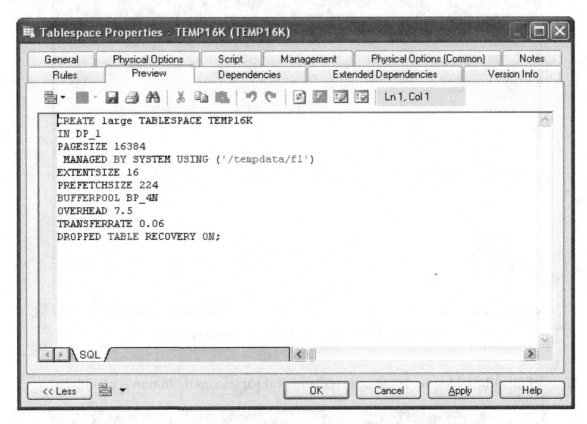

Illustration 121: DDL code to create a new tablespace (RDBMS DB2)

The procedure in Oracle database is effectively the same however the set of parameters differs from the parameters defined in DB2. The following is an example of a regular tablespace in Oracle database (Illustration 122):

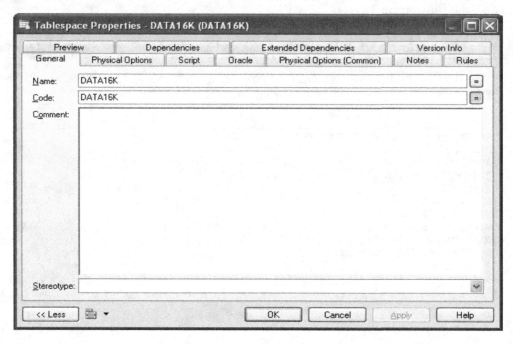

Illustration 122: Tablespace definition (RDBMS Oracle)

After defining the tablespace name and type, physical parameters definition is required.

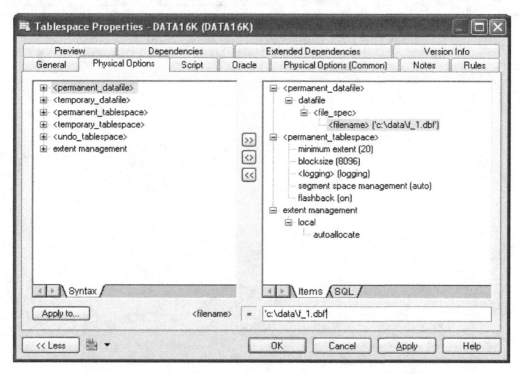

Illustration 123: Tablespace physical options definition (RDBMS Oracle)

Definition of the *datafile* in this example implies that the ASM is not used and explicit file definition is required. Other parameters explain various elements required for the tablespace definition.

Tablespace is associated with a buffer pool defined with a specific page size. Both Oracle and DB2 allows a tablespace of non-standard page size requiring existence of a buffer pool with the appropriate page size. The Illustration 124 shows an example of the code generated for the tablespace creation.

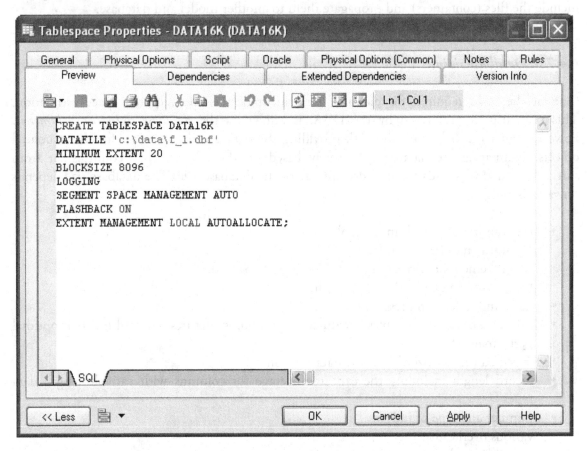

Illustration 124: DDL code to create the tablespace specification (RDBMS Oracle)

The DDL code, based on the tablespace specification is presented using the preview option in PowerDesigner.

The following is a summary of the tablespace design recommendations:

- the modeler and DBA have to work together to understand the elements relevant for the tablespace design:
  - □ data access patterns
  - □ data availability requirements
  - □ referential integrity implemented and enforced by the database
  - □ performance requirements
  - □ data movement requirements

- □ backup and recovery strategy
- it is more efficient for the DBA to implement designed tablespaces because of the toolset available for the database administration
- physical modeler should reverse engineer tablespaces into the model where these will be used in definition of the tables and indexes

In case of the ASM implementation the model by stores the names of the tablespaces only, without any reference to the underlying files. The modeler has to be careful not to accidentally include the files (containers) and propagate them to another model and database.

6.4.7.3. Database sizing

One of the tasks required for database implementation is the required space estimation. This task, usually performed by the DBA, is known as the *database sizing* or *volumetric*. PowerDesigner can help with this task providing the database size estimate for the structural objects. Estimating the database size solely based on the tables record count is far from sufficient and always leads to an underestimate of the database size. The database size depends on various factors:

- the number of records in the table:
  - □ initial number of records
  - □ increment per time-unit[158]
  - □ maximum expected records count
- table and index compression used[159]
- existence of aggregate tables[160] with corresponding structures required for their optimal performance[161]
- expected time horizon[162] for the data kept on-line
- record length including the expected average for columns with variable length data types[163]
- number and type of indexes
- various overheads:
  - □ table overhead
  - □ record overhead
  - □ large object overhead
- additional space required:
  - □ temporary space

---

[158] For instance: monthly, weekly, daily increment in terms of number of records

[159] Oracle provides block level while DB2 provides table level compression when compressing the data in the DB2 additionally provides column level compression that can be combined with the table compression

[160] Materialized views in Oracle or Materialized Query Tables in DB2

[161] For instance in Oracle, materialized view logs

[162] Example: data will be kept for 18 months

[163] VARCHAR data type

- ☐ logging space
- ☐ system space
- ☐ space for data import/export
- ☐ space for auditing
- ☐ space for monitoring
- ☐ space for various data dumps

The database sizing results have high visibility in the project and either overestimation or underestimation can lead to problems. Underestimates lead to undersized database that will ultimately run out of space. On the other hand space overallocation is impacting the cost of use for the database by having the extra space never used.

The DBA usually performs the database sizing by performing a spreadsheet calculation. This method, although common among the DBA is facing the following challenges:

- the list of objects has to be synchronized between the database and the spreadsheet. Although not an overly complicated task it is prone to errors and omissions by the person maintaining the list
- calculation method is always questionable and depends on the estimator's knowledge and understanding of the space allocation in the database
- factors used in calculation are constantly changing with the database version[164]
- it is difficult to take into consideration all the average variable column lengths when performing the calculation
- indexes and materialized views/query tables can be omitted (by mistake) from calculation
- physical implementation details such as table compression is not usually taken into consideration

The goal is not to have the storage space calculated to the exact byte; but to perform a quick, uniform, consistent and explainable estimate of space required. This goal can be achieved with PowerDesigner using the database size estimation functionality built in the tool. Calculation is based on the estimated number of records per table, specified in PowerDesigner.

Collection of input parameters pertinent to the sizing is the responsibility of the physical modeler:

- number of records in the table:
  - ☐ initial number of records
  - ☐ increment per time-unit
  - ☐ maximum number of records
- expected time horizon for data kept on-line
- record length including the expected average for columns with variable length data types

---

[164] For instance factors such as table overhead, record overhead etc. are constantly changing. This can significantly impact the estimates.

DBA has to provide the following:

- various physical object overhead factors:
  - ☐ table overhead
  - ☐ record overhead
  - ☐ large object overhead
- temporary space required
- logging space required
- system space required

CASE tools can do a pretty good job in storage space estimation by providing detailed calculation at the database object level. To start the process, record counts per table have to be specified:

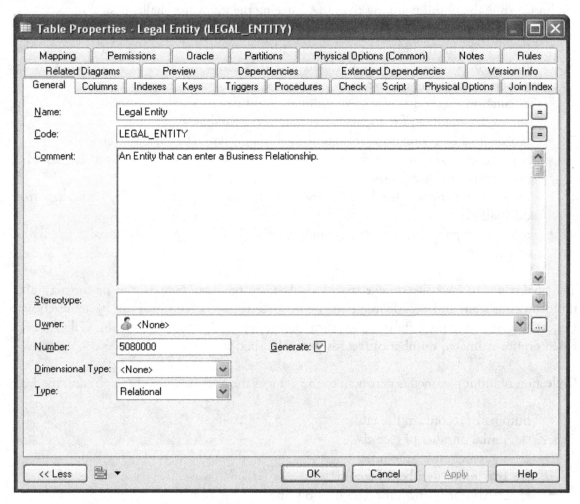

Illustration 125: Specification of the records count for the table LEGAL_ENTITY

The table LEGAL_ENTITY is specified to have 5,080,000 records. To perform the space estimate calculation, PowerDesigner requires that each table has a record count specified. After specifying the records count per table, the data can be reviewed using the following screen:

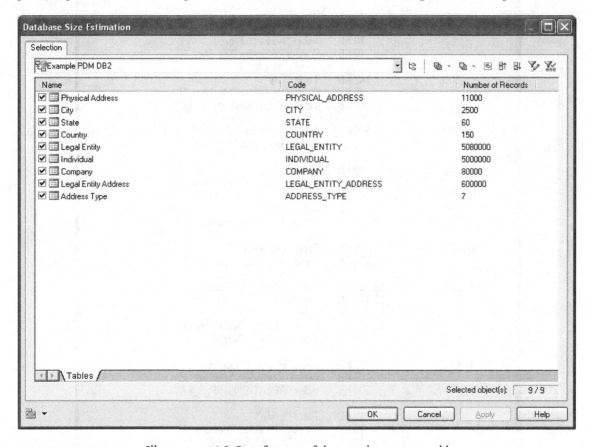

Illustration 126: Specification of the record counts per table

PowerDesigner performs the space calculation by estimating the required space estimate for the structural database objects:

- tables
- indexes
- MV/MQT

An example of the PowerDesigner's output for database sizing is shown in the Illustration 127.

```
Output                                                              [x]

Estimate of the size of the Database "Example PDM DB2"...

        Number      Estimated size    Object
---------------     ---------------    ---------------
            7            10 KB         Table "Address Type"
                         10 KB         Primary key index "Identifier_1"

        2,500           142 KB         Table "City"
                         48 KB         Primary key index "Identifier_1"
                         81 KB         Index "RELATIONSHIP_4_FK"

       80,000         2,585 KB         Table "Company"
                      1,710 KB         Primary key index "Identifier_1"

          150            10 KB         Table "Country"
                         10 KB         Primary key index "Identifier_1"

    5,000,000       336,672 KB         Table "Individual"
                     99,738 KB         Primary key index "Identifier_1"

    5,080,000       224,445 KB         Table "Legal Entity"
                     99,738 KB         Primary key index "Identifier_1"

      600,000        19,695 KB         Table "Legal Entity Address"
                     13,117 KB         Primary key index "Identifier_1"
                     13,117 KB         Index "RELATIONSHIP_5_FK"
                     13,117 KB         Index "RELATIONSHIP_6_FK"
                      8,738 KB         Index "RELATIONSHIP_7_FK"

       11,000           759 KB         Table "Physical Address"
                        208 KB         Primary key index "Identifier_1"
                        208 KB         Index "RELATIONSHIP_3_FK"

           60            10 KB         Table "State"
                         10 KB         Primary key index "Identifier_1"
                         10 KB         Index "RELATIONSHIP_1_FK"

---------------     ---------------    ---------------
                    834,186 KB         Total estimated space

Database size estimation successful.|

◄ ► \ Database Size /           ◄        IIII        ►
```

Illustration 127: Database size estimate in PowerDesigner

The space estimate is performed for the database instantiated structural object only. For each table and corresponding set of indexes the tool calculates the space requirements. Space calculated here represent the storage requirements for the structural database objects, however space for additional components have to be added:

- *temporary space*—usually calculated as a percentage of the estimated space required for the structural objects
- *logging space*—usually calculated as a percentage of the estimated space required for the structural objects

- *system space*—database dependent. The DBA can provide estimate for the system space required.
- *import/export data files*—database class dependent. In case of a transactional[165] database the size of the area for data export/import is relatively small. On the other hand, a DSS database can have requirements for a large space
- *audit files*
- *monitoring files*
- *various data dumps*

Total space required for the database must also include the size of components that are supporting special database features.

6.4.7.4. Creation procedure for the infrastructure database objects

Infrastructure database objects are the DBA's domain of responsibility. The DBA has expertise, knowledge, experience and specialized toolset to design, create and administer the infrastructure objects. Although the PowerDesigner can be used to design and implement the infrastructure objects, it is better to take an approach where the DBA implements them in the database and the modeler simply reverse engineers these into the model.

Implementation complexity varies with environments where the infrastructure objects are implemented. In development environment where the performance is not a critical factor, a simple implementation based on automatic management can be implemented. The goal is to minimize the database administration cost. The testing and production environments, on the other hand require careful design and involvement by both DBA and the modeler. Implementation is a team effort including the following participants:

- *infrastructure team*—teams that are administering the operating system and storage (e.g. SAN or NAS)
- *network team*—the team that is administering the network (e.g. LAN or WAN)
- *security team*—the team responsible for the corporate security

It is the DBA's responsibility to lead the design and implementation of the infrastructure objects. The DBA works with all teams mentioned in the process on a daily basis and relies on their support and cooperation so established inter-teams synergy can help significantly to solve the obstacles encountered.

---

[165] OLTP—On-line transactional processing

From the modeler's perspective, assuming that the implementation of the infrastructure database objects lies with the DBA, the creation procedure is essentially the same irrespective of the environment. The procedure is shown below:

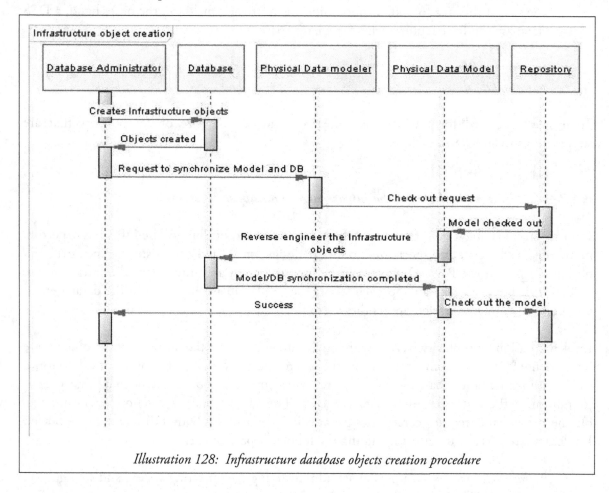

Illustration 128: Infrastructure database objects creation procedure

The DBA designs the infrastructure objects based on the requirements defined in the model as well as application specific requirements. After the objects implementation, the modeler synchronizes the model by reverse engineering the infrastructure objects from the database. The process is completed after model is validated against the database and no differences are reported. The final step is performed by the modeler who checks-in the model to the repository. After the model is successfully checked-in, the DBA is informed about successful completion which marks the process end.

Physical modeling process assumes that the infrastructure objects are reverse engineered into the model and subsequently used by the structural objects during the model design.

6.4.8. Database security

Database objects and data content must be safeguarded against unauthorized access or modifications using the *security model*.

DEFINITION: *The security model implements required permissions to control the ability to manage and access the database objects and their content.*

Database security is a complex topic that deserves a separate book, however for modeling purposes this book will provide an explanation of few basic concepts. There are two concepts important for the security, defined as follows:

- *authentication*—process of validating the user's identity
- *authorization*—process of ensuring that the user is allowed to perform specific action against the database objects

Implementation of authentication is dependent on the database. While DB2 relies on the authentication provided by the operating system, Oracle allows authentication by the database. When PowerDesigner's stores a *user* in DB2, the *user* is also a database schema. If Oracle database is used, PowerDesigner assumes the same (user is equal to the schema) except that the *user* can explicitly be defined in the database by specifying the password.

Authorization is implemented through the concepts of *permissions*[166].

DEFINITION: *Permission is a right to perform specific action against the database object.*

Permissions are implemented with a specific scope:

- *object level* or
- *database-wide permissions*

In DB2 the database-wide permissions are known as privileges.

Permission is related to a specific database object (e.g. table, view, sequence etc.) allowing specific operation against the object. For instance, in both DB2 and Oracle databases, the *SELECT, INSERT, UPDATE* and *DELETE* are permissions that allow the data *retrieval, creation, modification* and *removal* from the tables or views.

PowerDesigner can store and generate permissions (both object and system-wide) from the physical data model. Storing the security model (permissions and privileges for users, roles and groups) is a functionality that is not offered by many of the CASE tools on the market. PowerDesigner offers a comprehensive functionality in terms of storing and implementing the database security model.

The advantage of storing the security model in the data model is listed below:

- the DCL[167] code can be *uniformly deployed from the model*

---

[166] Reading the database documentation might be confusing sometime. DB2 is using the concept of remission and privilege to denote access to the database object and database resource (database wide access) respectively. In Oracle the object and system permission are used for these purposes

[167] Data Control Language (DCL) is the code that grants or revokes permissions in the database.

- security models (as part of the data models representing databases in different environments) can be *compared and synchronized:*
  - □ between the models
  - □ between the model and database
- object-level permissions and privileges (system-level permissions) can be *validated after deployment* by comparing the model with the database
- PowerDesigner provides a *formal model check* for the following:
  - □ *missing permissions*—objects without explicitly granted permissions are reported as warnings during the model check
  - □ *unspecified permissions*—users, groups or roles defined in the model are reported during the model validation check if the permissions are not present
- PowerDesigner's on-demand reporting capabilities can be used effectively to provide *comprehensive security model documentation*

Many times the data team is faced with a situation that object modification includes dropping and replacing a structural or behavioral database object. Complexity of this task, when working with the production database, is high and it is easy to forget to include all the required components in the code. Frequently, the developer responsible for creation of the delta code[168] omits or accidentally modifies the permissions, causing unnecessary application failure.

When the security model is stored and implemented from the physical model, the code produced from the model can[169] consistently include permissions. After the implementation, the model is validated against the database verifying that security model implementation.

6.4.8.1. Users

The concept of a *user* is defined as the lowest level in the security model's hierarchy. For the purpose of our discussion, the assumption is that the user and schema are equal[170] in both RDBMS.

When the user creates an object without explicitly stating the object's schema, the object is created by default in the schema with the name of a user that deploys the code[171]. At the schema level, the user that created the schema is specified as the object's *owner*.

In PowerDesigner the concept of a *user* can sometimes be confusing. So the following is the definition of a *database user* from a database perspective.

---

[168] The code that performs a database modification without data loss

[169] Permissions are not implemented by default so the modeler has to explicitly require their implementation

[170] Using the CREATE USER command in Oracle, the user can be created. This is not possible in DB2

[171] Providing that the user has the privilege to implicitly create a schema while creating the database objects

DEFINITION: *A database user represents a named identifier of an external entity authorized to use the database resources.*

In PowerDesigner the concept of a user is used in two ways:

- as the database user
- as the schema that owns the objects created in the database (e.g. tables, indexes, views, stored procedures etc.).

The following illustration demonstrates the user definition in PowerDesigner:

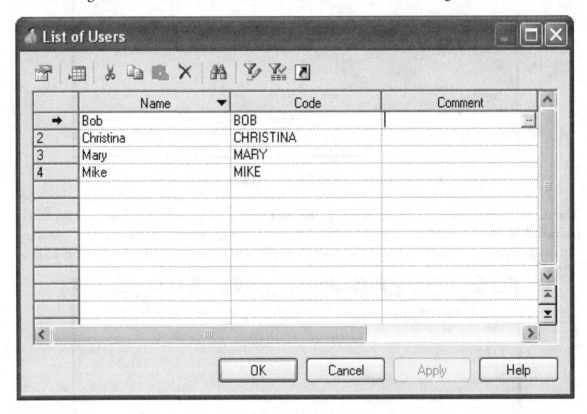

Illustration 129: List of database users defined in PowerDesigner

Users are defined by name. The naming conventions for the user names can significantly vary between the companies. Usual classification distinguishes between the *people* and *systems* defined as users. When the communication and data exchange is required between the database systems, the DBA needs to use specialized database concepts: *database links* (Oracle) or *nick names* (DB2). The names should be structured in a way to clearly distinguish between the systems and the business users.

Each user identified in the list potentially requires a password[172] for identification purposes as shown below:

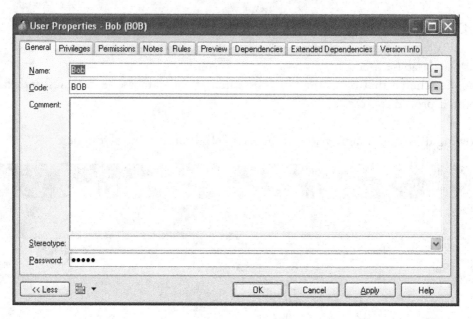

Illustration 130: User definition for Oracle database user

The Oracle database user is defined by the *user name* and corresponding *password*. The password is not exposed in a readable format for security reasons. However the generated statement that creates user will have the password specified as shown in the Illustration 131:

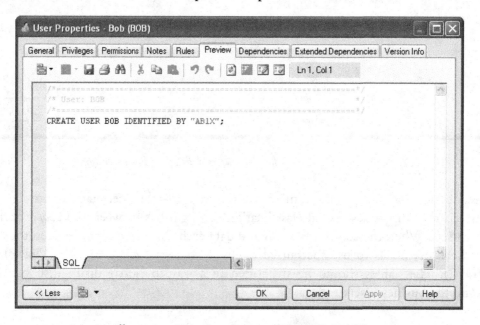

Illustration 131: Creating user (RDBMS Oracle)

---

[172] Depending on the user authentication implementation, the password is not always required. If the authentication is performed externally (not by the database) the user password is not explicitly required

The modeler can choose not to include the password in the model for security purposes. In that case the created DCL code has to be manually modified to include the password.

Although not advisable, the DBA can explicitly grant permissions to the user. Using PowerDesigner, the permissions can be specified at the user level. In this example the modeler can specify the privileges (database-wide permissions) for the user BOB, using the following dialog (as shown in the Illustration 132):

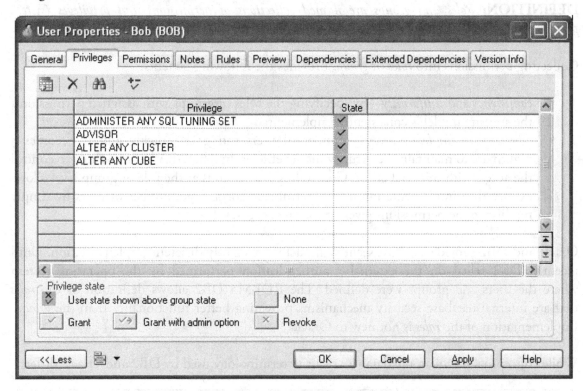

Illustration 132: Example of privileges explicitly granted to the user

Each privilege or permission can be granted to the user with the ability to transfer the permission to another user[173]. Good security practice is to limit or disallow the usage of ability to *transfer granted permissions*, because it becomes increasingly complex and time consuming to control and consistently implement the security model.

Maintenance of the security model as part of the physical model helps the modeler to perform the security model validation against the database.

---

[173] This option is known as 'with grant option'.

6.4.8.2. Roles and groups

It is a common practice to implement security model using roles and groups as collection of permissions[174]. Databases can have large user base that makes implementation of the security model at the user level extremely difficult, time consuming and prone to errors and omissions. Very quickly it becomes complex to control explicitly granter user permissions.

DEFINITION: *Roles and groups are named collections of permissions and privileges (system permissions).*

Collecting permissions into *roles* or *groups* provides the following benefits:

- *consistency* and *uniformity*—by specifying the roles or groups with assigned permissions, the security model is consistently implemented
- *efficiency in implementation*—number of users can grow quickly and it becomes a nightmare to maintain the security model efficiently. The DBA has to be able to control the access with minimal effort. Controlling permissions at the role or group level allows exactly this: implementation of the permission for a large number of users by simply modifying the permissions given at the aggregate level

Oracle and DB2 provide a robust security model with slightly different implementation. Until recently, DB2 relied on the external[175] authentication performed by the operating system where the users and groups were defined. The RDBMS DB2 allows definition of the *roles* that are internal database security mechanisms providing better functionality than the *groups*. Implementation of the *roles* is not new to Oracle.

While conceptually similar, the database security terminology used by DB2 and Oracle differs:

DB2	Oracle	Definition
Permission	Object permission	Structural or behavioral object access
Privilege	System permission	Database-wide resource access

Table 24: Differences in terminology between the DB2 and Oracle

Assuming that efficient implementation of the security model is using permissions assigned to the roles and groups, the question is how to control the consistent and efficient implementation of the security model in **various phases** of the system development life-cycle. Database has to be secured and access should be tightly controlled in every environment (development, testing, and production) and this is achieved by providing the security model that is controlled at the

---

[174] Assumption is that, along with permissions, the model implements the privileges (system permissions) too

[175] Authentication by the operating system or security software external to the database

group or a role level starting with database in the development environment all way to the production. At first, this approach might look excessively limiting for the following reasons:

- the development environment is perceived as an environment where the developers have full freedom to test their ideas and try various approaches before they chose the optimal one
- the testing environment requires testers to create temporary data structures for the intermediate testing results or test data
- the production environment requires the highest level of access control and data safety with clearly defined permissions based on the minimal required access[176]

To fully understand the approach we will start with diagram explaining the permissions granted in various environments (Illustration 133):

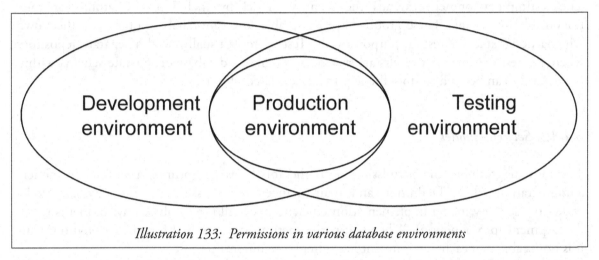

Illustration 133: Permissions in various database environments

Every environment shown here starts with permissions granted to the roles (or groups) in production environments. As the most secure, the production environment requires a minimum permissions granted. Production environment will have clear segregation between the roles that are responsible for:

- maintenance and
- database support and consumers roles

The development environment implements all permissions from the production environment including the role or group responsible for the application development. Enforcement of a strict security model in the development environment will usually cause many challenges for the data team. While the goal is to ensure disciplined development through enforcement of standards and disallow ad-hoc database object creation or modification, it is difficult to ensure that rules are followed if the role designated for development has excessive permissions. It is expected that developers need to test their ideas by introducing temporary solutions while assessing their

---

[176] The approach to the security model is actually relatively simple: user should have the minimal access to the database required to perform their work

benefits. New or modified indexes, de-normalized tables, views and various other optimization alternatives are available to tackle the database related challenges. One way to handle this is to establish specific naming conventions that will clearly separate temporary solutions from the valid objects implemented in database and controlled by the model.

Another approach is to create separate schemas and allow full object control at the schema level designated to a single user. This will distinguish the official development from the locally-owned schemas used by developers for their own testing.

In either case the model stays intact serving as a golden copy of the database objects required for development. At any point in time the modeler can create a code that can bring the database back to its original state by eliminating all modifications performed by the development team.

The testing environment extends the security model by including the groups or roles responsible for testing. These groups have to be able to create database objects in their own schema designated for testing purposes only. Testing tools usually need a separate repository where the test data and test results are stored. A designated database or separate schema within the database can be used to store the required test-related objects.

6.4.8.3. Security model

The idea of grouping the permissions into the roles[177] is to optimize the security model's administration effort. Definition and maintenance of permissions in the physical model makes the security model implementation efficient across all the database environments (from development to production). When comparing permissions required for various environments it is noticeable that each environment has different requirements.

Certain guidelines are required in regards to the permissions definition depending on the environment (development, testing or production). Users have different access requirements to the database. Depending on the database classification, the user access profiles can be categorized into the following classes:

- For the transactional databases (OLTP)
  - □ Regular users
  - □ Database administrators
  - □ Application support
- For the decision support systems (OLAP)
  - □ Regular users
  - □ Super users
  - □ Database administrators
  - □ Application support

---

[177] Further, we will use the role to reference both roles and groups due to their similar conceptual meaning.

The roles are assigned to users based on their requirement for data access. The data access classification is shown in the following illustration:

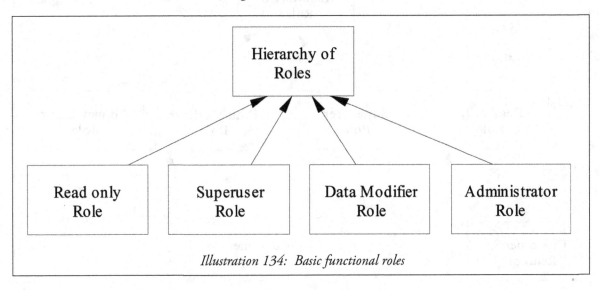

Illustration 134: Basic functional roles

- *read-only role* is limited to the read-only access to the database objects. A role can include subordinate roles[178] further limiting the data access to a specific subset of database objects
- *superuser role* includes specialized users that have knowledge and ability to modify the database objects. This is an exception that is typical for the DSS[179] where highly skilled analysts need to create database objects based on their on-going analysis requirements
- *data modifier role* allows the data modification in the database
- *administrator role* allows for structural modification of the database objects including creation and object removal from the database

These roles are further subdivided into roles specifically carved to include permissions targeting specific objects (e.g. schemas, tables etc.) as shown in the Illustration 135.

---

178 Other roles that segregate the read-only access to the specific subset of database objects
179 Decisions Support Systems-Data Warehouse

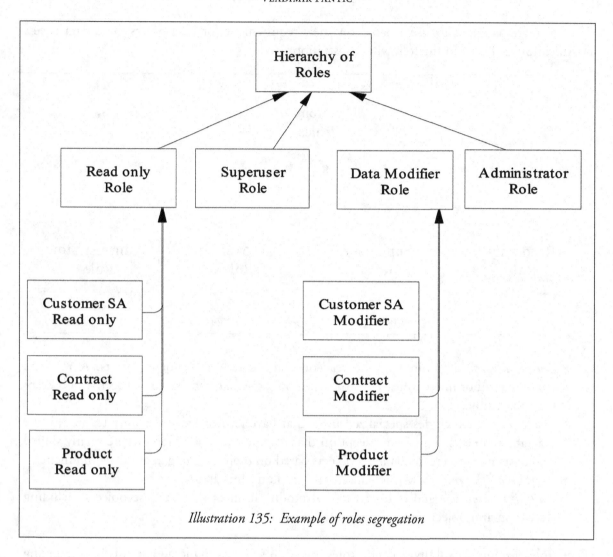

Illustration 135: Example of roles segregation

In this example the READ ONLY and DATA MODIFIER roles are further segregated into the roles that define the object access at the schema level. The database allows assigning of roles to other roles and in this example roles at the lower level are assigned to the higher level roles.

The roles design is dependent on the responsibilities assigned to specific job functions performed by business users. We are assuming that the database modifications are strictly controlled through the physical data model and only authorized people have the ability to modify the database.

Implementation of the security model has to start with the development environment and consistency, using the approach that was described previously, has to be kept across all databases. The following are the recommendations in regards to the security model implementation:

- maintain consistent security model in all environments (development, testing and production)
- assign permissions to modify the database objects to a limited number of users.
- establish communication channels to inform the development team about the database modifications

- implement auditing for the personnel authorized for structural database modifications
- assign user level permissions on an exception basis only

Although this might seem excessive for the database in the development environment, it will introduce the coding discipline for the developers and establish efficient database administration. An example of the security model based on the roles is provided below.

The first step is the definition of roles shown in the Illustration 136:

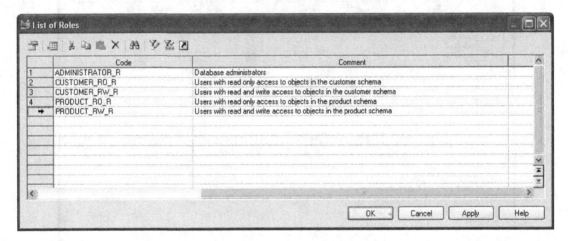

Illustration 136: Roles defined in the model

For each role the access type has to be defined. The following is an example of access specification for the administrator role using the Oracle as a target database:

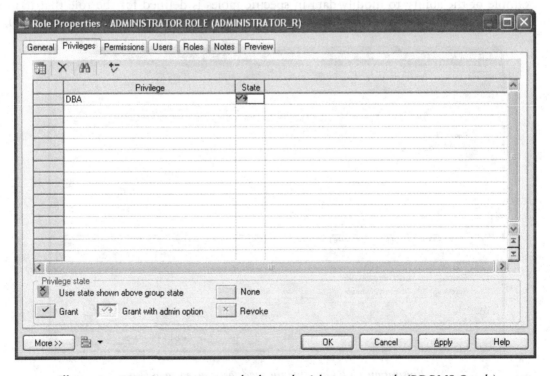

Illustration 137: Assigning required roles to the Administrator role (RDBMS Oracle)

For the ADMINISTRATOR role assigned is the Oracle's predefined DBA role so the users that have this role can perform regular database administration tasks.

For the CUSTOMER READ ONLY ROLE the permissions are based on the read-only access type to the objects in a specific schema:

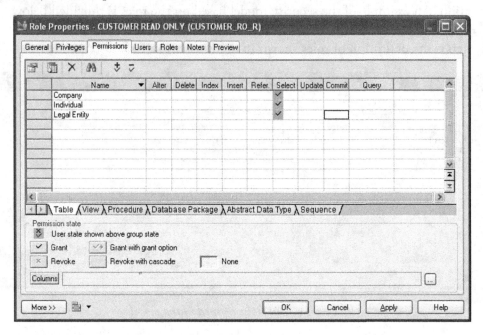

Illustration 138: Read-only access to objects in specific schema (RDBMS Oracle)

An example of the ability to modify data in specific tables is defined for the role that has the read and writes capabilities on the objects in specific schema as shown in the Illustration 139.

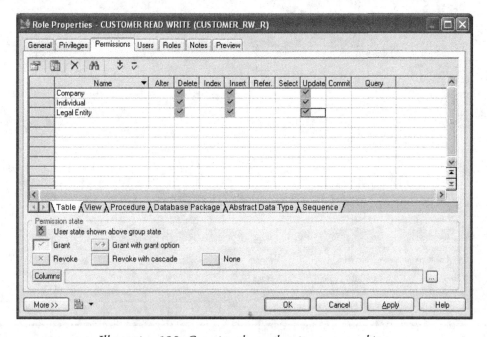

Illustration 139: Granting the read-write access to objects

The *select* permission is not granted explicitly to the role. Considering that the role can be granted to another role, the created CUSTOMER_RW_R role can inherit the read-only access permission to the tables via the previously defined CUSTOMER_RO_R role.

After the roles are defined, permissions are specified based on the job profile that will be using them (Illustration 140):

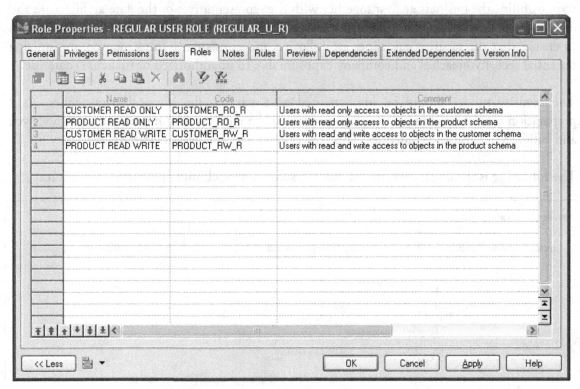

Illustration 140: Roles required for a regular business user

The final task is to assign the roles to the users. Granular access control is implemented through the roles making it relatively simple to control the security model. Storing the security model as part of the physical model allows tight control and consistent and uniform implementation of the physical model during the full database life-cycle.

6.4.8.4. Security model implementation procedure

Definition of the security model is handled by the security department at the corporate level. The data security is an important concept of the data architecture and it is handled very carefully in every organization. Large companies have specially designated teams responsible for all aspects of access, usage and data dissemination. The modeler, together with the DBA is responsible for implementation rather than detailed definition of the data security model. The data security model needs to be standardized across environments. Standardization of the security model provides efficient model implementation and simplified auditing. The security department has to provide the following guidelines:

- roles in every environment (from the development to the production environment)
- specification of required minimal permissions for each role
- role hierarchy
- data encryption requirements

While the corporate security model is the data architecture and data security team's responsibility, the business analyst together with the representatives of the data architecture and data security have to develop a customized security requirements for the project. The goal is to ensure that the security guidelines are followed and consistently implemented, minimizing potential security breaches and company exposure due to unauthorized or malicious data use.

The security model should be implemented as a part of the physical data model. As a preparation for the production, implementation of the data security model has to be reviewed and validated against the guidelines. This step is known as a *security walk-through*.

The following is the illustration that shows the security model implementation procedure:

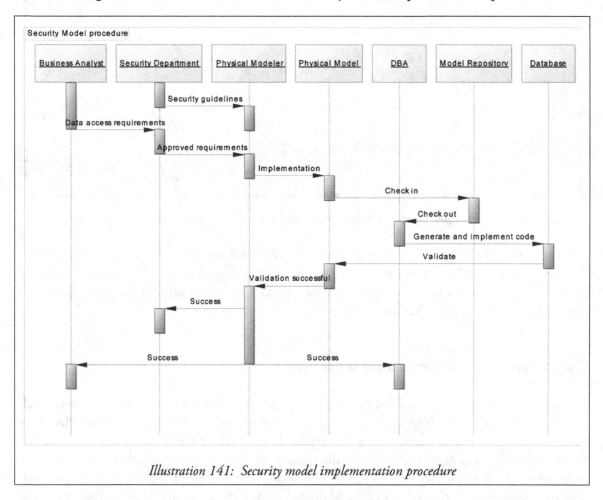

Illustration 141: Security model implementation procedure

The business analyst is responsible for a clear definition of the requirements for data access from the business perspective. The guiding principle is the functional requirements for each business role in the business process.

The business analyst's responsibility is to define the type of access required by the business user. The security requirements are submitted to the security department and data architecture for review and approval. After the requirements are approved the physical modeler is responsible for the security model implementation. This can be a lengthy process considering that the security in general is very sensitive topic in every company.

The security model should be implemented as part of the physical model by defining the roles[180], role hierarchy and users. After updating the model with required components the model is checked into the repository.

The DBA's responsibility is to generate the DCL[181] and implement it in the database. After the DCL implementation, the DBA informs the modeler about the code deployment and the modeler validates the physical model against the database. Team members are informed of the model implementation which marks the completion of the procedure.

The corporate security model sometimes leads to problems that can have severe impact on projects causing even project termination due to the constraints imposed by the security rules. The production environment has very restrictive rules intended to safeguard the data structures and data content against unauthorized or malicious use. To ensure that the data is safe, usual guideline is that the structures in the database must be static. In other words any dynamic alteration of the table structures is strictly forbidden. To be more specific, common security guidelines usually <u>do not allow</u> the following:

- dynamically dropping the table or view
- dynamically altering the table
- table content truncation[182]

The goal of the security model is to prevent data loss, unintentional or malicious data modification, however sometimes the strict implementation of defined rules can lead to unexpected problems. Large databases require implementation of advanced design techniques such as partitioned tables. An optimal strategy to load data into partitioned tables is to prepare the data in a separate table that is later attached as a new partition to the partitioned table. This task requires permission to alter the table structure as well as a permission to create table for the new partition. The technique is perfectly valid and recommended for large scale databases but it could violate the corporate data security standards that disallow the structural object modifications (e.g. ALTER tables).

To avoid these situations the recommendation is to include the security department early in the project and explain used design techniques. Failing to do so can jeopardize the project time-line

---

[180] Depending on the approach, we can proceed with definition of roles or Groups.

[181] Data Control Language is generic language that grants or revokes permissions and privileges to specific users or roles/groups

[182] While the DELETE statement is classified as a DML statement, the table truncation is classified as a DDL statement. The DDL statement do not need explicit COMMIT so their result is irreversible making them very dangerous in case of human errors

to the point where the security department does not authorize implementation of the solution effectively stopping the implementation.

6.4.9. Developing model in a multi-user modeling environments

Complex models require a team of modelers working on the model. A multi-user environment increases the complexity of model development and requires objects locking to prevent the model corruption. CASE tools are using the model repository to allow and coordinate multi-user access to the models.

Conceptually, concurrent access to the model assumes that only one user is allowed to modify an object while others can be allowed to read consistent version of it. While the object modification is in progress, it has to be protected from other users attempting to perform the modification. The object "protection" mechanism is known as the *object locking mechanism* and the concept of locking is further explained in the following illustration:

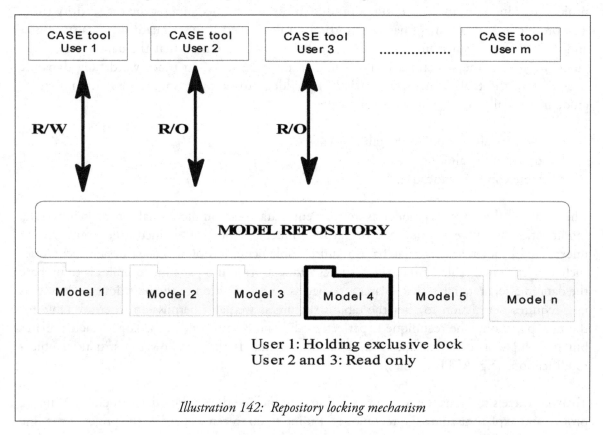

Illustration 142: Repository locking mechanism

The model repository allows multiple users to have access to the models stored in the repository. In this example the *user 1* has locked the *model 4* in exclusive mode. The lock allows the *user 1* to modify the model while disallowing other users to do the same. At the same time other users (*user 2* and *3*) have the ability to read the stored version of the model but not change it.

When working in a multi-user environment where users are concurrently accessing the model, it is important to understand the lock granularity.

Physical data model is treated as an integral object, so the lock is set at the model level when the model has been checked out of the repository. In other words, it is impossible to lock a specific object within the model, rather the whole model is locked using a specific lock type. When trying to derive the independent modeling units challenge is to organize the model into non-overlapping segments to simulate multi-user access while ensuring that no model corruption occurs. The approach is best explained using a simple example:

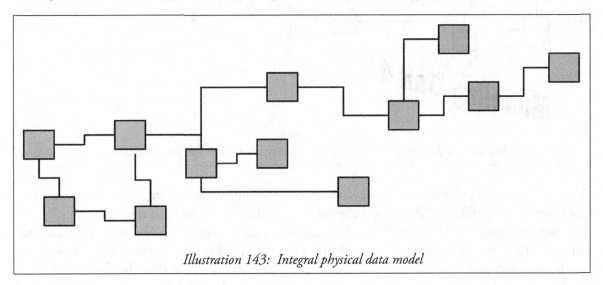

Illustration 143: Integral physical data model

The model comprises of tables related to each other. The modeler has to "carve" the model into subsets that will have minimal or no overlapping in terms of common tables. The modeling approach based on the subject areas can help the modeler achieve do this. Instead of working with a large model, the modeler should divide it into independent *modeling units*. The following has to be taken into consideration while creating the modeling units:

- each *modeling unit* has to *keep the logical cohesion*. This is best achieved following the boundaries of subject areas
- the modeling unit has to have *acceptable size* in terms of number of tables and complexity of relationships so that a single data modeler can handle it
- excessive number of modeling units will increase the complexity of model integration

Continuing with the example, let us assume that two modelers have to divide the modeling work. As an input for the *modeling units* creation, the *subject areas* created in the conceptual model can be used to help us create a **cohesive modeling unit**. The following illustration demonstrates the approach:

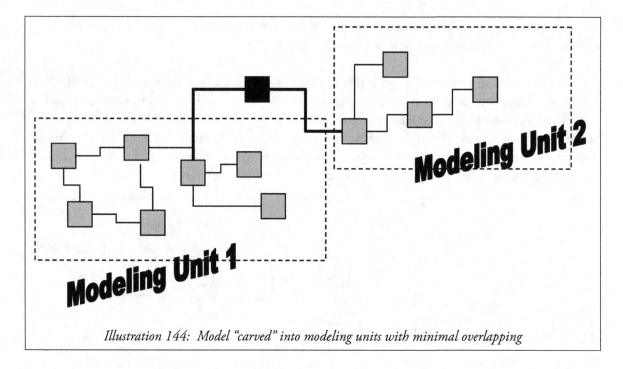

Illustration 144: Model "carved" into modeling units with minimal overlapping

Two sub-models are derived from the model using the subject areas defined in the conceptual data model. Each sub-model can be assigned to a modeler to work with the modeling unit in complete isolation. After the work on the modeling unit is completed, the model integration into the final model version occurs. Model integration takes the models representing the modeling units and uses the associative tables to "glue" the models into the final model. In PowerDesigner the *model merge* is used to integrate the models.

This modeling approach requires discipline and coordination in the modeling team. Exceeding the boundaries of the sub-model area can complicate models integration into the final version. The final step of sub-models integration is the responsibility of the data architect.

6.4.10. CASE tool standardization

Large projects sometimes include multiple modeling teams and the problem of CASE tool standardization sometimes arises. This is typical for companies that operate in different geographies or companies that grow through acquisitions. If the architect is faced with situation that data modelers are using different tools, the model integration becomes a serious problem.

Solving the CASE tools standardization problem is not a simple one. Large organizations have a challenge of strong resistance when introducing new tools. The following are the challenges to be considered when assessing the CASE tool standardization:

- *licensing costs*—CASE tools require significant investment that has to be justified by the size, complexity and number of models. If multiple tools are used, the vendor's volume discount is less possible

- *training*—efficient tool utilization requires extensive training. Multiple tools introduce requirements for increased cost of training
- *personal preference*—introduction of a standard tool might cause frictions in the modeling team due to personal preference of the team members. The risk of endless discussions which tool is better and for what reasons, should never be underestimated
- *legacy models*—the tools standardization will require a significant models conversion effort that is sometimes just partially possible due to differences in CASE tool's functionality[183]
- *repositories*—administration and licensing costs might be excessive if multiple CASE tools are used with different repositories
- *project time-lines*—changing the tool in the middle of a project might have a detrimental effect on the project time-line

Corporate data architecture team plays an important role in establishing and enforcing the standards. If the CASE standardization is not feasible the architecture team must come up with the model integration strategy.

Along with the CASE tool standardization across the enterprise, the data architecture team has to enforce uniformity of the modeling approach so that model integration results in a model with high level of consistency and uniformity.

6.4.11. Formal physical data model validation

Before the physical model is ready for implementation, the model has to be validated. Formal model validation assesses the model completeness and quality assuring successful implementation. PowerDesigner provides model validation to ensure that the rules of physical data modeling are consistently followed and model is implementable in the target database. However for auditing purposes it is required that the formal model quality assessment certificate is issued by the data architect who assesses the model.

The following is the model validation checklist that can be used by the architect to assess the model completeness and quality.

6.4.12. Physical data model checklist

The physical data model checklist has to ensure the completeness of the physical model prior to implementation. If the model is complex, components could be omitted by accident. The CASE tool independent checklist will help the modeler perform the final validation before the model is released as completed. The checklist could be extended or customized to include specific database features to be checked.

---

[183]   For instance, some CASE tools do not support storing the security model

Physical data model checklist

Model

- Author specified
- Version specified
- DB server specified
- Content defined
- Is validated by the CASE tool and no errors are reported
- Is checked into the repository
- Logical modeler has reviewed the transition from LDM to PDM

Table

- Schema owner specified
- Name specified according to naming conventions
- Class defined[184]
- Number of rows defined
- Comment specified
- Primary constraint specified
  - ☐ Primary Key is named
  - ☐ Supporting index is defined
- Alternate (business key) defined
- Physical attributes are defined:
  - ☐ tablespace
  - ☐ partitioning (if applicable)
  - ☐ compression (if applicable)
  - ☐ initial logging (if applicable)
  - ☐ Security policy (if applicable)
  - ☐ Data Capture (if applicable)
- Caching clause defined (if applicable)

Column

- Name specified according to naming conventions
- Data type specified
- Mandatory/optional indicator is specified
- In-line check specified (if applicable)
- Default value specified (if applicable) or GENERATED ALWAYS rule is specified (if applicable)
- BIT or CHARACTER semantic specified (if applicable)

---

[184] For instance in a DSS system the table can be classified as fact, dimension, outrigger or bridge

Reference

- Unique name assigned according to naming conventions
- Implementation strategy defined:
  - ☐ Declarative or trigger implementation
  - ☐ Enforcement specified
  - ☐ Referential integrity rule defined:
    - o DELETE rule
    - o UPDATE rule
- Cardinality specified:
  - ☐ parent to child
  - ☐ child to parent

View

- Schema owner defined
- Name defined
- Has an underlying SQL statement defined

Procedure

- Schema owner defined
- Name defined according to naming conventions
- Has an underlying SQL code defined
- Comment

Trigger

- Schema owner defined
- Name defined according to naming conventions
- Has an underlying SQL code defined:
  - ☐ event
  - ☐ scope
  - ☐ timing
  - ☐ atomicity
  - ☐ comment

Sequence

- Schema owner defined
- Name defined according to naming conventions
- Sequence is used by at least one table
- Physical attributes defined:
  - ☐ data type or domain
  - ☐ start value/max value/min value/increment
  - ☐ cycle clause

    ☐   caching
    ☐   order

Index

- Schema owner defined
- Name defined according to naming conventions
- Tablespace specified
- Index uniqueness defined
- Composition defined:
  - ☐ columns
  - ☐ column order is specified
  - ☐ partitioning clause (if applicable)

Alias/synonym

- Schema owner defined
- Same defined according to naming conventions
- Visibility defined
  - ☐ public
  - ☐ private

Permissions

- Users are defined
- Privileges are granted to users without ADMIN option
- Permissions are NOT granted explicitly at the DB object level

The following is the explanation of elements defined in the checklist:

Model

- *Author specified*—The modeler's name
- *Version specified*—Depending on the approach the version control can be handled via the repository or manually by the modeler. Explicit version and date should be stated in the model to avoid any confusion
- *DB Server specified*—physical data model is designed for a specific database so it is required to state the database name and version
- *Content defined*—short model definition and a brief explanation of the model
- Is *validated with no errors*—model should contain no formal validation errors when the validation is performed by the CASE tool
- Is *checked into the repository*—if a repository is used, the expectation is that the model is always checked in the repository
- *Logical modeler has reviewed the transition from LDM to PDM*—assuming that the logical data model is foundation for the physical model. It is required that the "first-cut" physical data model is reviewed by the logical modeler. The review has to

ensure that the model transition did not change the business rules stated by the logical model and all elements marked for transition are part of the resulting physical data model

Table

- *Schema owner specified*—explicit table ownership is required to avoid the table created in the default schema. Schema ownership can be implicitly defined by the user that is deploying the model at the time of DDL implementation but this is not considered a good modeling practice
- *Name specified according to naming conventions*—unique table name must be specified according to naming conventions
- *Class defined*—depending on the model class (DSS or OLTP) tables can have different classification. In the Star schema modeling technique tables are classified as facts, dimensions, bridges and outriggers. PowerDesigner has a provision to explicitly classify the table category
- *Number of rows defined*—PowerDesigner provides functionality to perform an <u>estimation</u> of the database size based on the number of rows[185]. This task was usually performed by the DBA using the spreadsheets. By using PowerDesigner to perform the calculation, the modeler can provide consistent, fact-based estimate
- *Table comments specified*—business description of the table content
- *Primary constraint (PK) specified*
  - □ *Primary Key is named*—Implementation of the referential integrity requires definition of the primary or unique constraints[186]. By SQL standard it is not required to explicitly define the name of the primary key constraint; the database will define the name automatically. The problem arises when the model is compared with the database and differences between the primary constraint names are reported
  - □ *Supporting index is defined*—Definition of unique index can precede creation of the unique or primary constraint. If a unique index already exists, the created primary or unique constraint will reuse the index
- *Alternate (business key) defined*—the definition of a business key is required if the primary key is based on strategy to use a surrogate key[187]. When designing a DSS system it is common to use surrogate keys as the primary key. In that case the business key is used to identify a record by its natural attributes
- *Physical attributes defined*—the following model components are required:
  - □ *tablespace*—specification where the table physically resides. In case of partitioned table, multiple tablespaces might be used

---

[185] AllFusion by the CA allows definition of the initial number of records, monthly increment and maximum number of records. Based on these values we can estimate the database size over time (e.g. 3, 6, 9, 12 and 24 months)

[186] Theoretically every table should have a PK defined. For the purpose of the referential integrity implementation a reference can point to a primary key or a unique constraint

[187] Surrogate key is an identifier that is system generated (sequence of GUID) and has no business meaning

- ☐ *partitioning (if used)*—if partitioning feature is used, partitioning strategy[188] must be defined along with corresponding partition-related details
- ☐ *compression (if applicable)*—specification if data compression is used to optimize the space utilization[189]
- ☐ *initial logging (if applicable)*—logging can be turned on or off. In case that *no logging* option is explicitly required (for performance reasons) the model reviewer has to ensure that this option is used properly[190]
- ☐ *security policy (if applicable)* -important for implementation of advanced security features (granular data access control)
- ☐ *data capture (if applicable)*—if data replication is used then the *data capture* definition is required
- • *Caching clause defined (if applicable)*—if table is accessed frequently and it is not large in size then the caching mechanism that will "pin" the table in the memory can improve the performance of data access

Column

- • *Name specified according to naming conventions—all objects stored in the model should comply with the corporate naming conventions. Enforcement of the naming conventions can be performed with the PowerDesigner automatically*
- • *Data type specified*—data type or user defined data type (domain) has to be defined for each column. In case that the data type or domain is not explicitly defined, the tool will replace it with the default data type that is defined at the model level (usually the VARCHAR data type with predefined length).
- • *Mandatory/optional indicator is specified*—specification if the column can accept the NULL value or not
- • *In-line check specified (if applicable)*—in-line check allows implementation of the business validation rule at the column level
- • *Default value (if applicable) or GENERATED ALWAYS rule is specified (if applicable)*—database allows the default value to be used automatically when the user does not provide the value. If value has to be calculated based on the in-line column values, the option GENERATED can be specified
- • *Sequence specified (if applicable)*—the sequence is a database object that can be used to generate sequential numbers. Usually this object type is used to generate the values for the primary key

---

[188] The modeler has to be aware of available Partitioning strategies for the database. For instance DB2 supports the Range and Hash partitioning while Oracle supports the Range, List and Hash as main partitioning methods. Partitioning strategy specification requires good understanding of advanced database features and this is why help from the DBA is required and expected

[189] Extensive use of compression might negatively impact the database performance and model review has to take this into consideration

[190] Common use of the no logging option would be when massive data load occurs for tables that are transient in nature. If something goes wrong and the load is interrupted the only option is to drop the table. Sometimes this is acceptable if the time to load the data is limited and data can be recreated without data loss

- *BIT or CHARACTER semantic specified (if applicable)*—specification of the semantic used, important when using languages with special, non-English character set

Reference

- *Unique name assigned according to naming conventions—uniqueness of the reference names in the model is required*
- Implementation strategy defined as:
  - □ Declarative or trigger implementation—enforcement of the referential integrity can be done using the triggers. PowerDesigner offers predefined templates for the triggers to enforce the referential integrity rules in the database.
  - □ Enforcement specified—although the reference exists we can opt to enforce it or not. If enforced, the reference will reject the records that violate the integrity rule defined. The references that are not enforced can be used for query optimization by the optimizer but the records that violate the reference will not be rejected by the referential integrity
  - □ Referential integrity rule been defined:
    - o DELETE rule—if the parent table instance is deleted, then this rule specifies what happens with the related child record. The behavior for the DELETE rule is specified by the ISO Standard.
    - o UPDATE rule—if the parent record is updated this rule specifies what happens with the related child record. Update rule behavior is specified by the ISO standard but not yet implemented *in the databases as an explicit referential integrity rule*
- Cardinality specified:
  - □ parent to child—number of instances in the child table related to one instance of the parent table
  - □ child to parent—number of instances in the parent table related to the instance of the child table

View

- *Schema owner defined*—each view has to have the schema defined
- *Name defined according to naming conventions*—unique name has to be assigned to each view
- *Underlying SQL statement defined*—view requires a SQL statement that is executed every time the view is invoked. Each view has to have a SQL statement defined

Procedure

- *Schema owner defined*—the schema name is required for each stored procedure
- *Name defined according to naming conventions*—unique name of the procedure is required unless the stored procedures are overloaded[191]

---

[191] Overloading is a technique that allows us to create set of procedures with the same name but different parameters (signature). By providing the Stored Procedure name and appropriate signature we can count on the database to execute the wanted procedure

- *Underlying SQL code defined*—each procedure must have the underlying code (e.g. PL/SQL[192], SQL/PL[193], JAVA or C) defined
- *Comment*—documenting the stored procedure is required for maintenance purposes

Trigger

- Schema owner defined—trigger has to have the schema name defined
- Name defined according to naming conventions—unique trigger name has to be provided
- Has an underlying SQL code defined:
  - □ event is defined—each trigger has to have an event (INSERT/UPDATE/DELETE) that will invoke execution of a trigger. DB2 allows only triggers that are "fired" on an INSERT, UPDATE and DELETE statements while Oracle includes additional trigger types invoked on various event types (e.g. DDL or system events)
  - □ scope is defined—triggers can be fired after execution of the statement[194] or after modification of each row[195]
  - □ timing is defined—trigger can be executed BEFORE or AFTER the triggering event
  - □ atomicity is defined—trigger can be executed as an autonomous transaction[196] or transaction that is nested within the calling statement's transaction
  - □ has an introductory comment—an introductory comment that explains the functionality and basic information about the trigger

Sequence

- *Schema owner defined*—the schema where the sequence is created
- *Name defined according to naming conventions*—the sequence must have a unique name within the schema
- *Sequence is used by at least one table*—validation that the sequence is used by at least one table
- *Physical attributes defined:*
- *data type or domain*—being independent object that will be used for the sequential number generation implies that the column data type must correspond to the range of the sequences defined. For instance, if the sequence has a range of 1 to 3,000,000,000 then the receiving data type cannot be an INTEGER since the maximum value can be up to 2,147,483,647. Depending on the relational database used, the appropriate data type must be specified. In DB2, for instance, we would use BIGINT rather than the INTEGER to accommodate the range specified by the sequence in our example

---

[192] Oracle

[193] DB2

[194] Statement level triggers

[195] Row level triggers

[196] Autonomous transaction is transaction that can be committed or rolled-back independently of the transaction that called it

- *start value/max/min/increment*—typical parameters for the sequence include the starting, ending and increment values
- *cycle clause*—the sequence generator can restart after reaching the maximum value or stop at the maximum value depending on definition of this parameter
- *caching*—the range of values cached for performance purposes
- *order*—invocation of the sequence can sometime give numbers that are not ordered. If it is required to have the generated numbers ordered, this option has to be specified

Index

- *Schema owner defined*—the schema where the index is located
- *Name defined according to naming conventions*—index name uniqueness is required
- *Tablespace specified*—the index can reside in the same or separate tablespace. The tablespace has to be explicitly specified if it is different from the tablespace defined for the table for which an index is created
- *Has the index uniqueness defined*—an index can be defined as a unique or non-unique index
- *Has its composition defined:*
  - *columns*—by deleting indexed columns from the table we might accidentally leave an index with no columns. Formal model validation would report this as an error that can be subsequently fixed by deleting the offending indexes (indexes with no columns defined)
  - *column order is specified*—the column order in a compound (multi-column) index has impact on performance so the column order has to be reviewed to ensure optimal performance
  - *partitioning clause (if applicable)*—the index partitioning is a design feature that can be implemented for performance purposes. In case that the index is partitioned, the partitioning strategy has to be explicitly defined

Alias[197]/synonym [198]

- *Schema owner defined*—the schema where the alias/synonym is created
- *Name defined according to naming conventions*—unique name for the alias/synonym
- *Visibility defined:*
  - *public*—alias/synonym visible by all users in the database. Definition of a public alias/synonym can pose a security problem by exposing the object to a wide audience
  - *private*—alias/synonym defined with limited visibility

Permissions

- *Users are defined*—list of database users has to be reviewed for security purposes
- *Privileges are granted to users without the ADMIN option*—the ADMIN option allows transfer of the permission to other users opening a potential breach in the security

---

[197] DB2
[198] Oracle

model. The model has to be reviewed for potential unnecessary use of the ADMIN option

- *Permissions are not granted explicitly at the DB object level*—all the permissions should be controlled at the role (or group) level instead of granting them directly to the user. This ensures consistency and uniformity of the implemented security model.

6.4.13. Physical data model documentation

The documentation required for the physical model differs in complexity from the documentation created for the logical data model. The audience for the documentation is mostly the technical personnel such as:

- DBA
- Developers
- Architects (data and application)

Depending on their role, the team members will have different documentation requirements. The documentation is created and produced directly from the model using the document layouts. PowerDesigner offers two reporting alternatives:

- list reports—these are operational reports intended to provide required information in tabular format
- professionally formatted reports—detailed reports intended to serve as a finalized project documentation

Report creation is relatively simple. Predefined report layouts are available in the tool that modeler can use to create reports of various complexity quickly. When new report definition is needed, the template can be dynamically created on demand and stored in the model for future use.

No matter how efficient reporting is, the report consumers should be trained to avoid using printed reports as the only source of information. When the report is created and printed, consumers tend to use them repeatedly running the risk of working with outdated reports. It is much better approach to use the reports created on demand, directly from the model when they are needed rather then create them and store them separately. Report generation on demand ensures that the report content is synchronized with the model content.

PowerDesigner can produce list and full reports. The difference is mostly the report formatting. Full reports include reporting on multiple model components allowing creation of a professional-looking document. List reports are more operational, tabular reports that provide a quick look into the meta-data for specific class of objects.

The following is a quick demonstration of PowerDesigner's reporting capabilities. After specifying the name of the report, the object class on which the reporting is required has to be specified (Illustration 145):

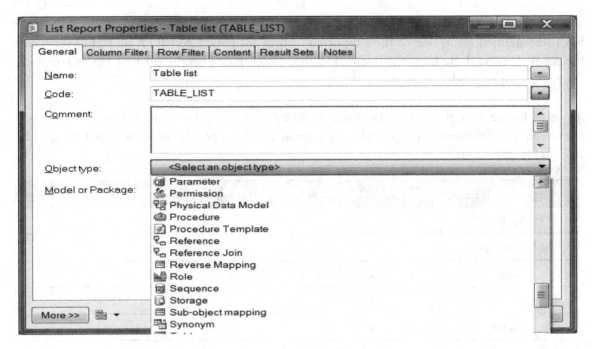

Illustration 145: Specifying the object class for which reporting is required

For the purpose of this example the table report is specified (Illustration 146):

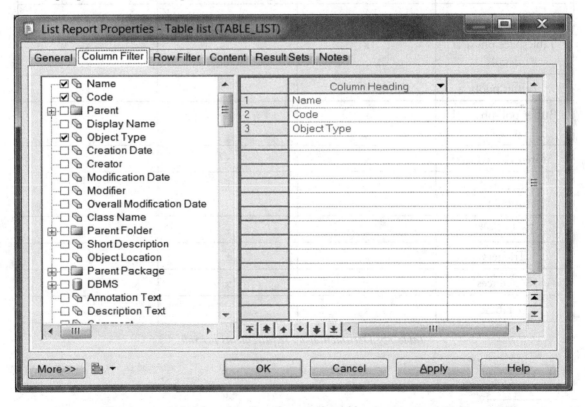

Illustration 146: Meta-data specification for table report in PowerDesigner

The report content is specified by simple click on the box. For each report the output format has to be defined using one of the supported output formats: CSV, RTF, and HTML. Once the report is created the template is stored in the model. Based on the existing report template, the report can be produced on-demand.

As noted before the reporting requirements in terms of the report content depends on the team members. The following table provides a proposal for the type of reports required by specific role (Table 25):

Report on/Role	DBA	Developers	Architect
Tables	x	x	x
Table-level details	x		
Indexes	x	x	x
Index-level details	x	x	
Views	x	x	
Materialized views (MV)	x	x	x
MV physical details	x		
Tablespaces	x		x
Tablespace physical details	x		x
Buffer pools	x		x
Buffer poll physical details	x		x
Stored Procedures	x	x	
User defined functions	x	x	
Packages[199]	x	x	
Triggers	x	x	
Sequences	x	x	
Database	x		x

Table 25: Documentation requirements per role

---

[199] DB2 and Oracle both use the concept of package but the meaning is different. In DB2 the package is the stored procedure that is bound with the optimizer plan. In Oracle the concept of package is related to the grouping of stored procedures and user defined functions (UDF) loaded together for execution.

The recommended approach is to create two flavors for each object report: a quick object snapshot including basic meta-data and a detailed report with comprehensive meta-data. For instance a quick *table report* might be limited to the following details:

- schema
- table name
- number of records in the table
- comment
- primary key
- unique key
- foreign keys

A detailed report might include additional elements:

- table organization (e.g. heap organized table, index organized table, clustered table)
- enforcement of the referential integrity
- partitioning strategy
- partitioning keys
- tablespaces
- table physical details (e.g. compression, caching, parallelism etc.)

Some companies establish a practice to publish model-related reports for wider audience. If this is the approach taken the preferred report format should be the HTML allowing users the report access via a standard internet browser (e.g. Internet Explorer, Opera, Safari, etc.). Although convenient, this approach might lead to some information consistency problems due to a report publishing cycle on the designated company intranet site.

6.4.14. Documenting the code

Producing code documentation is a task that takes time and sometimes it is perceived as an unnecessary overhead. At the point when coding is completed, the developers have thorough understanding of the code's functionality including all the little "tricks" included in the code. However, after few months the knowledge and understanding of the code's functionality decreases to the point where it is very difficult to remember the details[200]. The code documentation serves multiple purposes:

- records relevant code details
- helps the supporting personnel understand the code
- provides the knowledge transfer

---

[200] Personally the author experienced this when, after four years had opportunity to reviewed his own code

Assuming that reading the code is sufficient to understand the code's functionality is proves to be wrong. When the code is designed, the developer had thorough understanding of the problem he was trying to solve. Over time that knowledge simply dissipates leaving just a vague memory of the implemented solution. Even for an experienced developer, few months of not dealing with the code he developed, will have detrimental effects on understanding the code and being able to maintain it efficiently.

The problem is amplified when the maintenance team has to take responsibility for code maintenance.

Below are the guidelines for documenting the code:

- include a standardize script header included with the following details:
  - □ *information about the developer:*
    - o first and last name
    - o contact details (e.g. phone and e-mail address, secondary support person)
  - □ code *version and date*
  - □ *permissions needed for code invocation*
  - □ *special instructions.* Depending on the database this can include various details related to: compiling, binding, isolation level used etc.
- for each procedural construct[201] providing comments to explain the following:
  - □ functionality of the construct
  - □ specific coding details important for understanding the functionality

Documenting the code can be done in many different ways. The simplest and probably the most efficient way is to provide comments embedded in the code. Comments should be very concise, describing the necessary logic implemented in the code segment they are referring to.

Although it is expected that accurate code documentation exists, it is surprising how many applications operate without documentation. Developers sometime assume that the person responsible for the code maintenance is able to understand its functionality just by reading the code. This is usually not the case because of the following:

- *code complexity*—the code that involves complex logic requires time to understand. It is very difficult to get into someone's else logic quickly
- *coding approach*—modern databases allow implementation of sophisticated programming techniques that includes Object-Oriented paradigms. For instance both DB2 and Oracle include ability to overload stored procedures[202]. This technique can

---

[201] Without getting into programming theory we will mention that procedural code development uses constructs to implement the logic: sequential operations (e.g. various calculations, input, output), selections (e.g. if, case etc.), iteration or loops(e.g. WHILE, FOR, etc.), another procedure call, exit and finally procedure completion.

[202] Overloading is the Object-Oriented technique allowing two objects to have the same name but different parameter set (signature)

be useful in creating a flexible application solution, but it can be a nightmare for the maintenance team

- *developer's experience*

Many companies are outsourcing their production support. Efficiency of outsourcing can be greatly improved by providing the code that is well documented allowing the outsourcing company to understand the functionality in a shorter period of time.

Detailed code documentation is out of scope for this book. More details and useful techniques for code documentation can be found in database books for developers. The discussion here is focused on documenting the DDL and DCL code generated by the tool.

The DDL script for the structural objects produced by the tool is documented by the tool that generates the code. Structural database objects (e.g. tables, views etc.) are relatively simple for documentation considering that they do not include programming logic that needs to be understood. As a minimum from business meta-data perspective, structural objects should include the definition[203] that will be stored in the database as an associated object. The definition is stored in the tool and subsequently propagated through the code to the database.

The following is a header for the structural objects:

```
--==================================================================

-- Database name: <the name of the database>
-- DBMS name: <database version and release number>
-- Created on: <date and time of the script creation>
-- To be implemented on: <date and time of scheduled implementation>
-- Class: <script class: DDL>
-- Created by: <the name and contact info of the person that created the script>
-- Remarks: <explanation of the script's functionality>
-- Authorization required: <permissions required for the script implementation>


--==================================================================
```

Standard header for the structural objects

The following is the explanation of the required information:

- *database name*[204]-at minimum the database name has to be provided. However it is a good idea to provide additional details relevant for the connection to the database:
  - □ database server
  - □ port number

---

[203] Stored as a comment

[204] If the script requires implementation in multiple databases, all databases where the script needs to be implemented have to be specified

- *DBMS name*-the name of the database platform (e.g. Sybase, DB2, MS SQL Server etc.) along with the version and release number
- *created on*-the timestamp when the script was created
- *class*—DDL (Data Definition Language) script that will contain SQL statements to create or drop various objects
- *to be implemented on*-scheduled date and time of implementation. In case of multiple databases each database has to have corresponding date and time of implementation for proper scheduling
- *created by*—the name and contact details of the person that created the script
- *remarks*—the script can be very lengthy and, based on parameters specified in the tool, it can include various objects. It is required to briefly explain what the expected functionality of the script is so that the person that is executing the script knows and can verify that the expected functionality is in-line with the statements provided in the script. If the script implements the *change requests (CR)*, specific CR identifiers have to be listed
- *authorization required*—specification of the authorization required to run the script.

Following is an example of the header for DDL that will drop and re-create tables in the database:

```
--=======================================================================

-- Database name: DW01P
-- DBMS name: DB2 V9.7 Common Server
-- Created on: 01/18/2011 9:14:56 PM
-- Class: DDL only
-- Created by: Vladimir Pantic, Data Architect, myemail@company.com,
--             (416) 555-5555
-- Remarks: The script to drop and re-create all tables in schema ABC.
-- Authorization required: IMPLICIT_SCHEMA or ownership of the schema


--=======================================================================
```

Example of the header for the Structural objects

The header has to be included as a comment at the beginning of the script and the purpose is to provide basic script description.

Behavioral database objects (e.g. stored procedures, methods etc.) include the programming logic that needs to be well documented. Irrespective of the script classification (structural or behavioral code), the code produced by the tool has to include a standard header with a content that depends on the code classification. The following is suggested header for the behavioral objects:

--==

-- **Object class:** *<SP-stored procedure, TR-trigger, UDF-Function, MT-Method>*
-- **Object name:** *<the name of the object>*
-- **Short description:** *<textual description of the functionality>*
-- **Input parameters:** *<list of input parameters with their data types>*
-- **Output parameters:** *<list of output parameters>*
-- **Return status:** *<explanation of the return statuses when the code is externally*
-- *called[205]>*
-- **Purity level:** *<assessment if the code is changing the database state>*
-- **Special instructions:** *<instructions on how to compile or bind the code>*
-- **Preferred isolation level:** *<isolation level used>*
-- **Object created by:** *<the name of the developer that created the code>*
-- **Object creation date:** *<date when the code was created>*
-- **Object last modified by:** *<the name of the developer that last modified the code>*
-- **Object last modification date:** *<the date of last code modification>*
-- **Object invocation syntax:** *<syntax of the code invocation[206]>*
-- **Transaction behavior:** *<explain if the code is referencing other code>*
-- **Overloaded:** *<specify if the code is overloaded>*
-- **Required authorization:** *<specify required authorization to implement and execute*
-- *the code>*
-- **Remarks:** *<special remarks to the user/administrator>*

--==

Standard header for behavioral objects

The following is the explanation of the information required for the header:

Object class—object classified as:

- **SP**—stored procedures
- **TR**—triggers
- **UDF**—user defined functions
- **MT**—methods

Object name—unique object name according to naming conventions

Short description—functionality description of the code. The intention is to provide basic information about the code so that supporting personnel, during the maintenance phase, can quickly understand the behavioral object's functionality

---

[205] Applicable to the Stored Procedures only.
[206] Instructions on how to run

Input parameters—specification of the input parameters with their data types

Output parameters—specification of the output parameters for the stored procedures

Return status—return status indicating a success or failure triggering a predefined response at the integration level

Purity level—specification of the side effects in the code functionality. It is important to know if the code is or is not changing the state of the database

Special instructions—code compilation and binding instructions might differ and this is the place to specifies relevant instructions

Preferred isolation level—standard isolation levels are defined as: *serializable, repeatable read, read committed and read uncommitted*[207]. Based on the desired transaction required isolation level should be specified

Object created by—the name and contact details of the developer that created the object.

Object creation date—object creation date

Object last modified by—the name and contact details of the developer that last modified the object

Object last modification date—last modification date

Object invocation syntax—example of the object invocation (e.g. stored procedure call)

Transaction behavior—specification if the object calls other objects or not. If the object does not call other objects then the scope of functional modifications is limited to that object. In case that object calls other objects, the functional modification might have side effects on the functionality of called objects

Overloaded—overloading is a programming technique of providing different functionality using the same object name. Based on the object's signature[208] the database engine will invoke proper object for execution. By specifying that the code is *overloaded* the developer is stating that there are more than one object with the same name and different signature (parameters)

Required authorization—authorization required for the object creation and execution

Remarks—other specific details about the object

---

[207] Both Oracle and DB2 implement control of the Isolation levels. For instance in DB2 the transaction can use one of the following isolation levels: CS (Cursor Stability), RS (Read Stability), RR (Read Repeatability) and UR (Uncommitted Read)

[208] Specification of parameters set.

Here is an example of how the header is populated:

```
--=====================================================================

-- Object class: SP
-- Object name: LOAD_CUSTOMERS.SQL
-- Short description: This stored procedure loads records from the CIS database extract into
PARTY.CUSTOMER table.
-- Input parameters:
-- CUSTOMER_FIRST_NAME : VARCHAR (20) representing the first name.
-- CUSTOMER_LAST_NAME : VARCHAR (54) representing the last name.
-- BIRTH_DATE: DATE representing the date when the customer was born.
-- Output parameters:
-- P_MESSAGE_O : Descriptive text indicating the Stored Procedure completion status
-- P_RETURN_VALUE_O : Return status of procedure
-- Return status:
--      -1 => Exception occurred
--       0 => Successful Happy Path
-- Purity level: DML-Database content change
-- Bind instructions: REOPT ONCE[209]
-- Preferred isolation level: CS[210]
-- Object created by: Martin Frommer
-- Object creation date: 11-Apr-2011
-- Object last modified by: Gene Jao
-- Object last modification date: 14-Aug-2011
-- Object invocation syntax:
-- CALL AK.LOAD_CUSTOMERS
-- (<CUSTOMER_FIRST_NAME>,<CUSTOMER_LAST_NAME>,<BIRTH_DATE>,
-- <P_MESSAGE_O>,<P_RETURN_VALUE_O>)
-- Transaction behavior: CALL OTHER
-- Overloaded: NO
-- Required authorization:
-- EXECUTE on the following procedures in AK schema:
--      VALIDATE_CUSTOMER
--      VALIDATE RATING
-- Remarks: No special instructions.


--=====================================================================
```

Example of a standard header for a stored procedure defined in DB2

The example provided here is a header specifically created for a DB2 stored procedure. Although majority of details provided are the same, specific details such as: isolation level specification and object invocation, might be different for other databases.

---

[209] Example is for a Stored Procedure in DB2. This is specific instruction applicable to DB2 only.
[210] DB2 specific.

7. MODEL IMPLEMENTATION

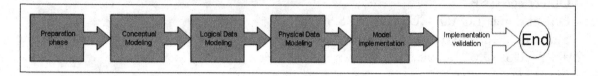

The physical data model implementation requires a rigorous process that ensures all elements defined in the model are properly propagated to the code and implemented in the database. This modeling phase involves the DBA and physical modeler in a joint effort to create and deliver the code. Historically, CASE tools were used to generate basic DDL code[211] that would be further modified by the DBA to include additional physical details typical for the database object created. This approach can lead to potential problems:

- the modeler is not aware of specific implementation decisions made by the DBA at the time of manual code modification
- modified code might go into the database implementation without review by the physical data modeler
- additional "last minute" modifications might be included directly in the script bypassing the model

If the script is modified by the DBA without going through the model, this can lead to inconsistencies between the database implementation and the model. The approach taken is to have the code fully generated from the model. The model implementation clearly requires both the DBA and data modeler working as a team. While the model, controlled by the modeler, is used to generate the code, the DBAs' involvement is to provide various technical details related to a particular database. The model will be updated to include technical details and parameters needed for the fully functional code.

The implementation phase starts with the model walk-through with the DBA. Purpose of the model walk-through is to allow the DBA's input in terms of implementation details that are missing or should be modified in the model. Model has to incorporate various technical details about the database objects. Once the model is completed with all objects and required details, the DBA should not need to modify the code generated from the CASE tool.

Implementation step itself can be conducted by the DBA or the modeler depending on the target environment where the model is implemented. Usually the development environment is not under the DBA's control and physical modeler can implement the model directly to the development database. Other environments (testing and production) are under different regimen and only the DBA can implement the code. The following table outlines the

---

[211] Usually limited to the tables, view and index creation

238

required types of the database access based on the type of environment where the model is implemented:

	Development DB	Testing DB	Production DB
Data modeler	Create/Drop objects	Read only access to validate the model	Read only access to validate the model
DBA	Create/Drop objects	Create/Drop objects	Create/Drop objects

Table 26: Required database access based on database environment

The model implementation phase is followed by the model comparison with the database and this task is performed by the modeler. To perform model validation against the database, the modeler has to have access to catalog tables in the database. Catalog tables access is required by the tool to gather the technical meta-data for the database reengineering.

7.1. Physical data model walk-through with the DBA

The model implementation starts with a model walk-through where the DBA reviews the model with the physical modeler. The DBA provides guidance and valuable input during the physical design. Before the model gets implemented, the DBA has to perform model validation to ensure that all required components are present and optimally designed.

The model walk-through has the following goals:

- assess completeness
- provide additional technical details to improve the performance and optimize utilization of database resources
- ensure that overall database solution is maintainable

Before the model walk-through the modeler has to prepare model for the walk-through by doing the following:

- perform the formal physical data model validation. This step is performed by PowerDesigner and it is fully automated
- assess the model completeness by validating it against the *physical data model checklist*
- segregate clusters of related tables into diagrams for easier review. Instead, the model is divided into smaller diagrams with cohesive groups of related tables to enable focused review of an isolated model segment at a time.

Prior to the model walk-through, the model has to be available to the DBA for an independent review. The DBA should have enough time to perform independent model assessment so that model walk-through is performed more efficiently. The walk-through is performed in at least two steps:

- *initial model walk-throug*h followed by model modifications performed by the physical modeler
- *final model walk-through,* required to review the modifications implemented in the model
- The following is the model walk-through agenda:
- *introduction*—the modeler has to give a quick model overview and conventions used in the model. This step is sometimes overlooked assuming that DBA is familiar with standards used in the model and the model itself
- *model components*—understanding of what is included in the model and what is not is crucial for the physical implementation
- *model components walk-through*—the modeler will explain to the DBA the design and included physical details of each component included in the physical data model
- *questions and answers*—the modeler will answer questions related to the model and the design approach taken
- *DBA's recommendations*—the DBA will provide recommendations for model optimization

During the model walk-through the DBA may provide valuable input to the modeler in terms of model optimization while at the same time asking questions related to the design. The modeler has to keep track of open issues and observations provided by DBA. After the completion of the initial model walk-through it is necessary to analyze all the recommendations provided by the DBA and answer questions related to specific design decisions included in the model. A word of caution here: ***the author has witnessed many situations where the input and especially questions asked by the DBA were perceived as an attack on the model. It is imperative to understand that the DBA is there to understand why certain design decisions were made because sometimes deviation from modeling principles is required in order to achieve the required performance levels. Asking questions about the model and providing input about re-design should not be perceived as an attack on the model or the modeler. This is rather an input of a team member that has knowledge and expertise to help improve the quality and efficiency of the implemented solution.***

Maximum performance improvements while minimizing the resources utilization is the ultimate design goal for the modeling team. The DBA will assess if the database design can be improved by using various techniques:

- table clustering
- vertical and horizontal table partitioning
- indexes
- materialized views
- parallelism
- database infrastructure objects design optimization (e.g. buffer pools, tablespaces etc.)

Model walk-through is a time of direct interaction between the modeler and DBA when the design details are explained and analyzed, preparing the model for closing and implementation. From the modeler's perspective, the model has to comply with the requirements specified in the logical data model and performance requirements specified in the Service Level Agreement[212]. The DBA, on the other hand, reviews the model from the performance optimization, resource utilization and implementation perspective. The DBA's goal is to stay within the boundaries defined in the SLA. This is why keeping the balance of both aspects (the modeler's and DBA perspectives) is important for the model's quality and functionality. Model modifications that favor performance to functionality might lead to a solution that is not maintainable in the long run. On the other hand, functionally perfect models are sometimes posing unsolvable challenge for performance optimization, so finding a balance between these is crucial.

7.2. Recommendations for efficient code deployment

Handling problems with code deployment is not trivial especially if the database is populated with data. Generally, after the initial deployment any modification of the database, irrespective of the class (development, testing, and production) is assumed to require a delta code. From time to time a full database refresh (dropping and recreating all database objects) might be required.

To alleviate challenges with code deployment, following are the recommendations:

- *clearly define roles and responsibilities*—*who* does *what*, *when* and *how* is important to know when the things go bad! Spend some time defining the roles and responsibilities in the process. This will help you to react quickly and decisively when the problem is encountered
- *good and concise documentation*—having a thick manual at 2:00 AM is not very helpful if the person solving the problem does not know where to find what he is looking for. The documentation should be designed to allow quick problem identification and resolution
- *appropriate training*—formal initial training is important but more important is to provide continuous training by repeating, testing and practicing the procedures. This will help the team to properly react to incidents with code deployment.

7.2.1.1. Initial database code deployment

The reviewed and approved physical data model marks the physical data modeling process completion. The code generation is performed directly from the tool. Before implementation to code should be review by the DBA.

The Illustration 147 describes the procedure.

After completion, the model is checked into the repository. Initial code deployment starts with the model checkout from the model repository. The model is then synchronized with the

---

[212] SLA

database to include all the referenced infrastructure objects. The purpose of the synchronization step is to bring the infrastructure objects to the model so that the model corresponds to the database. After the model synchronization with the database, the modeler creates the final version of the script. The model and corresponding script is then checked into the model repository.

Implementation continues by DBA checking out the model and script from the repository. The DBA performs an independent review before the code is implemented in the database. After implementation the DBA informs the modeler about successful implementation instructing him to compare the model to the database. If the comparison does not show any differences the deployment is deemed successful and the modeler informs the DBA that the procedure is completed. The model has to checked-in to the repository in case that there are some minor acceptable differences[213].

Initial full database implementation assumes that the database is empty, so the code deployed creates required database objects and implements the access control through script. From time to time it is required to wipe out the development database and do the full, clean database deployment. When the data model is stored in the tool, the full deployment can be done quickly using the following procedure:

- generate the DDL code that will drop all objects:
  - □ behavioral objects
  - □ structural objects such as: tables, synonyms etc.
- generate the DCL script

---

[213] Model comparison to the database might report some minor differences cause by implementation of the default database values. These are acceptable and should be included in the model as such

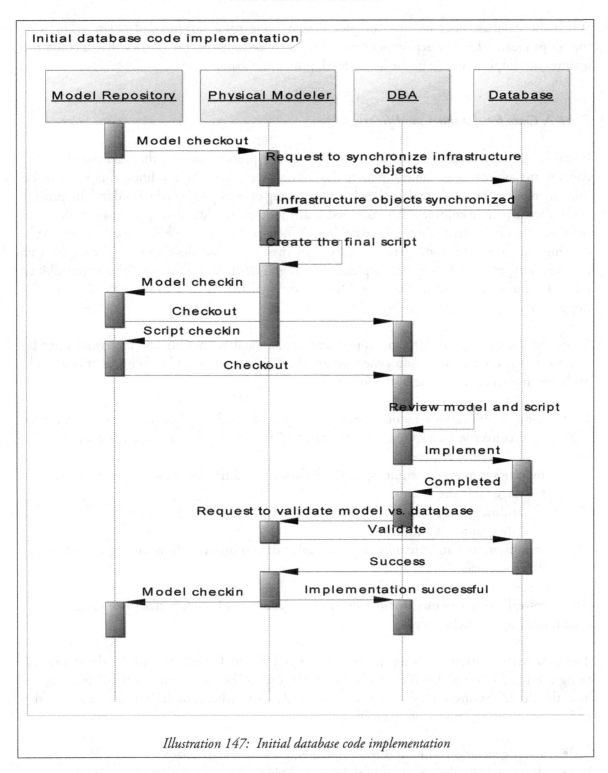

Illustration 147: Initial database code implementation

The full deployment script is intentionally broken into the DDL and DCL components so they can be run in sequence. It is a good idea to provide the script for full deployment each time there is a modification in the database because the script can be used by the developers to create a replica of the database on their local computer and independently perform various tests.

When the database does include complex design using some advanced database features[214], the script created for full deployment might need to exclude specific clauses that include the features not implementable in the local, development database.

7.2.1.2. Code for database modifications

Initial DDL deployment is relatively straight forward process because the database does not contain any objects (e.g. tables, indexes etc.). However when the modifications need to be implemented in the database that already have existing objects populated with data, the process is significantly more complex. It is assumed that modeler should create code that implements required modifications without the data loss. When performing modifications by manually creating the code, the DBA has a full control over the code development, hence he can choose an appropriate strategy to implement changes. With PowerDesigner the responsibility for code's functionality shifts from the DBA to the tool that is used to generate the code for implementation.

Given the various events that can happen during the database modifications it would not be realistic to expect that the code generated by the CASE tool provides fully functional code ready for implementation due to the following:

- some modifications require implementation of database specific functions for data type conversion and these are not standardized across the databases. A manual code modification is required
- modifications might require specialized database utilities for the following reasons:
  □ large table size
  □ requirements for high availability[215]
  □ table content sensitivity
- modifications might require more complex data transformations during the structural object change

When PowerDesigner is used for the delta code generation it is expected that some manual code modification might occur.

The database modification using the code generated by the CASE tool will be demonstrated using the model created for DB2 as the target database. The procedure starts by deciding on how the modifications will be propagated to the database when PowerDesigner generates the code. The following options are available:

- script generation without direct implementation in the database
- direct code implementation in the database via a "live" connection to the database

---

[214] For instance the table partitioning

[215] Special procedures are required when the table modification has to be done on-line while users are accessing the database. For instance, Oracle allows this using special package for on-line table re-definition

No matter how experienced you are with the tool, recommendation is to always create the script, review and implement it manually. This will help lower the risks of:

- accidentally dropping required database objects
- performing an incorrect object modification due to omissions or potential errors in the code

For the script generation the tool has to be connected to the database. The procedure goes through the following steps:

- connect to the database
- reverse engineer the database into a model
- compare the original to the database (reverse engineered) model
- report the differences
- modeler specifies which model components will be implemented
- PowerDesigner generates the script

The procedure is started by connecting to the database. The following is the illustration of the connection dialog:

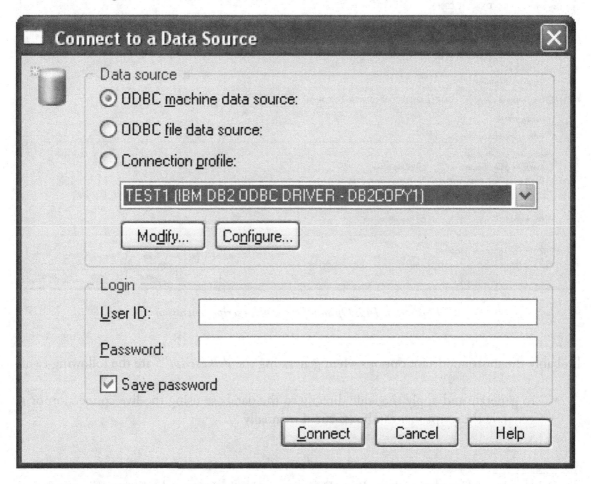

Illustration 148: Dialog to connect to the database (PowerDesigner)

The user name and valid password has to be specified to connect to the database. If the modeler is performing the code generation and deployment, proper permissions are required for the user to be able to perform required activities:

- for the reverse database engineering, the user must have read-only permission to access the system catalog tables where the database meta-data is stored
- permissions to create, drop or modify appropriate database objects are required to implement the script
- additional permissions related to the security model deployment are required if the DCL is part of the code deployment

To avoid security problems, choose the *not to save the password* option in PowerDesigner.

Once connected to the database, user has to specify the code generation options as shown in the Illustration 149:

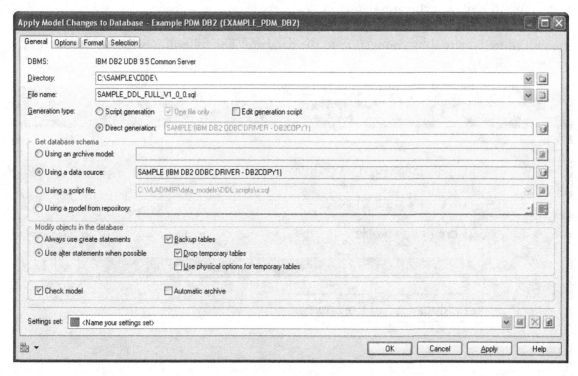

Illustration 149: Options for the delta script generation

Probably the most important options when generating the *delta script*[216] are the following two:

- to generate and apply the code directly to the database using the live connection or to generate the script that can be executed manually

---

[216] Delta code modifies the database. PowerDesigner can implement the database modifications with or without the data loss depending on options specified in the tool

- options related to how the structural objects are modified:
  - □ using the ALTER statements whenever possible or
  - □ using the approach where the intermediate tables are created and data is transferred from the original table (as explained later)

Instead of implementing the code directly from the model, better approach is to do the following:

- create the script
- review the script[217]
- run the script manually

Another important decision is if the modifications have to be performed with or without data loss. When database is created and used, the tables are populated with data and any modification might impact the data content. Modifications introduced in the script can structurally change the table requiring it to be dropped and re-created. Procedure is quite different when modifications are implemented without the data loss as shown in the table 27:

Table modification **with** data loss	Table modification **without** data loss
Drop the referential integrity	Drop the referential integrity
Drop the table	Rename the table[218]
Re-create the table with the new structure	Create table with the new structure
Create related database objects (e.g. primary and unique constraints, indexes, comments)	Load the data from the (original) renamed table
Re-establish the referential integrity	Create related database objects (e.g. primary and unique constraints, indexes, comments)
Grant permissions	Re-establish the referential integrity
	Grant permissions
	Drop the (original) renamed table[219]

Table 27: Comparison of the delta code procedures
implemented with and without the data loss

The complexity of delta script modifications *without data loss* is higher compared to the complexity of code that implements modification *with data loss*. Many challenges will be encountered when modifying the database populated with data. The following are typical types of problems that have to be handled in the delta scripts:

- if the data has to be converted from the source data type that is not compatible to the target data type (for instance from character to a number) special data type conversion

---

[217] Having the script reviewed before its implementation decreases the risk of accidentally modifying or dropping a database object

[218] PowerDesigner will provide the temporary name for the table.

[219] This step is optional and recommendation is to drop the original, renamed table manually.

function has to be used. PowerDesigner will not automatically generate the code with explicit function specification. The tool will warn that the script generated is not directly implementable and manual intervention is needed before the script is fully functional

- if the data has to be constantly available, the modeler and DBA has to modify the script to use database-specific solutions
- modification of large tables require significant script modifications to include phase data off-load and re-load to decrease pressure on the logging space

These situations might cause a lot of problems if the script is not carefully reviewed before the execution especially in environments where the data volumes are high and any accidentally dropped tables need hours to restore. This is the main reason why the advised approach is to have the script generated by the CASE tool, reviewed and then run in the database manually rather than performing the direct execution via the live database connection.

Each database object has a specific set of properties stored in the model. When PowerDesigner performs comparison between the model and the database prior to delta code generation, the modeler explicitly specifies the scope for comparison i.e. what is and what is not included in the object comparison between the model and the database. The Illustration 150 provides an example of the database object properties that will be included in the model and database comparison.

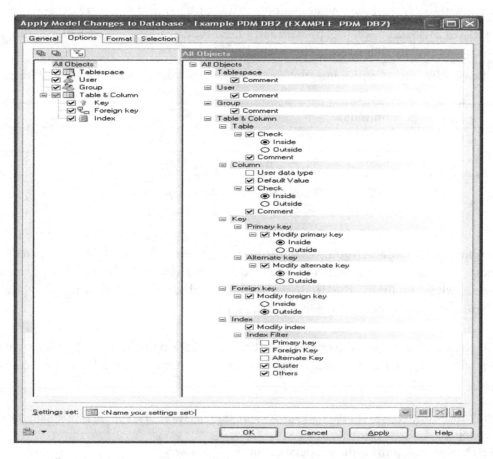

Illustration 150: Specification of object components to be included in the code

For databases that do not use the table and index partitioning the comparison is straightforward. The structure is constant and specification of the object properties does not include any variable elements. However, when the table partitioning is involved the object might be constantly changing. Partitions can be added or dropped constantly changing the table structure. The table's structure recorded in the model might be different than the one that is currently in the database. Performing modifications on the partitioned table[220] require model synchronization (to include the partitions) with the database prior to performing modifications in the model. This increases complexity and introduces a risk for potential accidental damages to the table that has to be modified. Therefore it is necessary to be cautious in case of the partitioned table modification.

The Table 151 shows the code formatting page that allows specification of common elements pertaining to the character set (encoding), case (upper, lower or mixed) and object schema specification (ownership). To provide the business meta-data, PowerDesigner can also generate the table-level comments with the table name when the comment is not explicitly defined.

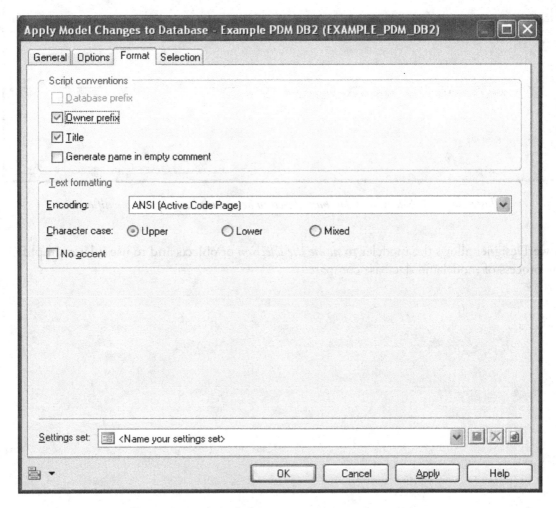

Illustration 151: Code formatting options in PowerDesigner

---

[220] Index or both

The list of objects included in the model can be extensive. There is a possibility that some objects, although in the model, are excluded from code generation. PowerDesigner allows for explicit specification of the objects to be included into the model and database comparison as shown in the Illustration 152:

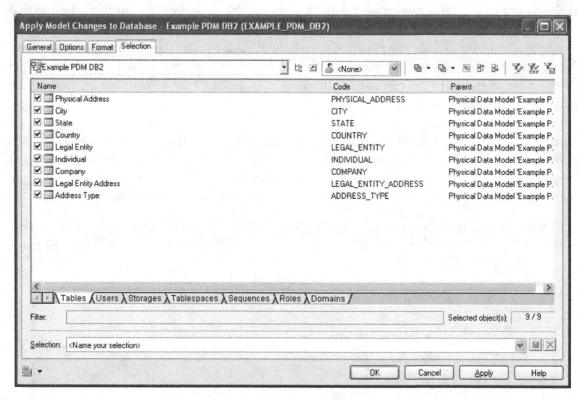

Illustration 152: Selection of database objects to be included in scope for modifications

PowerDesigner allows the modeler to *name the selection* of objects and re-use it later simplifying the process of model and database compare.

7.2.1.3. Final code packaging

The database code implementation requires specific sequence. When code is manually created, the DBA has to pay special attention to the database object inter-dependencies and this is not trivial as shown in the Illustration 153:

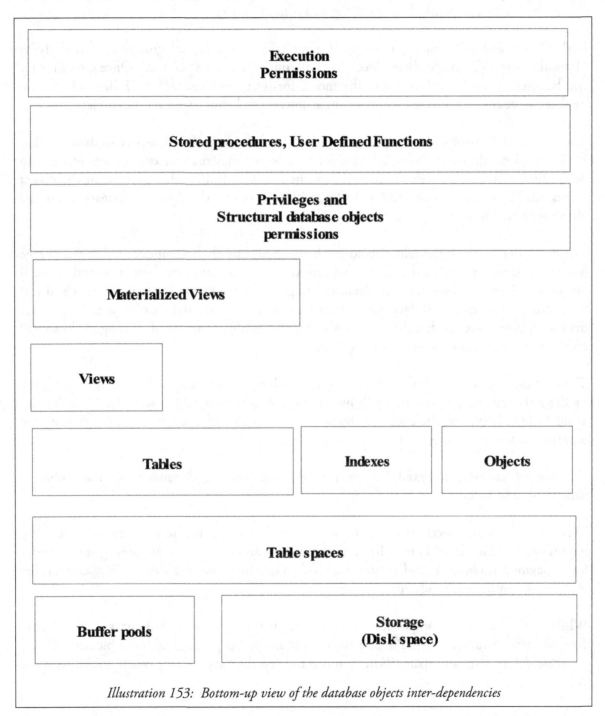

Illustration 153: Bottom-up view of the database objects inter-dependencies

The process of database implementation starts with the database creation. The infrastructure objects are created next. The infrastructure objects required are:

- *database storage* (disk space)
- *buffer pools*—segment of the server's central memory where the data is read and written before user consumption or writing to a disk respectively

Both Oracle and DB2 have a concept of a tablespace as a logical grouping of underlying physical storage. Generally, these object types are under the DBA's control. Once created, they will be re-engineered and brought to the model for future reference. If the DBA and physical modeler agree then the infrastructure database objects can be managed via the model.

The structural database objects (e.g. tables, indexes etc.) reside in the tablespace so their creation is directly dependent on the tablespace existence. Sometimes the concept of dependence can be confusing because it is not necessarily required to specify the tablespace when the object is created. For instance both DB2 and Oracle use a concept of a *default tablespace* where the object is created if the tablespace is not specified.

The default tablespaces generally should not be used because the assumption is that the storage has to be carefully designed and maintained to gain maximum performance and optimal utilization. A single tablespace with default settings can rarely satisfy the requirements and it is used mostly in development databases. When creating structural database objects the tablespace definition is required so that the objects placement is explicitly specified. Failing to do so will result in object creation in the default tablespace.

To avoid the use of the default tablespace when explicit tablespace specification is missing, the modeler should run a report that will list all objects with their tablespaces. The modeler can avoid accidently placing the database objects in the *default* tablespace by simply reviewing the report for offending objects.

Creation of tables is followed by creation of corresponding dependent database objects: constraints and indexes.

Views are structural objects that rely on underlying tables, so before the view is created the requirement is for the table to exist. The database is automatically maintaining the integrity by managing the object inter-dependencies. If the table included in a view is dropped then the view is automatically invalidated.

While a regular view is implemented as a data dictionary object without a physical data content instantiation, a materialized views are instantiated as physical tables implemented with automated[221] or semi-automated[222] mechanism to keep the data content synchronized with the

---

[221]   Materialized view refreshed ON COMMIT
[222]   Materialized view refreshed ON DEMAND

underlying tables. Materialized vies are created after the tables included in the view are defined in the database.

The next step is to implement the database permissions. When the full deployment script is generated from the tool, the DDL and DCL can be segregated in two different scripts. However, this is not the case with the delta script generation as it is easier to produce an integral script rather than separate DDL and DCL scripts.

Once all the structural database objects are in place, behavioral database objects can be implemented. The last step in model implementation is granting the right to execute the behavioral object (e.g. functions or stored procedures). The implementation of the execution rights for the stored procedures requires understanding of additional details pertaining to the way the stored procedure is compiled. In Oracle and DB2 there is a concept of the *definer's* and *invoker's* rights. The *definer* is the user that created procedure and if the stored procedure is compiled with the definer's rights then, by giving the execution rights to the end user, the user is authorized to access the underlying structural objects. In other words, the end user does not need explicit authorization to have access to the underlying structural objects. If the stored procedure is compiled with the *invoker's* rights then explicit grants for the access to the underlying structural objects is required.

The following is proposed code packaging:

1. DDL—create:
   1. infrastructure objects
      1. buffer pools
      2. storage
   2. tablespaces
   3. tables and triggers[223]
   4. indexes
   5. objects and methods
   6. views
   7. materialized views
2. DCL—grant:
   1. privileges
   2. permissions for the structural database objects
3. DDL—create:
   1. user defined functions
   2. stored procedures[224]
4. DCL—grant:
   1. execution permissions for behavioral database object

---

[223] Although the trigger is classified as a behavioral database object type it relies on the table (unless we are creating a specialized trigger type available in Oracle).

[224] Considering that there is a possibility that the Stored Procedure uses a UDF (User Defined Function) it is logical to create the UDF before the Stored Procedure that utilized the UDF is created.

In case of an integral code (a single script) that includes all required components for code generation the tool performs the code packaging based on the database object inter-dependency. When multiple scripts are created, the modeler must understand the object's dependencies to create a correct script.

7.2.1.4. Code generation

The code generation using PowerDesigner is an automated process. Once properly set, the code generation allows for uniform script creation. However, automated script generation can be dangerous if the modeler is not fully aware of options specified. Just by choosing inappropriate option the modeler can literally wipe out the whole database with a press of a button.

Based on the physical model, PowerDesigner can generate a single script (integrating the DDL and DCL scripts) or multiple scripts, as per modeler's specification. The script generation requires the following to be specified:

- object types to be created (e.g. tablespaces, tables, indexes, constraints etc.)
- object physical properties to be included

As mentioned before the starting point is definition of the database object types to be created. An example of objects specified for creation is given in the illustration below:

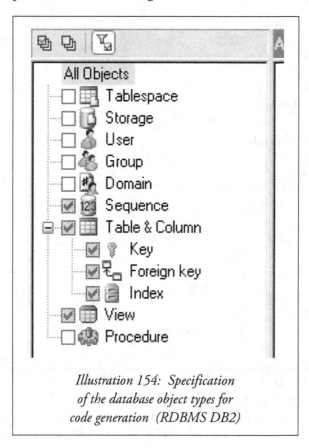

Illustration 154: Specification of the database object types for code generation (RDBMS DB2)

The target RDBMS in this example is IBM's DB2 database. For each object type in the list (e.g. table, index, view etc.) physical properties can be defined, as shown below:

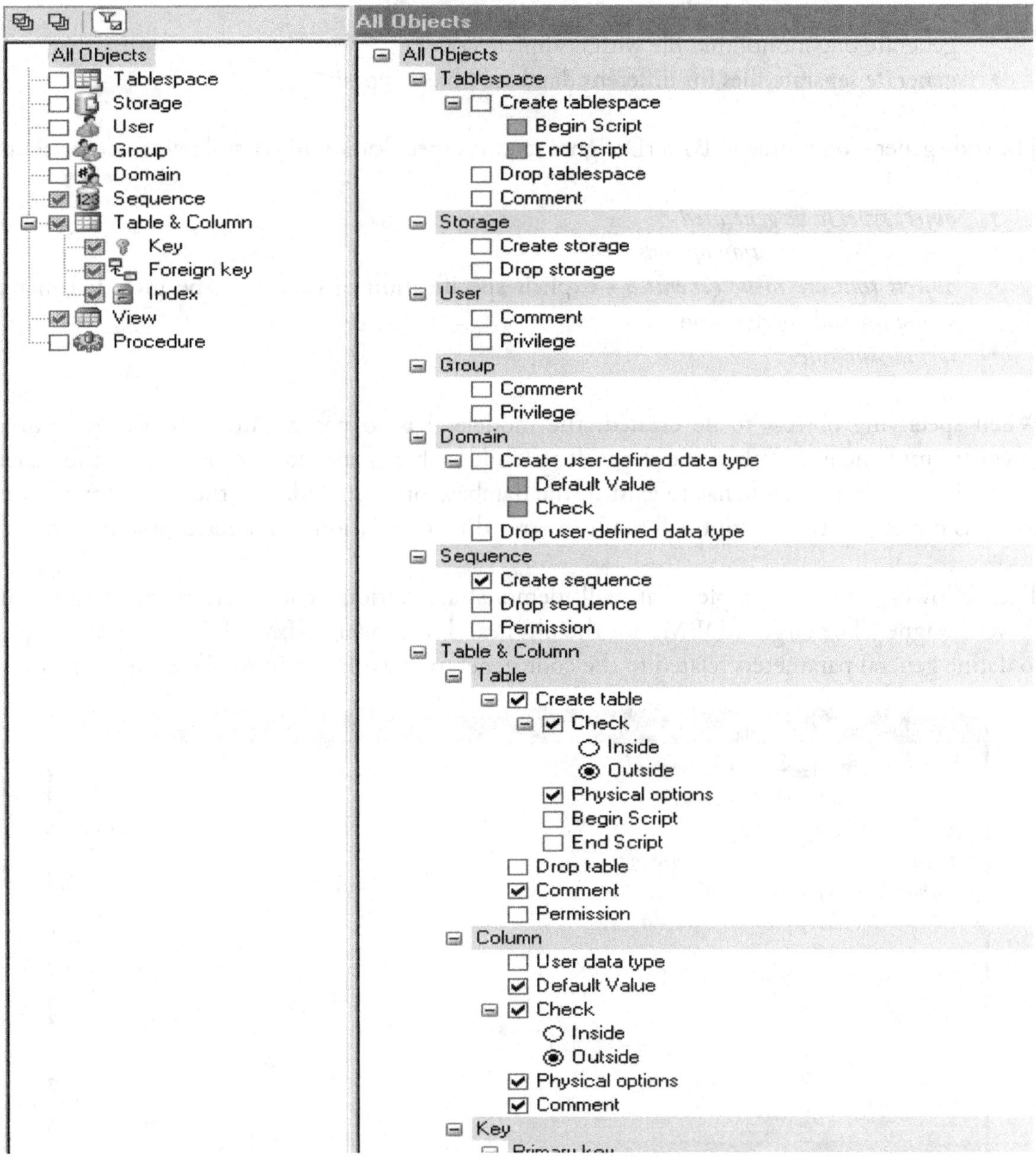

Illustration 155: Physical properties for various database object types in PowerDesigner

A convenient way to optimize the code generation is to prepare the tool by implementing the code generation profiles. Profiles are predefined options saved in the model or externally in the file. At modeler's disposal are two alternatives:

- generate one monolithic file with complete code[225]
- generate separate files for different database object types[226]

The code generation profile in PowerDesigner requires specification of the following components:

- *object types to be generated*
- *specific code generation options*
- *objects that are to be generated*—explicit specification of objects to be included in the scope for code generation
- *formatting rules*

When specifying objects to be created, the modeler has to pay attention to the referential integrity implemented. When the dependent (child) table is specified to be in scope for code generation, the parent table has to exist in the database or be included in the script generation. If this is not the case, the script will result in error due to violation of the referential integrity.

The following is an example that will demonstrate various code generation options in PowerDesigner. The target RDBMS for the physical data model is IBM's DB2. The first step is to define general parameters related to the code generation as shown in the Illustration 156:

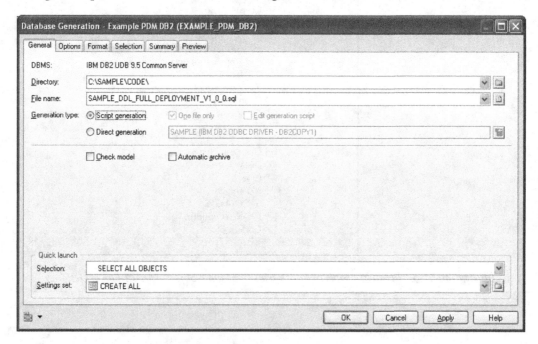

Illustration 156: General options for code generation

---

225 DDL and DCL including all the behavioral objects
226 For instance one file for tables, another for Indexes etc

The modeler is provided with two options:

- *script generation into a file*—this option will create a script that has to be executed manually. The file name and location (directory) has to be specified. The modeler should ensure that generated file name complies to the file naming conventions
- *direct generation into the database*—this is the option that will create script and proceed with database implementation via a live database connection

Code generated by PowerDesigner can include the statements that can drop the database objects. Although both Oracle and DB2 allow for dropped tables to be recovered[227], generally it is a good idea to avoid using the direct code generation and implementation via the live database connection to decrease the risk of accidentally dropping the database objects. It is better to generate code into a file, review it and run it manually in the database. The author had experienced this first-hand by accidentally dropping populated tables. The next step is specification of the database object types to be included in the code generation (Illustration 157):

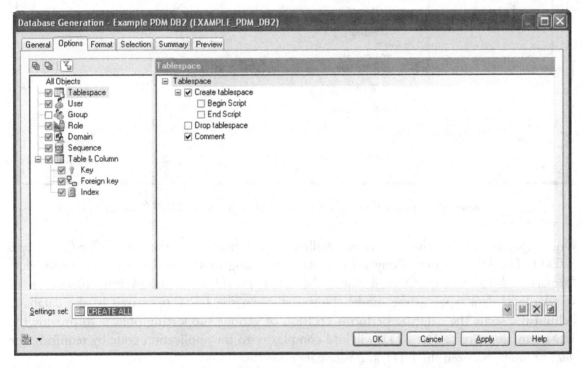

Illustration 157: Database object types included in the code generation

In this example the objects in scope are the following:

- tablespaces
- users
- roles

---

[227] Oracle is using the FLASHBACK feature while the DB2 is able to recover the table by creating the tablespace with DROPPED TABLE RECOVERY option. Alternatively the database backup can be used to restore specific objects

- user defined data types (domains)
- sequences
- tables and table related objects (keys, indexes)

For each object type the user can also specify additional options. The following illustration shows elements that can be specified for a table (Illustration 158):

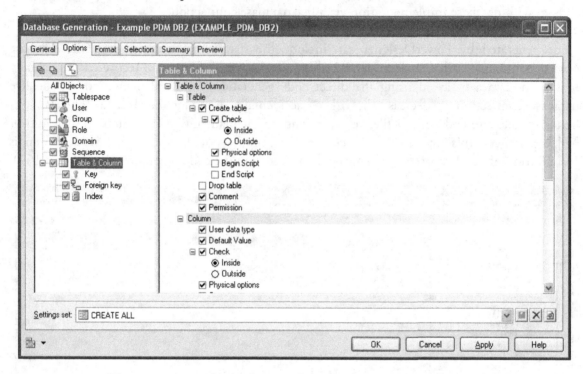

Illustration 158: Table-level options for code generation (RDBMS DB2)

One important option that can cause challenges is utilization of the *user defined data types* (UDT). The UDT is extensively used in data modeling to standardize the data types, data formats and constraints. Once defined, the UDT provides a uniform implementation of standardized data types in the model. However, when the UDT is created in the database, behind the scene the database performs creation of various supporting objects to provide the UDT functionality[228]. The UDT will add complexity to the application code by requiring the *data casting*[229] between the UDT and base data type[230].

When the UDT is used in the physical model, the modeler has an option to implement the UDT as such or use the base data type instead. By specifying the option to use the *user data type* in the column options, PowerDesigner will generate code to create the UDT before it is used for the column data type.

---

[228] As explained when the UDT are discussed in details

[229] Data type conversion

[230] For instance if the UDT AMOUNT is defined as DECIMAL (10,2), the casting converts the decimal number to the UDT AMOUNT or vice verse

If the table's *permission* options is chosen, when the table is generated the script will include both the DDL and DCL statements.

Another important segment related to the table is the constraints definition:

- primary
- foreign
- unique
- in-line

When the constraints are defined, the following rules should be taken into consideration:

- when creating a primary or unique constraint, the underlying index does not need to be created. The index is created by default-automatically by the database. Furthermore if the constraint supporting index creation is explicitly specified, the RDBMS will report that the index with exact definition (structure) already exists
- when the foreign key reference is established, the index creation on the column included in the foreign key, is optional. Recommendation by the database vendors is to create an index on the column (or columns) included in the foreign key[231]

The script is further customized by specifying the schema where the object resides, code page and character case[232] as shown in the Illustration 159.

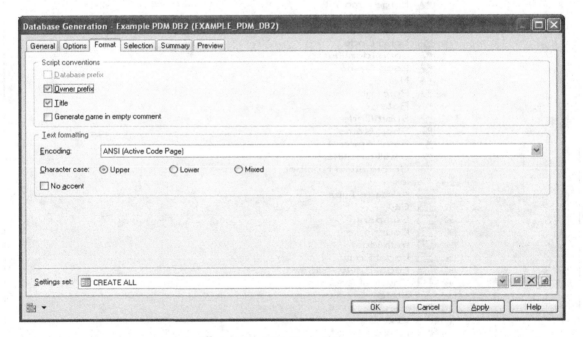

Illustration 159: Formatting options

---

[231] This is required to speed up the database access, help the optimizer optimize the access plan and avoid potential locking problems. For further details please refer to the database manuals

[232] For instance, if the database is specified to be case-sensitive, the objects CUSTOMER and customer would represent two different tables

The third step is to explicitly specify the objects included in the code generation. The model can include objects that are not ready or not intended to be implemented so PowerDesigner allows the object exclusion from the code generation. Once specified the list of objects in scope for code generation can be reviewed as shown in the Illustration 160:

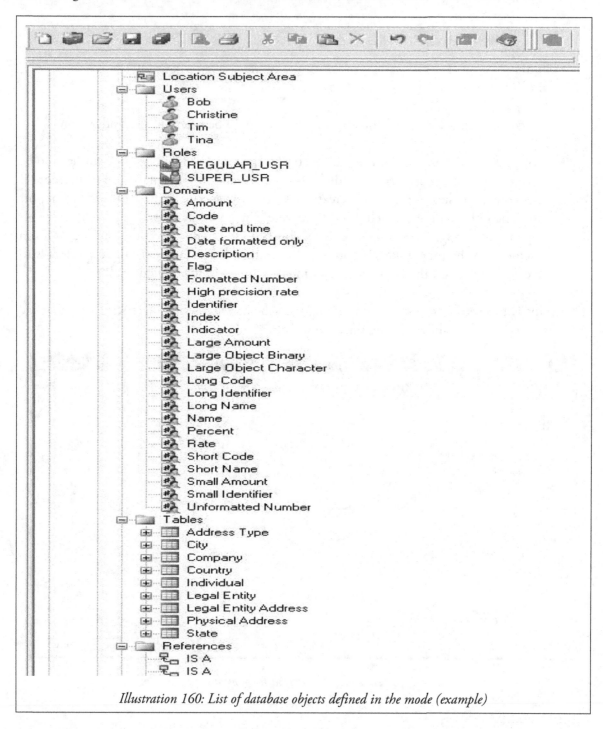

Illustration 160: List of database objects defined in the mode (example)

The screen snapshots (Illustrations 161, 162, 163, 164 and 165) show the database objects explicitly included in the script generation:

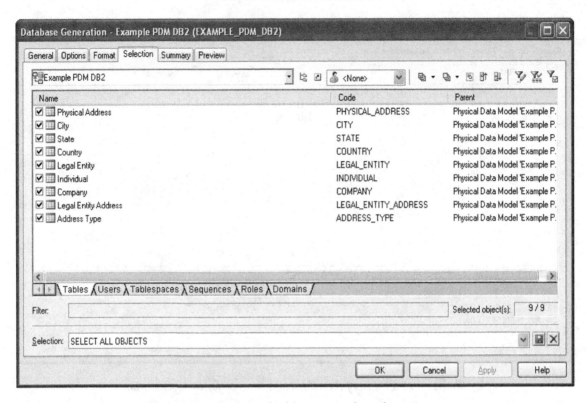

Illustration 161: List of tables in scope for code generation

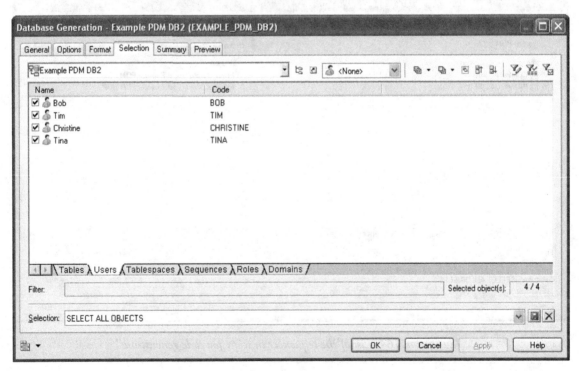

Illustration 162: List of the users in scope for code generation

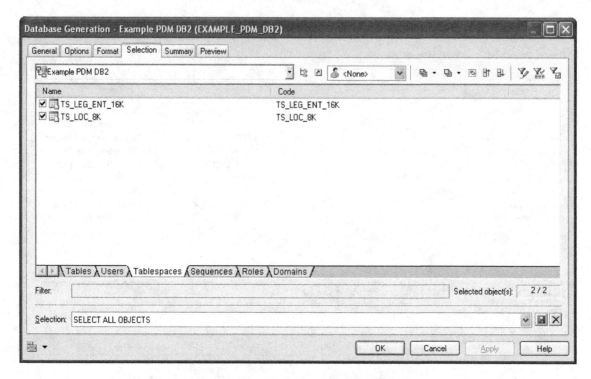

Illustration 163: List of the tablespaces in scope for code generation

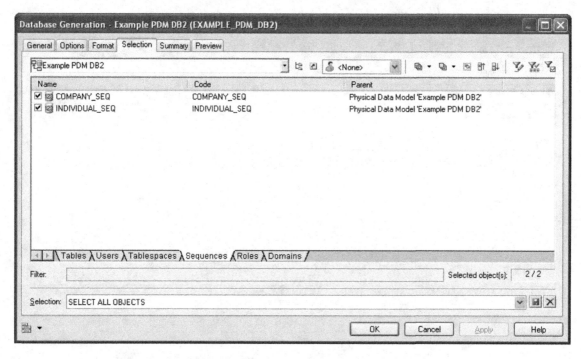

Illustration 164: List of the sequences in scope for code generation.

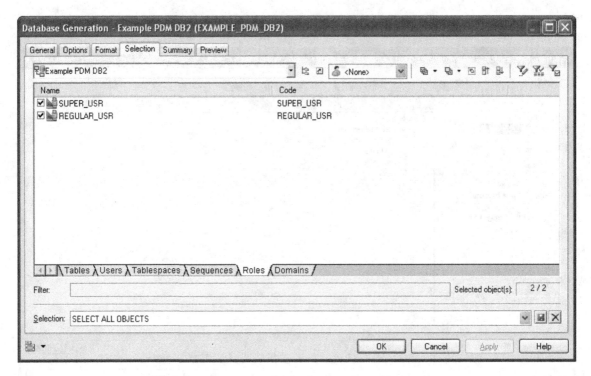

Illustration 165: List of roles in scope for code generation

Each screen allows specification of the objects to be included in the script that will be generated. The modeler can specify objects in scope, every time it is required or, by naming the selection (in this example the name of the selection is *SELECT ALL OBJECTS*) the set of objects in scope will be automatically predefined. At this point the tool is ready for code generation and by pressing the *OK* button the modeler will generate the code.

Let us look at the code generated by PowerDesigner to understand the results of choices made. The target RDBMS is IBM's DB2.

The code generation starts with definition of the tablespaces.

CREATE large TABLESPACE TS_LEG_ENT_16K;

CREATE large TABLESPACE TS_LOC_8K;

The assumption is that the *automated storage management (ASM)* is used, therefore the only requirement is to generate the tablespaces by name. Underlying data files[233] (containers[234]) are automatically managed by the database.

---

[233] In Oracle
[234] In DB2

These tablespace creation statements are triggered by the following specification:

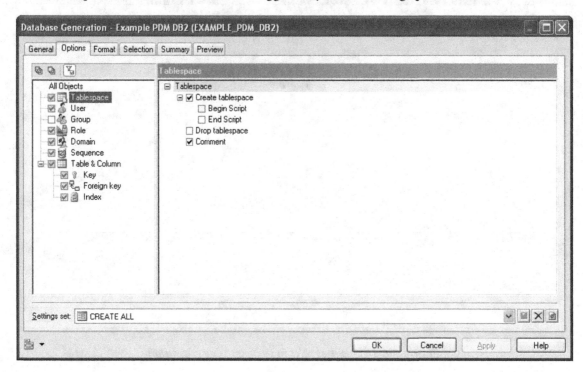

Illustration 166: Tablespace physical options (RDBMS DB2)

The roles are created next:

```
--============================================================
-- ROLE: REGULAR_USR
--============================================================
CREATE ROLE REGULAR_USR;


--============================================================
-- role: SUPER_USR
--============================================================
CREATE ROLE SUPER_USR;
```

The roles creation is controlled by the following options as shown in the Illustration 167:

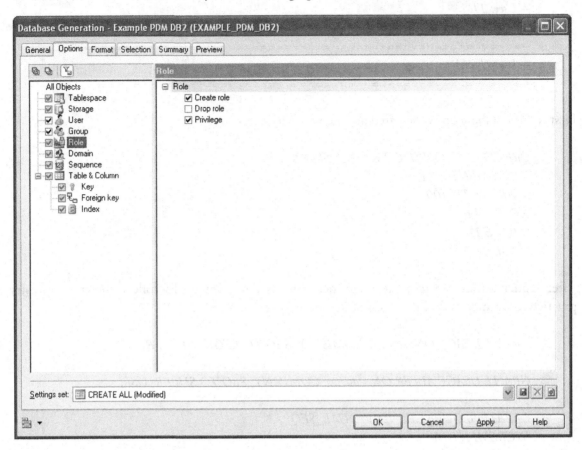

Illustration 167: Role generation options (RDBMS DB2)

Each role has the *privileges* assigned, requiring that the modeler specifies the option to grant privileges to the roles after their creation.

The users in DB2 are created externally because DB2 is using the operating system's (O/S) authentication[235]. Therefore the DB2 users cannot be explicitly defined (created) in the script. Specification of users in the model corresponds to the schema definition, however a placeholder exists to denote that one of the options we specified is the users creation:

```
-- ==========================================================
-- User: BOB
-- ==========================================================
-- ==========================================================
-- User: CHRISTINE
-- ==========================================================
```

---

[235] In Oracle the user can be defined in the database, so the script would include set of statements to create users with their passwords

```
--===========================================================
-- User: TIM
--===========================================================
--===========================================================
-- User: TINA
--===========================================================
```

First set of database objects created are the sequences:

> *CREATE SEQUENCE COMPANY_SEQ*
> *INCREMENT BY 1*
> *START WITH 100*
> *NO CYCLE*
> *CACHE 120*
> *ORDER;*

After sequences are created, the usage permissions are granted. To follow the best industry practice recommends that permissions are granted to the roles[236]:

> *GRANT USAGE ON sequence COMPANY_SEQ TO REGULAR_USR;*

> *GRANT USAGE,ALTER ON sequence COMPANY_SEQ TO SUPER_USR;*

> *CREATE SEQUENCE INDIVIDUAL_SEQ*
> *INCREMENT BY 1*
> *START WITH 1*
> *CYCLE*
> *ORDER;*

> *GRANT USAGE ON sequence INDIVIDUAL_SEQ TO REGULAR_USR;*

> *GRANT USAGE,ALTER ON sequence INDIVIDUAL_SEQ TO SUPER_USR;*

---

[236] As specified in the model

The sequences generation is controlled by options specified in the Illustration 168:

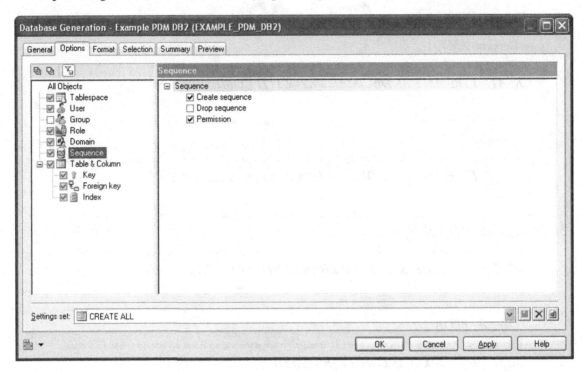

Illustration 168: Code generation options for the sequences (RDBMS DB2)

The model includes definition of the *user defined data types.* Assuming that the modeler decides to implement the UDT in the database, the following options have to be specified (Illustration 169):

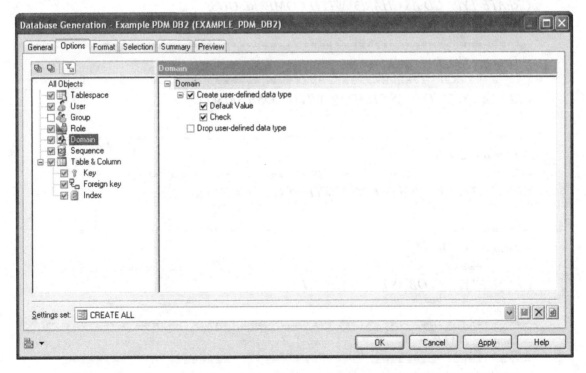

Illustration 169: Specification of the code generation options for UDT (RDBMS DB2)

The *user defined data types* are created accordingly:

```
--=================================================
-- Domain: AMT
--=================================================
CREATE TYPE AMT AS DECIMAL(14,2) WITH COMPARISONS;


--=================================================
-- Domain: AMT_L
--=================================================
CREATE TYPE AMT_L AS DECIMAL(24,2) WITH COMPARISONS;


--=================================================
-- Domain: AMT_S
--=================================================
CREATE TYPE AMT_S AS NUMERIC(8,2) WITH COMPARISONS;


--=================================================
-- Domain: BLOB
--=================================================
CREATE TYPE BLOB AS LONG VARGRAPHIC;


--=================================================
-- Domain: CD
--=================================================
CREATE TYPE CD AS CHAR(3) WITH COMPARISONS;


--=================================================
-- Domain: CD_L
--=================================================
CREATE TYPE CD_L AS CHAR(10) WITH COMPARISONS;


--=================================================
-- Domain: CD_S
--=================================================
CREATE TYPE CD_S AS CHAR(1) WITH COMPARISONS;


--=================================================
-- Domain: CLOB
--=================================================
CREATE TYPE CLOB AS LONG VARCHAR;


--=================================================
-- Domain: DATE_F
--=================================================
CREATE TYPE DATE_F AS DATE WITH COMPARISONS;
```

```
--===========================================================
-- Domain: "DESC"
--===========================================================
CREATE TYPE "DESC" AS VARCHAR(120) WITH COMPARISONS;


--===========================================================
-- Domain: FLG
--===========================================================
CREATE TYPE FLG AS CHARACTER(1) WITH COMPARISONS;


--===========================================================
-- Domain: ID
--===========================================================
CREATE TYPE ID AS INTEGER WITH COMPARISONS;


--===========================================================
-- Domain: ID_L
--===========================================================
CREATE TYPE ID_L AS BIGINT WITH COMPARISONS;


--===========================================================
-- Domain: ID_S
--===========================================================
CREATE TYPE ID_S AS SMALLINT WITH COMPARISONS;


--===========================================================
-- Domain: INDIC
--===========================================================
CREATE TYPE INDIC AS CHAR(3) WITH COMPARISONS;


--===========================================================
-- Domain: IX
--===========================================================
CREATE TYPE IX AS DEC(12,3) WITH COMPARISONS;


--===========================================================
-- Domain: "NAME"
--===========================================================
CREATE TYPE "NAME" AS VARCHAR(20) WITH COMPARISONS;


--===========================================================
-- Domain: NAME_L
--===========================================================
CREATE TYPE NAME_L AS VARCHAR(40) WITH COMPARISONS;
```

```
-- ===========================================================
-- Domain: NAME_S
-- ===========================================================
CREATE TYPE NAME_S AS VARCHAR(20) WITH COMPARISONS;


-- ===========================================================
-- Domain: NUMB_F
-- ===========================================================
CREATE TYPE NUMB_F AS VARCHAR(12) WITH COMPARISONS;


-- ===========================================================
-- Domain: NUMB_U
-- ===========================================================
CREATE TYPE NUMB_U AS VARCHAR(12) WITH COMPARISONS;


-- ===========================================================
-- Domain: PCT
-- ===========================================================
CREATE TYPE PCT AS DEC(6,3) WITH COMPARISONS;


-- ===========================================================
-- Domain: RTE
-- ===========================================================
CREATE TYPE RTE AS DECIMAL(8,4) WITH COMPARISONS;


-- ===========================================================
-- Domain: RTE_HP
-- ===========================================================
CREATE TYPE RTE_HP AS DEC(20,12) WITH COMPARISONS;


-- ===========================================================
-- Domain: TSTMP
-- ===========================================================
CREATE TYPE TSTMP AS TIMESTAMP WITH COMPARISONS;
```

The code generation proceeds with generation of the following objects:

- tables
- constraints
- indexes
- comments

Based on the option to generate the DDL and DCL together when creating a table, PowerDesigner will generate the code for each table using the following sequence:

- create table

- create table and column-level comments
- create indexes
- grant permissions

The table creation segment is shown below:

```
--===========================================================
-- Table: ADDRESS_TYPE
--===========================================================

CREATE TABLE ADDRESS_TYPE
(
   ADDRESS_TYPE_CD      CD         NOT NULL,
   ADDRESS_TYPE_DES     "DESC"     NOT NULL,
   CONSTRAINT P_IDENTIFIER_1 PRIMARY KEY (ADDRESS_TYPE_CD)
)
IN TS_LOC_8K
COMPRESS YES
NOT LOGGED INITIALLY;

COMMENT ON TABLE ADDRESS_TYPE IS
'The address classifier.';

GRANT SELECT ON table ADDRESS_TYPE TO REGULAR_USR;

GRANT DELETE,INSERT,REFERENCES,SELECT,UPDATE ON table ADDRESS_
TYPE TO SUPER_USR;

--===========================================================
-- Table: CITY
--===========================================================
CREATE TABLE CITY
(
   CITY_CODE           CD         NOT NULL,
   ISO_COUNTRY_CD      CHAR(3)    NOT NULL,
   STATE_CODE          CD         NOT NULL,
   CITY_NAME           "NAME"     NOT NULL,
   CONSTRAINT P_IDENTIFIER_1 PRIMARY KEY (CITY_CODE)
)
IN TS_LOC_8K;

COMMENT ON TABLE CITY IS
'Named urban area.';

COMMENT ON COLUMN CITY.ISO_COUNTRY_CD IS
'Unique code assigned by ISO to designate a Country.';
```

COMMENT ON COLUMN CITY.STATE_CODE IS
'Unique code identifying the State.';

COMMENT ON COLUMN CITY.CITY_NAME IS
'Name of an urban area.';

```
--==============================================================
-- Index: RELATIONSHIP_4_FK
--==============================================================
CREATE INDEX RELATIONSHIP_4_FK ON CITY (
    ISO_COUNTRY_CD        ASC,
    STATE_CODE            ASC
);
```

GRANT INSERT,SELECT,UPDATE ON table CITY TO REGULAR_USR;

GRANT UPDATE,SELECT,REFERENCES,INSERT,DELETE ON table CITY TO SUPER_USR;

```
--==============================================================
-- Table: COMPANY
--==============================================================
CREATE TABLE COMPANY
(
    LEGAL_ENTITY_ID       ID          NOT NULL,
    LINE_OF_BUSINESS_CODE CD,
    EMPLOYEES_COUNT       INTEGER,
    CONSTRAINT P_IDENTIFIER_1 PRIMARY KEY (LEGAL_ENTITY_ID)
)
IN TS_LEG_ENT_16K;
```

GRANT DELETE,INSERT,UPDATE,SELECT ON table COMPANY TO REGULAR_USR;

GRANT DELETE,INSERT,REFERENCES,SELECT,UPDATE ON table COMPANY TO SUPER_USR;

```
--==============================================================
-- Table: COUNTRY
--==============================================================
CREATE TABLE COUNTRY
(
    ISO_COUNTRY_CD        CHAR(3)    NOT NULL,
    ISO_COUNTRY_NAME      "NAME",
    CONSTRAINT P_IDENTIFIER_1 PRIMARY KEY (ISO_COUNTRY_CD)
)
IN TS_LOC_8K
```

COMPRESS YES;

COMMENT ON TABLE COUNTRY IS
'Named territory of a Nation according to ISO standard.';

COMMENT ON COLUMN COUNTRY.ISO_COUNTRY_CD IS
'Unique code assigned by ISO to designate a Country.';

GRANT SELECT ON table COUNTRY TO REGULAR_USR;

GRANT DELETE,REFERENCES,INSERT,SELECT,UPDATE ON table COUNTRY
TO SUPER_USR;

```
--================================================================
-- Table: INDIVIDUAL
--================================================================
CREATE TABLE INDIVIDUAL
(
   LEGAL_ENTITY_ID          ID           NOT NULL,
   LAST_NAME                "NAME",
   BIRTH_DATE               DATE_F,
   CONSTRAINT P_IDENTIFIER_1 PRIMARY KEY (LEGAL_ENTITY_ID)
)
IN TS_LEG_ENT_16K;
```

GRANT DELETE,INSERT,SELECT ON table INDIVIDUAL TO REGULAR_USR;

GRANT DELETE,INSERT,REFERENCES,SELECT,UPDATE ON table
INDIVIDUAL TO SUPER_USR;

```
--================================================================
-- Table: LEGAL_ENTITY
--================================================================
CREATE TABLE LEGAL_ENTITY
(
   LEGAL_ENTITY_ID          ID           NOT NULL,
   LEGAL_ENTITY_TYPE_CODE CD,
   LEGAL_ENTITY_NAME    "NAME",
   CONSTRAINT P_IDENTIFIER_1 PRIMARY KEY (LEGAL_ENTITY_ID)
);
```

COMMENT ON TABLE LEGAL_ENTITY IS
'An Entity that can enter a Business Relationship.';

GRANT INSERT,DELETE,SELECT ON table LEGAL_ENTITY TO REGULAR_USR;

```
GRANT DELETE,INSERT,REFERENCES,SELECT,UPDATE ON table LEGAL_
ENTITY TO SUPER_USR;


--===========================================================
-- Table: LEGAL_ENTITY_ADDRESS
--===========================================================
CREATE TABLE LEGAL_ENTITY_ADDRESS
(
    LEGAL_ENTITY_ID         ID          NOT NULL,
    PHYSICAL_ADDRESS_IDENTIFIER ID   NOT NULL,
    ADDRESS_TYPE_CD         CD          NOT NULL,
    CONSTRAINT P_IDENTIFIER_1 PRIMARY KEY (LEGAL_ENTITY_ID,
    PHYSICAL_ADDRESS_IDENTIFIER)
)
IN TS_LEG_ENT_16K;

COMMENT ON TABLE LEGAL_ENTITY_ADDRESS IS
'The address by type used by a Legal Entity';

COMMENT ON COLUMN LEGAL_ENTITY_ADDRESS.PHYSICAL_ADDRESS_
IDENTIFIER IS
'Unique identifier of the Physical Address.';


--===========================================================
-- Index: RELATIONSHIP_5_FK
--===========================================================
CREATE INDEX RELATIONSHIP_5_FK ON LEGAL_ENTITY_ADDRESS (
    LEGAL_ENTITY_ID         ASC
);


--===========================================================
-- Index: RELATIONSHIP_6_FK
--===========================================================
CREATE INDEX RELATIONSHIP_6_FK ON LEGAL_ENTITY_ADDRESS (
    PHYSICAL_ADDRESS_IDENTIFIER     ASC
);


--===========================================================
-- Index: RELATIONSHIP_7_FK
--===========================================================
CREATE INDEX RELATIONSHIP_7_FK ON LEGAL_ENTITY_ADDRESS (
    ADDRESS_TYPE_CD         ASC
);


GRANT DELETE,INSERT,SELECT,UPDATE ON table LEGAL_ENTITY_
ADDRESS TO REGULAR_USR;
```

GRANT DELETE,INSERT,REFERENCES,SELECT,UPDATE ON *table* LEGAL_
ENTITY_ADDRESS TO SUPER_USR;


```
--=============================================================
-- Table: PHYSICAL_ADDRESS
--=============================================================
CREATE TABLE PHYSICAL_ADDRESS
(
    PHYSICAL_ADDRESS_IDENTIFIER ID    NOT NULL,
    CITY_CODE                   CD    NOT NULL,
    STREET_NUMBER               NUMB_F,
    STREET_NAME                 "NAME",
    POSTAL_CODE                 CD,
    CONSTRAINT P_IDENTIFIER_1 PRIMARY KEY
    (PHYSICAL_ADDRESS_IDENTIFIER)
)
IN TS_LOC_8K;
```

COMMENT ON TABLE PHYSICAL_ADDRESS IS
'Exact geographic location within an urban area.';

COMMENT ON COLUMN PHYSICAL_ADDRESS.PHYSICAL_ADDRESS_
IDENTIFIER IS
'Unique identifier of the Physical Address.';

COMMENT ON COLUMN PHYSICAL_ADDRESS.STREET_NUMBER IS
'Numeric designation within the street.';

COMMENT ON COLUMN PHYSICAL_ADDRESS.STREET_NAME IS
'The name of the street within an urban area.';

COMMENT ON COLUMN PHYSICAL_ADDRESS.POSTAL_CODE IS
'Mailing code system within the Postal organization.';

```
--=============================================================
-- Index: RELATIONSHIP_3_FK
--=============================================================
CREATE INDEX RELATIONSHIP_3_FK ON PHYSICAL_ADDRESS
(
    CITY_CODE                   ASC
);
```

GRANT INSERT,SELECT,UPDATE,DELETE ON *table* PHYSICAL_ADDRESS TO
REGULAR_USR;

```
GRANT DELETE,INSERT,REFERENCES,SELECT,UPDATE ON table PHYSICAL_
ADDRESS TO SUPER_USR;


--==========================================================
-- Table: STATE
--==========================================================
CREATE TABLE STATE
(
   ISO_COUNTRY_CD          CHAR(3)      NOT NULL,
   STATE_NAME              "NAME"       NOT NULL,
   STATE_CODE              CD           NOT NULL,
   CONSTRAINT P_IDENTIFIER_1 PRIMARY KEY (ISO_COUNTRY_CD,
   STATE_CODE)
)
IN TS_LOC_8K;

COMMENT ON TABLE STATE IS
'Constitutional unit within a country.';

COMMENT ON COLUMN STATE.ISO_COUNTRY_CD IS
'Unique code assigned by ISO to designate a Country.';

COMMENT ON COLUMN STATE.STATE_NAME IS
'Unique code designating a Constitutional unit within a Country.';

COMMENT ON COLUMN STATE.STATE_CODE IS
'Unique code identifying the State.';


--==========================================================
-- Index: RELATIONSHIP_1_FK
--==========================================================
CREATE INDEX RELATIONSHIP_1_FK ON STATE (
   ISO_COUNTRY_CD          ASC
);

GRANT SELECT ON table STATE TO REGULAR_USR;

GRANT DELETE,INSERT,REFERENCES,SELECT,UPDATE ON table STATE TO
SUPER_USR;
```

The data integrity includes definition of the following constraints:

- primary keys
- foreign keys
- unique constraints

The script that defines references is positioned at the end of the generated code. The modeler can choose between the two alternative approaches for the data integrity constraints code generation (Illustration 170):

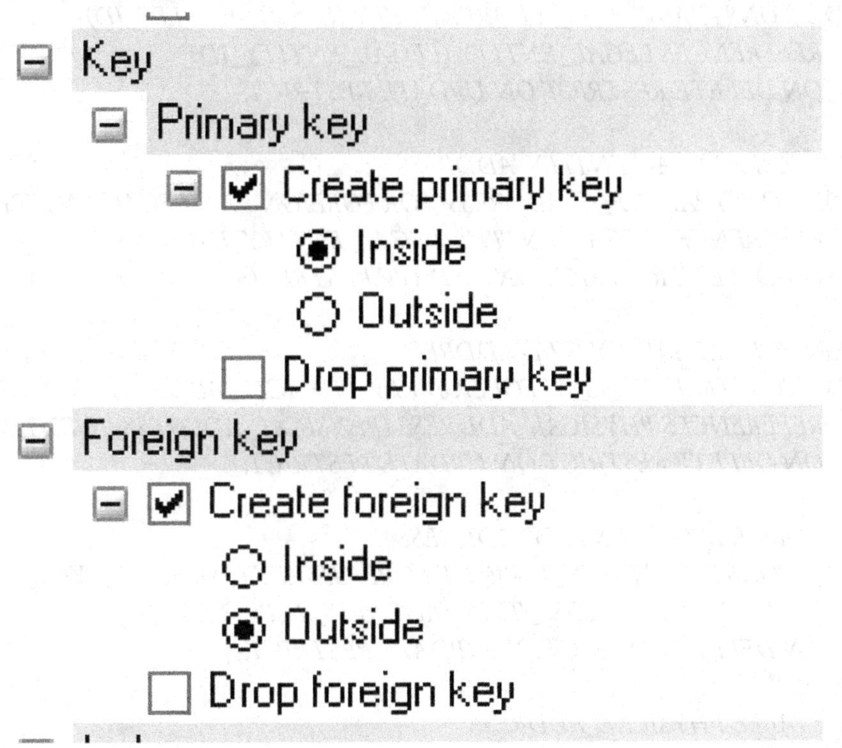

Illustration 170: PowerDesigner options for the data integrity constraints generation

Based on the option specified, the code generated for the primary key constraint can be positioned within the CREATE TABLE statement if the *create primary key **inside*** option is chosen. Otherwise the constraint is created using the ALTER TABLE statement.

Similarly, if the option to generate foreign key constraints *inside* the table is chosen, the *CREATE TABLE* statement will include the definition of the keys. By specifying the *outside* the table option, PowerDesigner will generate set of *ALTER TABLE* statements to add the referential integrity constraints:

```
ALTER TABLE CITY
    ADD CONSTRAINT F_WITHIN_THE FOREIGN KEY (ISO_COUNTRY_CD,
STATE_CODE)
        REFERENCES STATE (ISO_COUNTRY_CD, STATE_CODE)
        ON DELETE RESTRICT ON UPDATE RESTRICT;

ALTER TABLE COMPANY
    ADD CONSTRAINT F_IS_A2 FOREIGN KEY (LEGAL_ENTITY_ID)
```

REFERENCES LEGAL_ENTITY (LEGAL_ENTITY_ID)
ON DELETE RESTRICT ON UPDATE RESTRICT;

ALTER TABLE INDIVIDUAL
ADD CONSTRAINT F_IS_A FOREIGN KEY (LEGAL_ENTITY_ID)
REFERENCES LEGAL_ENTITY (LEGAL_ENTITY_ID)
ON DELETE RESTRICT ON UPDATE RESTRICT;

ALTER TABLE LEGAL_ENTITY_ADDRESS
ADD CONSTRAINT F_IS_ADDRESS_FOR FOREIGN KEY (LEGAL_ENTITY_ID)
REFERENCES LEGAL_ENTITY (LEGAL_ENTITY_ID)
ON DELETE RESTRICT ON UPDATE RESTRICT;

ALTER TABLE LEGAL_ENTITY_ADDRESS
ADD CONSTRAINT F_IS_AT FOREIGN KEY (PHYSICAL_ADDRESS_IDENTIFIER)
REFERENCES PHYSICAL_ADDRESS (PHYSICAL_ADDRESS_IDENTIFIER)
ON DELETE RESTRICT ON UPDATE RESTRICT;

ALTER TABLE LEGAL_ENTITY_ADDRESS
ADD CONSTRAINT F_IS_TYPE_OF FOREIGN KEY (ADDRESS_TYPE_CD)
REFERENCES ADDRESS_TYPE (ADDRESS_TYPE_CD)
ON DELETE RESTRICT ON UPDATE RESTRICT;

ALTER TABLE PHYSICAL_ADDRESS
ADD CONSTRAINT F_LOCATED_AT FOREIGN KEY (CITY_CODE)
REFERENCES CITY (CITY_CODE)
ON DELETE RESTRICT ON UPDATE RESTRICT;

ALTER TABLE STATE
ADD CONSTRAINT F_IS_IN FOREIGN KEY (ISO_COUNTRY_CD)
REFERENCES COUNTRY (ISO_COUNTRY_CD)
ON DELETE RESTRICT ON UPDATE RESTRICT;

It is a matter of personal preference to generate the referential integrity within or outside the table creation statement. The outcome is essentially the same. However, the recommended approach is to generate a set of ALTER statements to implement the referential integrity, for the following reasons:

- clear segregation between the structural objects (tables) and referential integrity constraints
- referential integrity implementation is positioned at the end of the generated script and it can be easily extracted and used to change the enforcement or drop references. Dropping and recreating the references might be an option to improve the performance of massive data load

Code generated from PowerDesigner will be stored in file. Before implementation the code has to be reviewed by both the modeler and the DBA. The code review becomes critically important when the database is loaded with data and structural modifications require no data loss. The following is more detailed discussion on code review.

7.2.1.5. Code review

Before implementation, a thorough review is required to ensure that the code is safe and provides an optimal performance. Complexity of generated code increases when the populated database has to be structurally modified assuming no data loss. In some situations constant database availability is required while the structural modifications are implemented which adds additional complexity to the code[237].

To ensure that the code is the deployment ready, review has to be performed by the DBA. The review has to ensure the following:

- the *code is properly generated*. The reviewer should concentrate on potential syntax errors or imprecision in code generation. Over time, the modeler and DBA will become aware of specific problems with code generation that require minor manual intervention
- the *chosen options do not have unwanted effects on database.* It is not difficult to make a mistake when generating code. By choosing the option to DROP tables before recreating them, the modeler can literally wipe out the whole database. The code review must ensure that chosen options do not have any side effects on the database content
- the code offers an *optimal* solution from *performance and data safety perspective*

The review procedure is described in the following illustration:

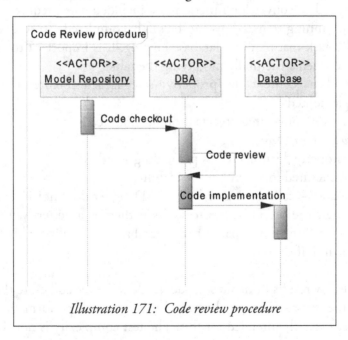

Illustration 171: Code review procedure

---

[237] Not all database engines allow for structural modifications while the objects are available. Oracle provides this functionality with their on-line table re-definition

The review starts with the DBA checking out code from the repository. The scope for the code review includes the following elements:

- *code completeness* review has to validate the following:
  □ objects approved for implementation are included in the script with required attributes
  □ cleanup is performed after the code implementation. The script that assumes *no data loss*. For that purpose the script creates tables, temporary in nature, which should be dropped after successful script execution. The script for temporary tables cleanup (drop) can be automatically generated by PowerDesigner by specifying the *drop temporary tables* option when generating the delta script shown in the Illustration 172:

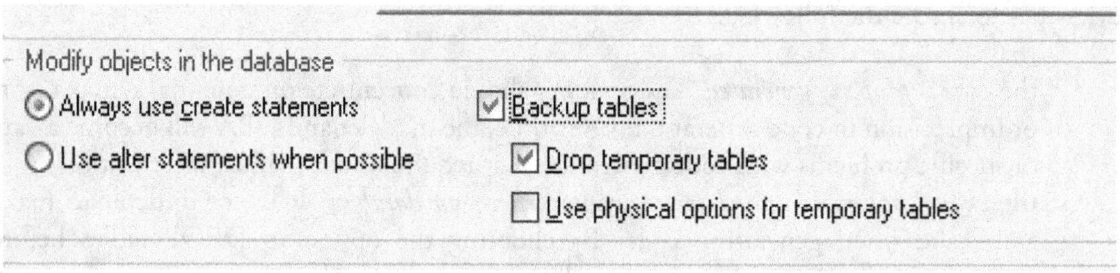

Illustration 172: Option to drop temporary tables when applying database modifications

  □ the code is safe for implementation:
    o proper data conversion functions are included when required
    o long running transactions can be safely completed. Structural modification is a DDL task that requires database logging. It is important to assign sufficient log space when structurally modifying the table
    o the data content is properly safeguarded before the modification is implemented
    o there is no unwanted objects drop or modification
- *adherence to the standards:*
  □ code is properly documented as per coding standards
  □ code is structured for maximum readability
- *code optimization*—code generated by PowerDesigner does not include special database utilities[238], therefore the DBA has to assess if there is a better way of implementing a modification to limit the impact on the database availability. This frequently requires manual code modifications

A successful code review results in finalized code, ready to be tested before the implementation. Responsibility for the testing is assigned to the DBA who will perform the functional test in the isolated database specially intended for this. The test complexity is not the same for the full

---

[238] These are database-specific

code compared to the delta script deployment. The full script deployment assumes *deployment with data loss*. The objects in the database will dropped (if they exist) and recreated using the script generated from PowerDesigner. On the other hand, the delta script assumes that there is *no data loss*, so the test should include a small data set to ensure that implemented script does not have any side effects.

The code testing is not explicitly shown in the diagram assuming that it is a part of the code deployment. After testing, the final code version is checked into the repository and subsequently implemented by the DBA in the database.

7.2.1.6. Code implementation

The DDL and DCL code implementation using PowerDesigner can be performed in two ways:

- from PowerDesigner directly to the database using the live database connection or
- by generating the scripts with manual implementation in the database

In order to avoid any unexpected side effects caused by errors or omissions, the recommendation is that the code should never be deployed directly using the live database connection.

Code implementation can be classified as:

- *full database deployment*—database objects are deployed into a brand new database or the deployment assumes that objects will be dropped and recreated
- *delta code deployment*—database modifications

Depending on the environment, the responsibility for the code deployment may vary:

Code deployed by	Development DB	Testing DB	Production DB
Physical Data Modeler	x		
DBA	x	x	x

Table 28: Responsibility for the code deployment

The script deployment should really be the responsibility of the DBA, however in the development environment the script can be deployed by the physical modeler to speed up the implementation process. Generic script deployment procedure is presented in the Illustration 173:

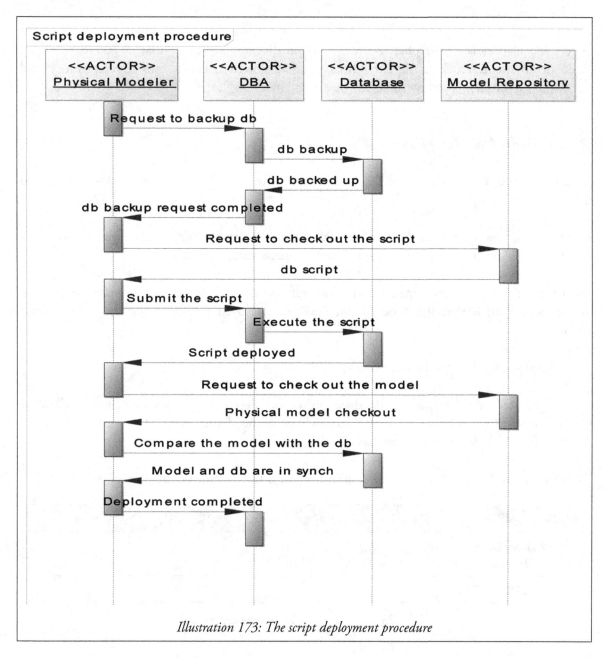

Illustration 173: The script deployment procedure

The deployment starts with the physical modeler submitting the request for the database backup to the DBA. After successful database backup, the DBA informs the modeler that the database is ready for modifications. <u>Do not proceed with modification unless you have a clear confirmation that there is a database backup that can be used to roll-back modifications if something goes wrong.</u>

The modeler proceeds with checking out the script from the repository[239] and submitting the script to the DBA for deployment. This procedure can be modified by DBA doing the script check-out from the repository, however recommendation is for the modeler to check-out the script and submit it for implementation. This extra step ensures that the correct script is executed by having a double checked by the modeler and the DBA before the execution.

After receiving the script the DBA proceeds with execution by running the script in the database. It is important that the script execution log is reviewed for any critical exceptions. If the script is properly tested before implementation, exceptions should not occur, therefore critical exceptions reported during implementation would be considered urgent and must be handled accordingly by the modeler and the DBA.

The script execution is followed by model and database comparison by the physical modeler. If the script implementation was successful, the comparison should not report any differences between the model and the database. Successful comparison marks the completion of the script deployment process.

---

[239]   Assumed here is the manual script deployment

8. Implementation validation

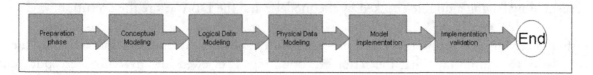

The database code deployment requires independent validation to verify successful implementation. Manual code validation implementation is not practical for the following reasons:

- the code complexity and size
- limited time available for validation
- knowledge and understanding of the database system catalog

As the project progresses towards the production environment the code control becomes more stringent. The goal of the implementation validation is to ensure that there are no discrepancies between the physical model and the database after the deployment.

From the DBA perspective the deployment is successful as long as there are no critical exceptions[240] or accidental object drops or modifications. Success of the data model deployment might be compromised for various reasons:

- *errors in the code*—the code generated by the tool is usually implementable without any problems. Unfortunately, like in any software, bugs can cause problems generating incorrect code. Code validation, performed by the DBA, should discover potential errors but, realistically, probability to find an error in the document with few hundred pages of code is relatively small
- *sub-optimal or missing code*—some modifications require implementation of some database-specific functions or methods to optimize performance and database availability. The code generated by PowerDesigner does not include advanced, database-specific utilities that can improve performance or allow for high availability. In case of data type conversion functions, PowerDesigner will inform the user that the code must be manually modified to include the data type conversion
- *incorrect code*—when specifying various parameters, the modeler or the DBA can make a mistake by specifying incorrect parameter or incorrect parameter settings in the tool which will result in incorrectly generated code. Validation process provided by PowerDesigner does not always include the physical parameter validation causing an error in the generated code. For instance in DB2 there is a rule that the primary key must include all the columns used in the table's hash partitioning. If this is not the case the DDL code execution will result in an error. PowerDesigner does not perform this

---

240 Some exceptions are acceptable if they are classified as informational or warnings

type of model validation hence incorrect hash partitioning key specification will cause an error during the code deployment

- *problems with permissions*—implementation of some database objects requires specialized permission. If these are not granted to the person deploying the code, the code implementation will fail. This problem is not necessarily a code-related problem but can cause lots of headache during the code deployment
- *database related problems*—some database operations related to structural modifications require complex processing that intensively uses database resources. For instance, altering a table by dropping or adding a column is an operation that requires logging. For large tables additional log space might be needed to successfully complete this operation and if the log space is not available, modification will fail
- *the code size and complexity*—a visual review of the code implementation log might simply miss some exceptions[241] resulting in an incomplete code deployment

The final step of code deployment is verification by comparing the model with the database. Once this step is successful the model deployment is completed.

The process of implementation validation is shown in the Illustration 174:

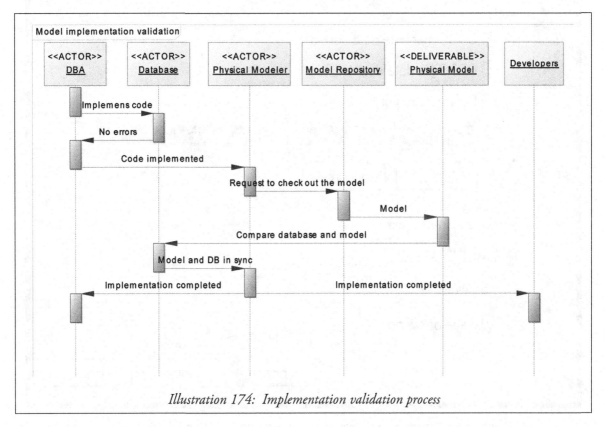

Illustration 174: Implementation validation process

The process starts with the script implementation. Information about successful deployment is sent to the modeler who checks out the model and proceeds with the model comparison against the database. If comparison is completed without any differences reported, the deployment process is considered successful. The DBA and developers are informed of successful process completion.

Comparing the model against the database can sometime result in differences that in reality do not exist. Typical discrepancies found during the validation, might include the wording in different case (e.g. database records certain options in the upper case format and model records it in mixed case), keywords ordering (e.g. granted permissions are recorded in different order than they are stored in the model) etc. These are not errors and they are reported by the PowerDesigner as warnings.

To demonstrate model validation against the database a simple example will be used. The script has already been implemented in IBM's DB2 database so the modeler proceeds with model comparison to the database.

The first step is to connect to the database (Illustration 175):

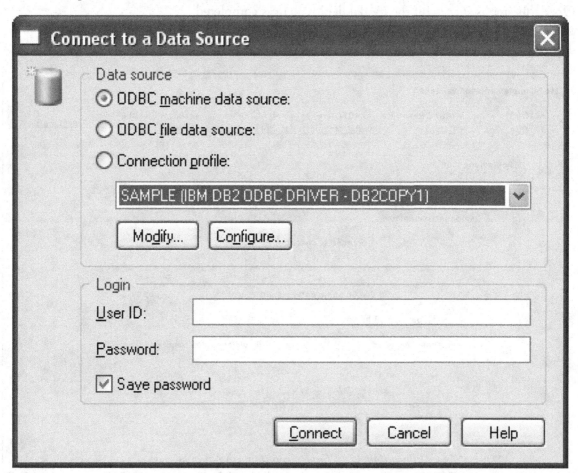

Illustration 175: Initial database log-in screen

The user must specify the connection details with the database name, authorized user name and the password. For model validation purposes the user does not need to have permissions to modify database objects—read only access to the catalog objects is sufficient to perform the validation.

The deployment validation is performed using the following steps:

- the user specifies the database object types to be compared with the model
- the database is reverse engineered into the physical model
- two models[242] are compared side-by side

Objects to be compared between the model and database are specified in the next step (Illustration 176):

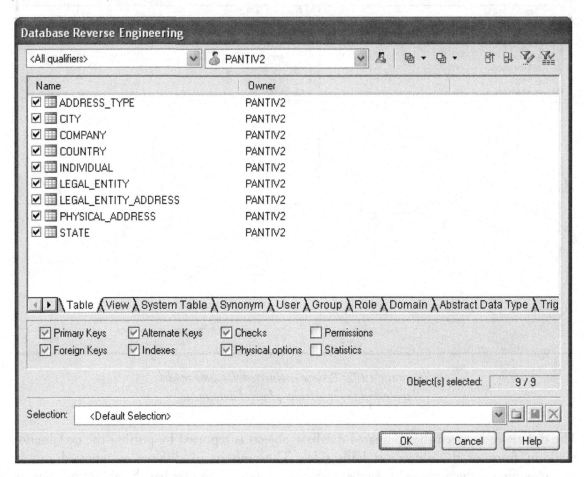

Illustration 176: List of database objects to be included in model/database comparison

The comparison can explicitly include or exclude the database object components. For instance, in case of database table the user can include:

- constraints (primary, unique and foreign keys)
- in-line checks
- indexes
- physical options (e.g. tablespaces)

---

242   The original physical data model and model created by database reverse engineering.

287

- permissions
- table statistics (number of rows in the table)

After the reverse engineering step is completed, models are compared side by side (Illustration 177):

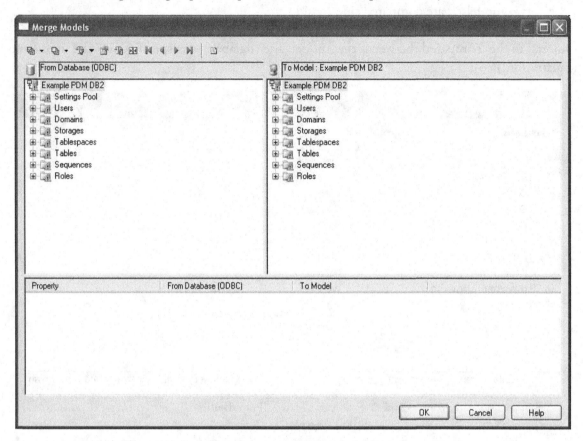

Illustration 177: Reverse engineered database model
compared to the original physical data model

The difference between the compared database objects is reported by putting the exclamation mark in front of the object on both sides. The amount of differences reported can be overwhelming if the number of database objects is large so the user has the ability to limit the information showed by the comparison. The recommendation is to filter *only the differences between the objects* while leaving out the objects that are identical.

By clicking on the plus (+) sign, the user can expand the sub-tree and view the details for a specific component (Illustration 178):

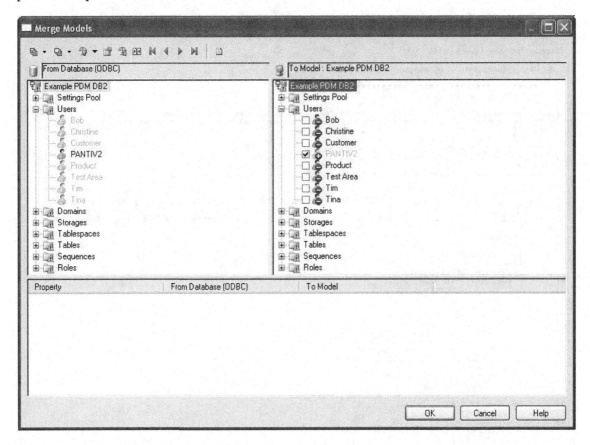

Illustration 178: Detailed differences in the list of users defined in the model and database

When the object does not exist, PowerDesigner shades the object on the side where it does not exist. For instance, the user *BOB* does not exist in the database while it is in the model. Considering that model/database validation actually assumes that the original model is balanced (synchronized) with the database, the minus sign (-) reflects that, if we want to synchronize the model with the database, the user *BOB* has to be removed from the model.

On the other hand, the user PANTIV2 exists in the database but not in the model. So, to bring this user to the model, the user has to be added. By clicking on the box beside the plus sign (+) the user PANTIV2 will be propagated from the database to the model.

To fully document the model and database comparison, PowerDesigner provides the formatted report of differences found during the process. Sample is shown in the Illustration 179:

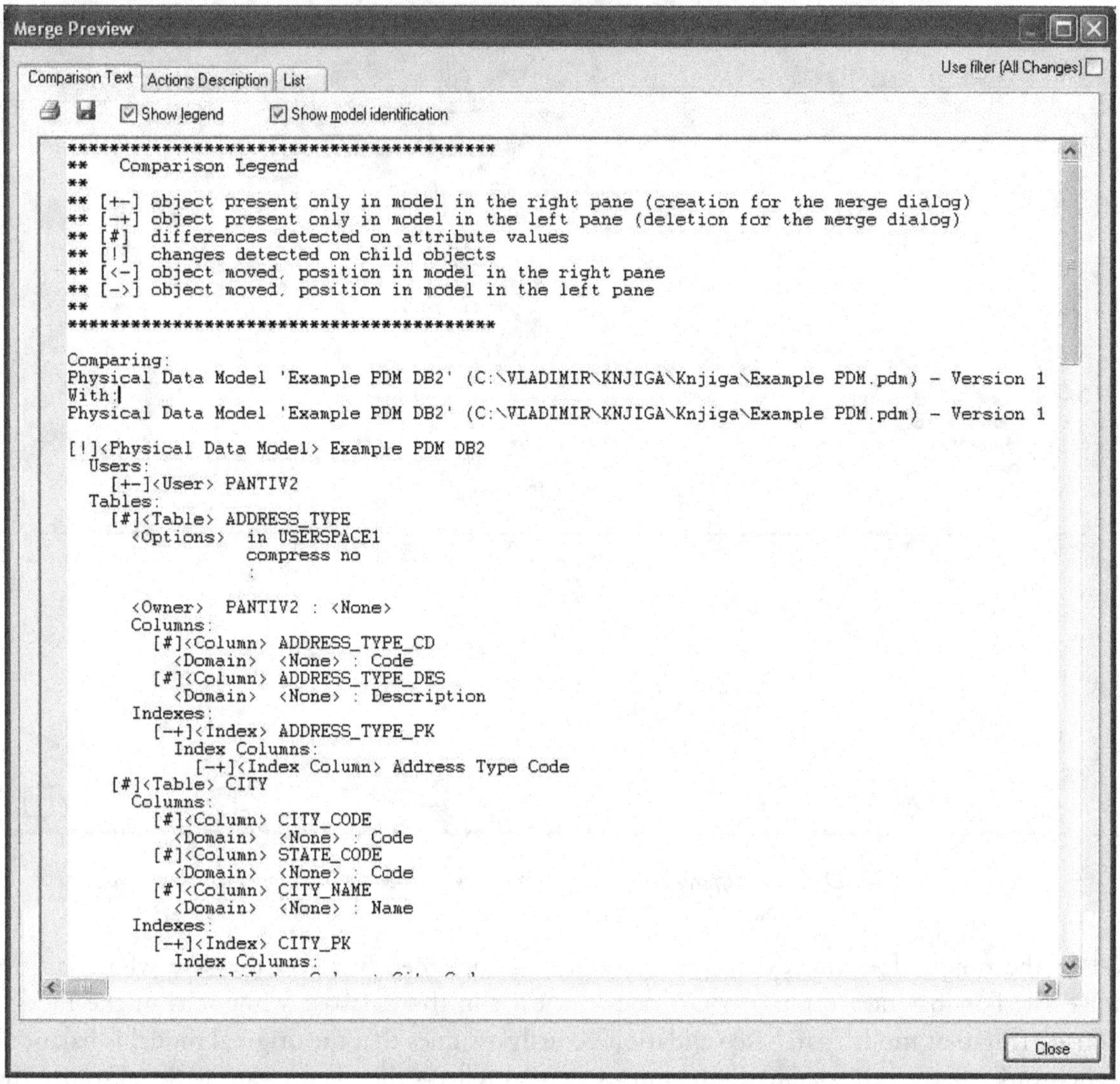

Illustration 179: Sample report of database/model comparison using PowerDesigner

This report is available whenever the model is compared to one of the following:

- another model
- database
- DDL/DCL script

As part of the change control process, the report should be published along with the model, documenting the findings of the comparison process.

The comparison process has the following advantages over a manual deployment validation:

- *fully automated*—the model/database comparison does not need a user intervention. PowerDesigner will perform the reverse engineering and compare specified objects automatically
- *fast*—even large databases with few hundreds of tables will require short period of time to do the comparison
- *repeatable, uniform and comprehensive*—number of database objects with their properties can be quite large. When PowerDesigner is used, the validation scope and objects with their properties is clearly defined and the process can be uniformly repeated when needed
- *customizable*—the modeler can always customize the objects and their properties included in the comparison

Although it is possible to perform the deployment validation manually, PowerDesigner offers significant increase in productivity by decreasing the time required to perform validation. This becomes obvious when the deployment is time-boxed and the modeler has literally minutes to ensure that the implementation is successful. Historically, code deployment was facing problems related to validation. Over time, the DBA developed numerous procedures to ensure that deployment went well. Unfortunately, even with the best intentions to keep the scripts up-to-date, they get outdated with the new database version. The functionality and script quality depends on experience and knowledge of the system catalog, so the quality of manual validation varies. By introducing PowerDesigner in the deployment validation, the trust in the deployment process by making sure that deployment went as expected.

9. WORKING WITH THE MODEL REPOSITORY

Success of the Model Based Environment heavily depends on the tools and their usage. During the modeling process, multiple models are created, each with multiple versions, accompanied with code and supporting documentation. What initially starts as a simple model ends up as a massive and complex set of inter-related artifacts that have to be maintained and synchronized.

Keeping track of documents and their dependencies using spreadsheets is just a futile attempt to solve this Gordian knot. Sooner or later the process based on manual tracking fails for the following reasons:

- procedures are cumbersome and time consuming so people try to become "inventive" by deciding how to customize them
- people get tired of maintaining data in multiple spreadsheets
- new team members involved in the process are not sufficiently trained causing errors and omissions and impacting the overall quality and integrity of maintained artifacts

In essence, no one is excited to maintain multiple spreadsheets for every modification of the model or database, hence the goal is to introduce a tool that can automate and control this process. PowerDesigner provides a specialized model repository that can be used to maintain other types of documents.

The discussion is started by providing the definition:

DEFINITION: *The repository is software that maintains documents in chronological order offering the following functionality:*

- *document version control*
- *document check-in*
- *document check-out*
- *document locking*
- *document comparison*
- *reporting capabilities*
- *robust security control*

The basic object, controlled and maintained by the repository is a *document*. Generically defined, a *document* can be any file stored in the repository: model, SQL code, DDL code, textual document, spreadsheet etc. The repository is responsible for maintaining the document versions and integrity by implementing a robust safety[243] and security[244] mechanisms.

---

[243] By implementing the locking mechanism
[244] Via the security model

9.1. Version control

The document[245] version is a snapshot of the document's content at a specific time and PowerDesigner repository provides mechanism to track the history of document snapshots over time. The version control implemented in PowerDesigner's repository works with the following document version concepts:

- *major version.* From the SDLC perspective this would be a significant model modification.
- *minor version.* This is the modification that is relatively limited in scope
- *(emergency) bug fix*[246]. The version increment due to bug fixes.

The Illustration below depicts the versions time-line (Illustration 180):

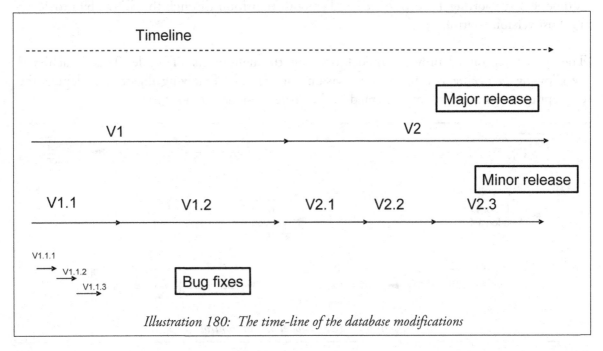

Illustration 180: The time-line of the database modifications

The major versions represent the base on which the development progresses and are created when significant modifications occurs. In software development, where the database design is just one of the components, the new version is related to the new software release introducing a major functionality modification. Depending on the approach taken the new versions can be scheduled regularly (e.g. each year) or irregularly. It is not easy to exactly quantify the number of modifications that will trigger the new version, but from the database perspective we can assume that the new version requires modification to at least 10% of the database's structural objects.

---

245   As mentioned before, from the repository perspective every file is a document-irrespective of its content
246   EBF

The major software release might not be directly related to the major database release because the software modifications for the new version might not necessarily require corresponding database modifications. However, major database modification will usually trigger significant software modifications resulting in new version for both.

Within the major release there might be one or more minor releases where less than 10% of the database objects are modified.

A bug fix is a situation, from a data model perspective, when the problem is discovered that requires a model modification.

As the model progresses through the SDLC, the need for control over model modifications will increase. The Model Based Environment emphasizes the tight coupling between the target database and corresponding physical data model. The model repository is the focal integration component supporting a synchronized and smooth transition through the SDLC by providing a robust version control.

The model repository provides model tracking throughout its life-cycle. This is achieved by allowing *branching* as a form of a revision control. The following illustration depicts the concept of version control implemented in the PowerDesigner's repository:

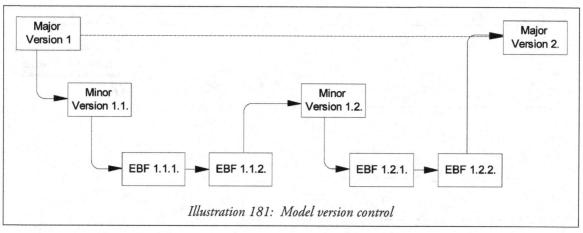

Illustration 181: Model version control

Assuming that the time-line goes from left to the right, the illustration shows two major model versions[247] (1 and 2). The model version 1 branches into the minor version 1.1 which further branches showing the two emergency bug fixes (EBF 1.1.1. and 1.1.2.). The EBF branch merges into the minor version 1.2. Within the minor version 1.2. there are two EBFs', 1.2.1. and 1.2.2. The minor version 1.2. merges into the major version 2.

The main branch (major version) is also known as a trunk containing always the latest and most stable version of the model. The version control uses the decimal classification based on monotonically increasing values to track the chronological model modifications.

---

[247] Usually referred as trunks

9.2. Implementation of the repository version control

An assumption of the Model Based Environment is that a model always corresponds to the database. The DDL produced from the model has to include all the objects that are required for implementation. Model version control is implemented usually via the model repository and versions are maintained automatically by the repository.

Database modifications might result in code changes, further what is a minor modification in the database might require significant code change on the application side. The distinction between the major and minor might be purely subjective. Provided here are few guidelines[248] to help distinguishing between the major and minor database modifications:

- *major modification*—a model modification of at least 10% of database objects[249] such as:
  □ tables related to more than one parent table
  □ referential integrity implementation
  □ implementation of complex data structures (e.g. super-type/sub-type tables, nested tables etc.)
  □ large table redesign by introducing:
    o table partitioning
    o modification of column data types
    o modification of physical characteristics that require data off-load and re-load
  □ materialized views
- *minor modification*—a model modification less than 10% of the database objects such as:
  □ columns in small or medium tables
  □ constraints that are not enforced
  □ indexes
  □ views
  □ small tables

DDL version number consisting of three components:

1. *major version number*—reserved for major modifications
2. *minor version number*—reserved for minor modifications
3. *bug fix number*—reserved for specific solutions to problems discovered in various phases of SDLC

Version number starts with a value of 1 and incremented by a value of 1 whenever a modification gets implemented. The version number is prefixed with the letter *V* that denotes the word VERSION.

---

[248] Quantitative measures provided here are purely empirical

[249] This is just an attempt to quantify the number of modifications so that reader can use it to classify the modification. For large databases even small modifications might require significant implementation effort

For instance:

V1.1.1

this version is the ***initial DDL*** version intended for the deployment into an empty database.

Minor modifications[250] will increase the minor version number for 1:

V1.2.1

The major version number is increased by one when the new development cycle starts and major enhancements or functional modifications are introduced into the database.

Database deployment includes the DDL to create database objects and the corresponding DCL to control access. The conventions for the version control are the same for both classes of the database code.

From the timeline perspective the minor are nested within the major modifications and bug fixes are nested within the minor ones. The following picture illustrates the modifications time-line (Illustration 182):

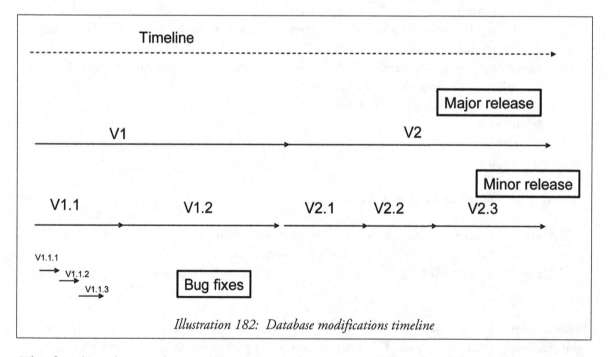

Illustration 182: Database modifications timeline

The first line depicts the overall time line. The second line in the diagram denotes major release. The initial deployment of the model is using the version number one (V1). The third line in the diagram describes the *minor release number* reserved for the modifications that change less than 20% of the database objects. Typically the major release reflects significant

---

[250] For instance adding few columns to a small table.

database modifications that have to be carefully planned because of potential down time for the database, while the minor releases are used to improve existing functionality and rectify discovered problems.

The last line in the diagram is reserved for bug fixes. When a solution to a critical problem is issued, the bug fix number within the minor version is assigned.

Essentially, any database modification has to be assessed for impact on availability. It should not be assumed that a small modification is simple one and has no impact on the database availability. In production databases the Service Level Agreement[251] defines very precise requirements for database availability so the modifications must be planned to avoid violation of the agreement.

9.3. File naming conventions for the database code

The physical data model will be used to produce the fully functional DDL and DCL code. The file naming conventions should create the name comprising of components that uniquely and unambiguously specify the following:

- the name of the database targeted for implementation (code deployment)
- the code class (DDL, DCL or both)
- the type of deployment (FULL or DELTA DEPLOYMENT)

The following is the proposal for the code naming conventions:

DBNAME_CLASS_TYPE_Vx_y_z.SQL

where:

DBNAME—the name of the database where the code is deployed

CLASS—the code classification as a Data Definition Language (DDL) or Data Control Language (DCL). The class is required only if the code is generated for full database deployment. In case of database modifications the classifier is not applicable because the code combines the two

TYPE—the type of deployment:

- *FULL deployment* assumes that the script will start with an empty database. The data loss is assumed if the existing database objects are populated with data

---

[251] The SLA is an agreement between the service provider and service user that defines the terms of usage and availability of the resources. The database availability is one of the major elements of each SLA.

- *DELTA deployment* where the deployed code modifies existing database objects. This type of code deployment assumes no data loss.

Vx_y_z—version information (x—major version number, y—minor version number, z—bug fix number)

SQL—standard file extension denoting the content of the file

The following is an example of the file name that contains the DDL code for initial deployment in database SAMPLE:

SAMPLE_DDL_FULL_V1_1_1.SQL

where:

SAMPLE—database name where the code will be deployed

DDL—code class: Data Definition Language

FULL—type of deployment. The FULL deployment assumes that the database is empty and all objects specified in the file will be created

V1_1_1—version

SQL—standard file extension for a file that contains the SQL statements

9.4. Repository safety mechanism

The repository is using a back-end database to maintain models and other stored documents. In the repository the models are stored in a decomposed form. The repository provides a locking mechanism that prevents users from accidentally overwriting each other modifications. Without getting into details about the locking strategies, the repository allows only one user to lock the object in exclusive mode and change it. The repository maintains the model locking explicitly requested by the user so that model integrity is not compromised. Locking granularity is at the model level, treating the whole model as an integrally locked unit.

The modeler can lock the model when:

- the model is explicitly checked-out or
- manual lock is explicitly requested

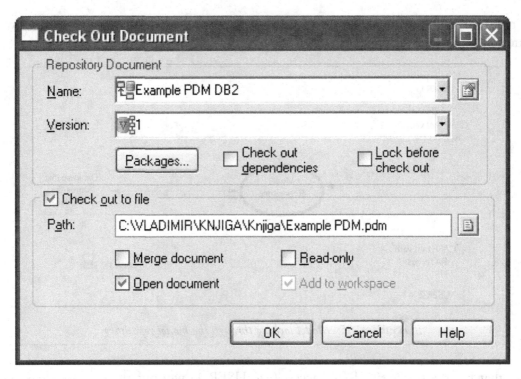

Illustration 183: Model check-out in read/write mode

The above illustration shows the PowerDesigner's model check-out window. By clicking on the *lock before check out*, the modeler will lock the model while working with it locally.

The following illustration shows a request for an explicit model lock in the repository:

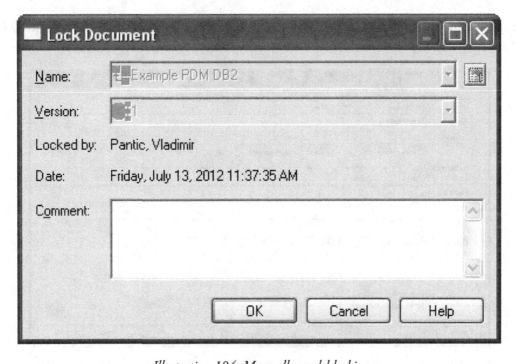

Illustration 184: Manually model locking

The repository allows multi-user access while keeping the model's integrity. The following illustration depicts the locking mechanism implemented in the repository:

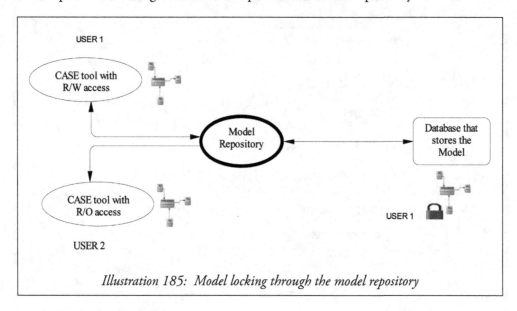

Illustration 185: Model locking through the model repository

A user that has the *read/write* (R/W) access (e.g. USER 1) will put the exclusive lock on the model in the repository while checking the model out. Other users (e.g. USER 2) can perform the model check-out in *read-only* (R/O) mode.

When the model is locked by a user others can access the model in read-only mode allowing them to read the model without modifying it. The locking mechanism implemented by the repository allows USER 1, in the example above to have full control over the model's content.

After completing the model modifications, the model can be checked-in to the repository using the check-in procedure as shown in the Illustration 186:

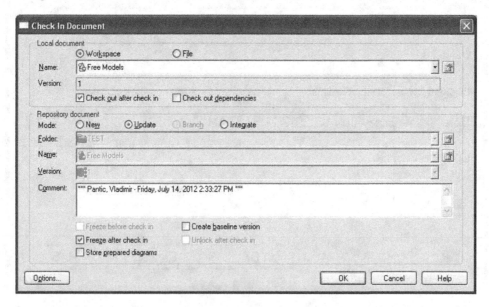

Illustration 186: Model check-in to the repository

When checking the model into the repository, the user has the following options:

- *create a new model*—if this option is chosen, a new model is created starting with version one
- *update existing version* of the model—the model in the repository increases the version number. If a branch of a minor version or EBF is created, the repository will automatically assign the corresponding version number
- *integrate into another model*—model integration assumes that the local model is synchronized[252] with an arbitrary repository model

Any model modification in the repository is automatically timestamped for audit purposes. It is a good practice to provide a textual description of the modifications (change requests) implemented in the model so that the information is readily available for each model version in the repository.

If the model version in the repository is frozen, the model cannot be updated. Every model update or integration into the repository will automatically update the model version. The model can have a status of *open* or *locked* depending on whether the model modifications are allowed or not. An example of a locked model is shown below:

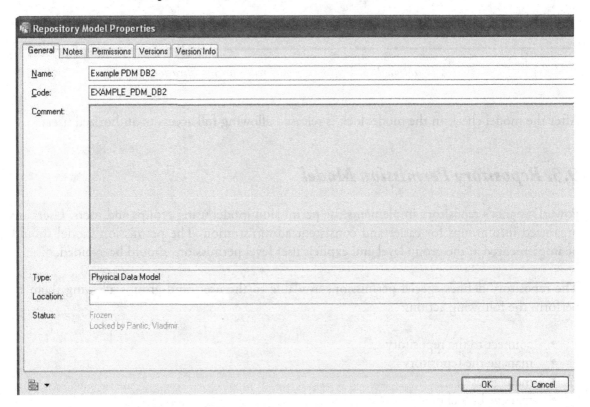

Illustration 187: Frozen model locked by user Vladimir Pantic

---

252 Local model is merged into a repository model

If the model is frozen, modifications are not allowed, however an authorized user can *unfreeze* the model by explicitly changing the status in the model repository (Illustration 188):

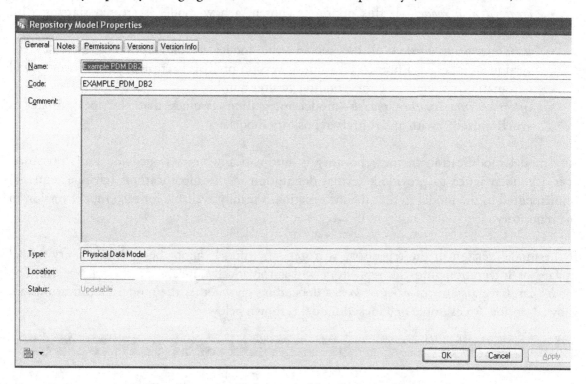

Illustration 188: Unfrozen model ready for modifications

After the model check-in the model lock is released allowing full access to authorized users.

9.5. Repository Permission Model

PowerDesigner's repository implements the permission model using groups and users. Users are organized into groups for easier and consistent administration. The permission model should be implemented at the group level and explicit user level permissions should be avoided.

The repository defines special permissions available to the users and groups allowing them to perform the following actions:

- connect to the repository
- manage the repository
- manage users
- manage branches
- manage configurations
- lock document versions
- freeze document version

From a document management perspective the permission model is based on two groups of users:

- users/groups with read/write (R/W) access
- users/groups with read-only (R/O) access

Establishing model ownership is always a challenging task. Responsibility for models depends on the model class[253] and for each class a single user role is assigned as the owner. The model owner is responsible for the model maintenance and synchronization with other models requiring the full read/write permission.

The following table shows the type of access required by specific role (Table 29):

Role	Conceptual data model	Logical data model	Physical data model
Business analyst	R/O	R/O	N/A
Logical data modeler	R/W	R/W (owner)	R/O
Physical data modeler	R/O	R/O	R/W (owner)
DBA	N/A	R/O	R/O
Developer	N/A	R/O	R/O
Data architect	R/W (owner)	R/O	R/O
Application architect	R/O	R/O	R/O

Table 29: Type of model access required by a role

where:

- **R/O**—user is able to access the model in **read-only** mode. The model cannot be modified by the user
- **R/W**—user is able to access and **modify the model**. The model (including branches) can be explicitly locked by the user
- **N/A**—the user **does not need explicit to access the model**. If required, a model access can be granted on exception basis

In the case of a conceptual model, both the data architect and logical modeler have the R/W access to the model. The model owner is assigned to the data architect while the logical modeler is given the R/W access to manage the model on the data architect's behalf.

---

[253] Conceptual, logical or physical model

The physical data model is owned by the physical modeler and the DBA has R/O access to it. This prevents the "back door" for minor modifications that are usually propagated by reverse engineering the database into a model. The ownership by the physical modeler forces all modification to go through the model before they are implemented in the database and regular comparison between the model and database ensures that there is no manual database modifications not recorded in the model.

9.6. Structuring the repository content

Depending on the modeling approach taken, the directory structure (folders) within the model repository may vary. Previously, we discussed the directory structure for maintaining the physical model with corresponding scripts (DDL and DCL code). The repository folders structure has to allow management of model-related artifacts so the structure has to be extended to take these into consideration. The directory structure can be further enhanced to enable efficient tracking of various project-related artifacts. However, this book is limited to the model-related artifacts only.

The repository directory structure layout depends on the approach that is taken when setting up the Model Based Environment:

- project-based
- subject area based

The repository structure for each approach will be further explained.

9.6.1. Model repository set-up for the project-based approach

The project-based approach requires a directory structure that supports a project. Therefore each project should have its own directory structure tailored to support efficient management of the project artifacts. The Illustration 189 presents a proposed repository directory structure for the *project-based approach*:

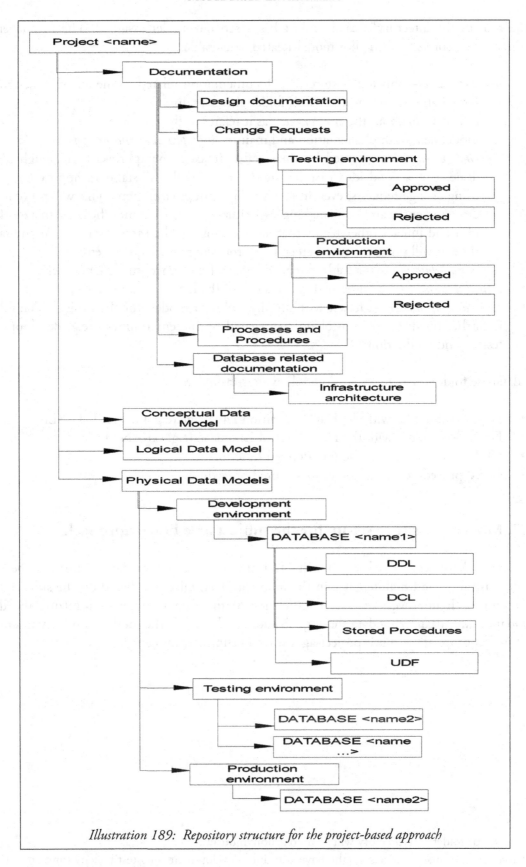

Illustration 189: Repository structure for the project-based approach

At the root of the directory[254] each project has a separate folder assigned. The first layer of sub-directories represents the major model-related deliverables:

- *documentation*—this folder stores the documentation related to the analysis, design an implementation of the models. This folder also contains:
  - □ information about the *environment* as it relates to the database
  - □ model design, implementation and maintenance *processes and procedures*
  - □ *change requests* segregated by their status (rejected or approved). Although rarely done, it is a good idea to track modification with the standard approval process using change requests, even in the development environment. This will prevent the development team from making experimental database modification to test their idea and impact other teams that are working on the same database. At the same time, it will prevent a scope creep by introducing new requirements
- *conceptual data model*—a folder for all versions of the conceptual data model
- *logical data model*—a folder with all versions of the logical data model
- *physical data model*—a folder with all physical data models for the project. The folder is further divided into sub-folders, segregated by the environment (e.g. development, testing and production[255])

The database folder further contains the following sub-folders:

- DDL—sub-folder with the Data Definition Language (e.g. CREATE TABLE)
- DCL—sub-folder with the Data Control Language (e.g. GRANT)
- UDF—sub-folder with the user defined function
- stored procedures—sub-folder with stored procedures

9.6.2. Model repository set-up for the subject area based approach

Modeling each project in isolation inevitably introduces redundant data, increasing the cost for administration and maintenance in the long run. Centralization based on the subject area centric approach improves the overall efficiency of the data team by minimizing the data redundancy and maximizing data sharing. To support this effort the model repository has to be structured appropriately so it is project-agnostic and subject areas centric.

---

[254] The words folder and directory will be used synonymously

[255] Large and complex projects might have multiple development and testing environments. Each database in each environment must have a corresponding data model

Below is a proposed model repository folder structure for the *subject area based* approach:

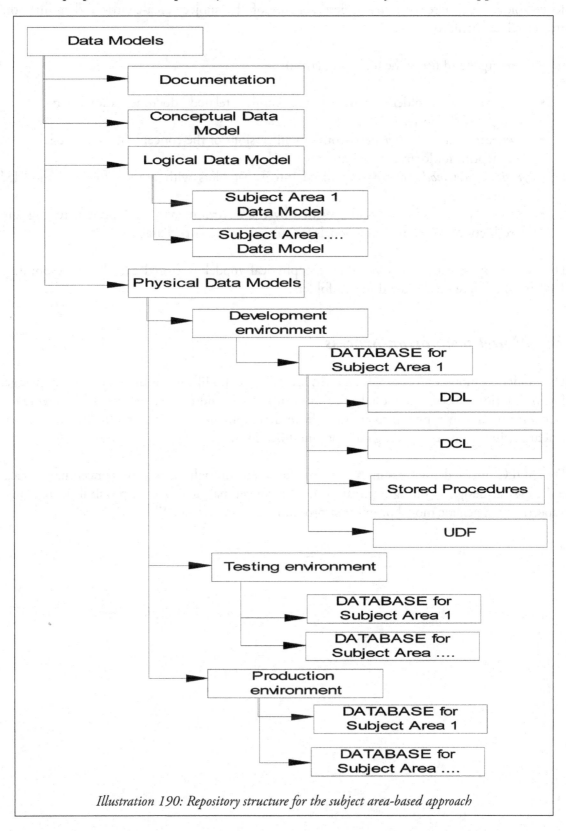

Illustration 190: Repository structure for the subject area-based approach

Instead of having a project at the root level, the repository structure separates folders by major deliverables. The content of the folders consists of the subject area-centric rather than the project-related artifacts.

Folders are organized using the following layout:

- *documentation* folders—contains the model related documentation (e.g. model comparison reports etc.)
- *conceptual data model folder*—contains all versions of the conceptual data model used as a blueprint for logical modeling
- *logical data model folder*—organized into sub-folders with models for each modeled subject areas
- *physical data model folder*—segregated by the environment (development, testing and production) containing the models for subject area-centric databases

The repository structure requires that the physical model is stored for the corresponding database and related code stored in sub-folders.

9.7. Model promotion process

The model promotion process defines steps for database modifications driven by model change. The promotion process has to establish a uniform, simple and consistent process of moving the model from one environment to another (from development to testing and finally production) synchronizing the corresponding database modifications.

The SDLC methodology assumes that model goes through phases of conceptual, logical and physical design resulting in creation of the conceptual, logical and physical data models respectively. A generic model promotion procedure is shown in the Illustration 191:

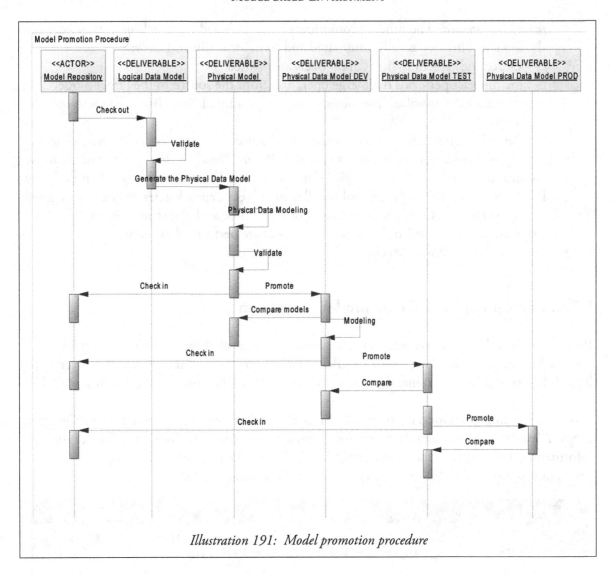

Illustration 191: Model promotion procedure

Assuming that conceptual model is relatively static and maintained at the corporate level, the promotion procedure, shown here, starts with the logical model.

The following is an explanation of the steps involved in the model promotion procedure:

- *model is checked out of the model repository*
- *model validation is performed.* Formal validation using PowerDesigner is performed and the output is analyzed for potential problems. If the validation is successful the model can be promoted. It is good idea to review and analyze the impact of warnings reported during the model validation considering that these can sometimes seriously impact the database's performance[256]

---

[256] For instance modern databases allow ability to use subsets of compound indexes for data access. What this really means is that if a compound index on columns A+B+C+D is defined, additional indexes on A or B or C or D may not be required. The database will use a compound index for data access

- *model is promoted.* The model promotion process is based on synchronization between the models. This step is fully automated and steps are outlined below:
  - □ source and target physical data models are opened
  - □ the modeler performs the merge operation from the source to the target model
  - □ the modeler specifies the objects to be promoted (synchronized between the models)
  - □ PowerDesigner performs the source model objects propagation to the target model
- after promotion, the *model is compared with its "base" version.* The model *merge* (synchronization) is deceivingly simple operation completely handled by PowerDesigner. Although the tool handles the object dependencies, it is always a good idea to perform subsequent comparison of the source and target models ensuring that specified modifications to the target data model are performed as required
- *model is checked into the repository*

9.7.1. Logical to physical data model promotion

Promotion from logical to the physical data model is controlled by the automated generation process implemented in PowerDesigner. Behind the scenes, a complex process converts the logical data model into relational database-specific constructs recorded in the physical model.

When performing generation of the physical model based on the logical model, PowerDesigner keeps relevant version meta-data for each modeling object providing the object lineage information. For instance, the *version info* tab will display the creation and last update user and timestamp in the INDIVIDUAL entity properties (Illustration 192):

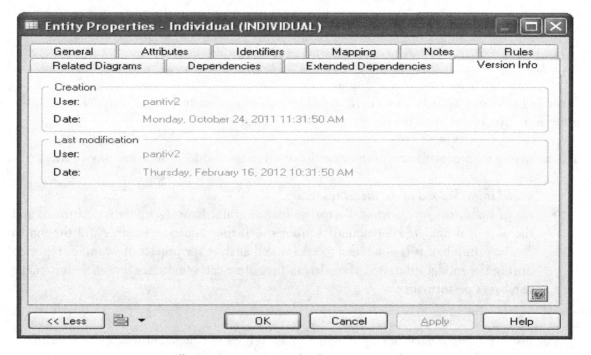

Illustration 192: Entity-level version meta-data

When the logical to physical model transition is completed, PowerDesigner stores additional lineage info for the derived object (the table INDIVIDUAL):

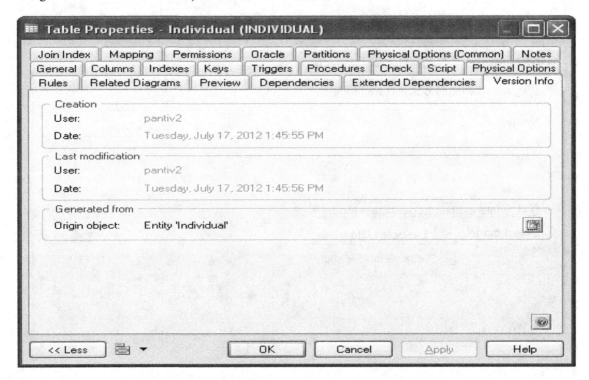

Illustration 193: Version information for generated table INDIVIDUAL

Table INDIVIDUAL is generated as part of the model transition from the entity INDIVIDUAL as shown in the *generated from* section of the screen. For each object created by the model transition process the name of the source object is kept as part of the lineage meta-data.

PowerDesigner provides the following model transitions:

- *derivation of a new physical based on the logical model* (model promotion)
- *update of the logical data model based on modified physical data model* (logical model synchronization)

Deriving the physical based on the logical model was previously analyzed. When the physical model is modified during the modeling process, it is required to retrofit the changes into the logical model. Not all modifications are required to be included in the logical model. The physical model is a detailed model of the database including structural components required for the applications functionality (e.g. audit columns in the table's structure) and these are the physical modeling constructs that will stay in the physical model only. Structural modifications that have a business connotation should be retrofitted into the logical model.

When the physical data model is modified, the modifications can be retrofitted to the logical data model used as a foundation for the generation of the physical model:

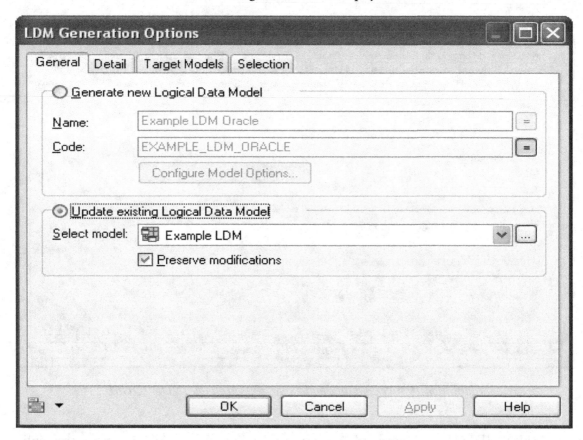

Illustration 194: Logical data model synchronization based on the physical data model

PowerDesigner keeps the information in the source logical data model that will be used as the target for propagating the modifications from the physical model.

The logical model is database agnostic. Having multiple physical data models based on a single logical model is fairly common for companies that provide support for multiple RDBMS. PowerDesigner can be efficiently used to maintain multiple physical models in synchronicity with the logical data model and vice verse. However, the reader should know that a logical model is not always kept in-sync with the physical model. In the case of a data warehouse design, modeling techniques are based on a dimensional model that is highly denormalized. Trying to maintain normalized logical in balance with the denormalized physical data model would be challenging in this case.

9.7.2. Physical data model and database promotion process

Promoting the logical to physical data models requires transition from one model type to another, the synchronization between the physical models is relatively straightforward. When the physical model needs to be promoted from one environment to another, the physical models synchronization is performed by propagating the meta-data attributes between two compatible model types. However, performing model promotion is a task that requires thorough understanding of the process as well as all the details pertinent to the database objects in scope.

DEFINITION: *Model promotion is a process of moving the model forward through the phases of the life-cycle from the development environment to the production environment.*

The basic assumption of the promotion process is that the physical model represents the database. Therefore, the model and database promotion goes hand-in-hand as shown in the Illustration 195:

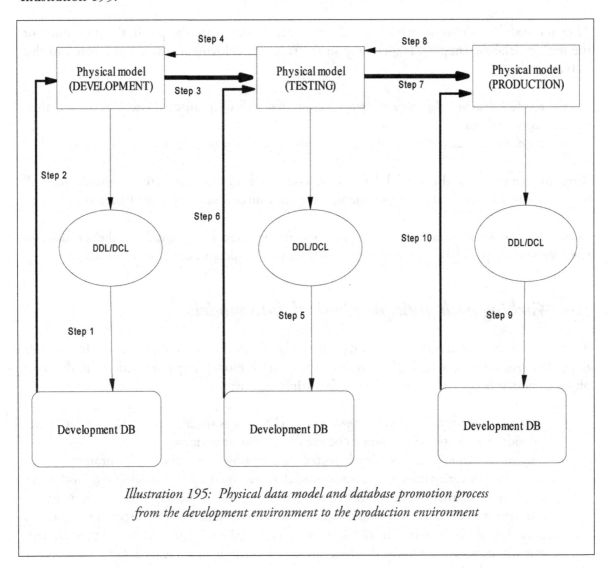

Illustration 195: Physical data model and database promotion process from the development environment to the production environment

Model implementation starts with the code generation (step 1). The physical model stored in PowerDesigner is used to generate the DDL and DCL code. After the script implementation, the model is validated against the database (step 2) and the implementation is deemed successful if the model corresponds to the database. The next set of steps in the promotion process is promoting the development model to the testing database. The development and test physical models are merged and changes ready for testing are moved to the test model (step 3). After the models are merged the development and testing data models are compared (step 4). Acceptable differences between the development and testing models arise from:

- *differences in the permission model*—considering that testing is getting close to the production environment, implemented permissions will differ from the development environment where they more relaxed
- *differences in the modeled database object state*—some of the development database objects are not ready for promotion to the testing environment so the development model contains objects that are not propagated to the testing data model

After successful model synchronization, the script is created from the physical data model for the testing database (step 5). Depending on the type of deployment, the script created in this step might be:

- *the full database deployment script*—script that will drop all database objects and then recreate them
- *the delta database script*—script assumes implementation of modifications with no data loss

After implementation the model has to be compared to the database to ensure that all modifications (or full database deployment) have been successfully completed (step 6).

Essentially the same process is performed when the model is moved to the production environment (steps 7-10) making this process uniform irrespective of the environment.

9.8. Working with multiple physical data models

A logical data model can serve as a foundation for the physical models implemented in multiple RDBMSs. Although theoretically possible, the logical model implementation in different physical models is not a trivial task for the following reasons:

- *data types are not fully standardized*—each RDBMS has specific non-standard data types providing a functionality that can be used in certain situations
- *referential integrity is not implemented consistently*—the type and enforcement of referential integrity rules is not standardized across the databases forcing the modeler to implement alternative enforcement mechanisms to ensure the required functionality
- *database features are not standardized*—due to implemented architectural solutions, databases differ in terms of object types and functionality that can be implemented. For instance in the Oracle database there is a concept of a *nested table*[257] while other databases don't have any such concept

---

[257] Special structural construct in Oracle RDBMS allows storing the columns that can hold an entire sub-table

To stay competitive the companies that are developing commercial software are forced to offer multiple target database platforms. The software architecture is designed generically to work with multiple databases assuming that each database offers:

- *structurally equivalent objects*—structural database objects such as tables and views offer the same composition and ability to store and present the same data content
- *equivalent functionality*—for instance the referential integrity rule implementation and enforcement should behave the same irrespective of internal implementation (declaratively or via the triggers)

Maintenance of large database models is complex by itself and having multiple models for different RDBMSs' further complicates the process. A manual solution to the databases synchronization is not impossible but it is time consuming and error prone requiring significant effort to keep the models and databases synchronized.

An alternative approach to any manual solution would require a single logical data model and multiple physical database-specific data models as shown in the Illustration 196:

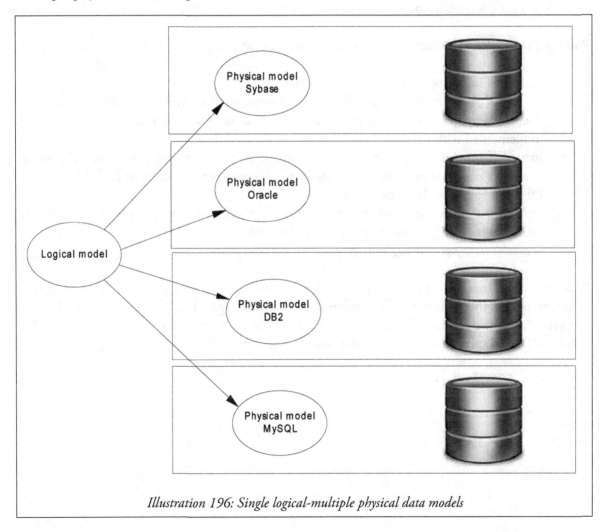

Illustration 196: Single logical-multiple physical data models

Based on a single logical data model, the modeler maintains multiple physical data models. Each physical model is designed for a specific RDBMS. All modifications must go through the logical model before they are implemented in the physical model. Prior to propagating modifications from the logical to the physical models, each modification has to be reviewed by the physical modeler who specializes in the specific RDBMS. Some modifications cannot be directly propagated and uniformly implemented in different databases due to differences in functionality offered by the RDBMS. Porting the application code can be challenging if the functionality implemented in database differs. The modeler has two alternatives:

- choose not to implement the required functionality in the database
- chose to have a database-specific implementation

If the functionality is not offered by the database or it is offered with certain limitations, the modeler can recommend implementation through the application. In that case all the databases should conform to the alternative solution. Alternatively the modeler can choose to have a database-specific solution implemented on a case-by-case basis which will complicate the database maintenance process requiring specialized code that is aware of the specific functionality implementation.

Potential areas where significant database differences could be expected are:

- *data types including the user defined data types* (UDT)
- *referential integrity implementation and enforcement* (for instance in MySQL certain database engines do not support the referential integrity so the model cannot be implemented with it)
- *structural constructs* (e.g. Oracle has a construct of an *external table* while the same construct does not exists in DB2; tablespace is construct common to both Oracle and DB2 but some databases do not have it)
- *indexes and index types* (for instance in Oracle there is a bitmap index type while in DB2 this index type cannot be explicitly specified)
- *available data partitioning strategies*

It is important that the physical data modeler is aware of specifics for each target database platform before the logical model modifications are propagated to the physical model. To mitigate the risk, each modification has to be reviewed by a specialist who specializes in the specific RDBMS, prior to the physical data model implementation.

The following illustration demonstrates the procedure for implementing the logical model to two databases (DB2 and Oracle) as shown in the Illustration 197:

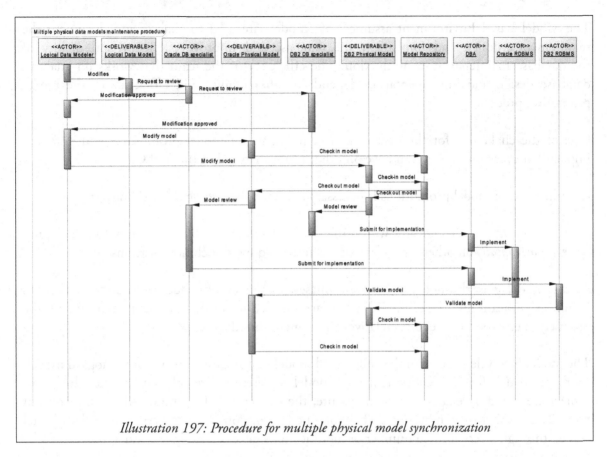

Illustration 197: Procedure for multiple physical model synchronization

The logical model, maintained by the logical modeler, is used as a generic model for the physical database-specific data models. To simplify the illustration only two target databases are chosen, however the same principles apply to the situation when more physical data models are required. Each physical data model, derived from the logical model, is synchronized with modifications implemented in the logical model. Before the modifications get propagated to the physical models, a specialist for each RDBMS has to review the requested changes. In the case that a modification is not implementable as required due to a lack of functionality in the target RDBMS, the physical modeler has to discuss and find a solution with the target database specialist, to implement required modification.

Standard model maintenance using the repository is in place and the model is checked-in to the repository after the physical modeler updates the models. Before the implementation, the specialist for the target RDBMS reviews the model and submits to the DBA for implementation. For simplicity, the illustration shows a single DBA where in practice each database has a DBA that specializes in the target RDBMS. After the model is implemented, the database and model are compared and maintenance is completed where there are no discrepancies reported. The model is subsequently checked into the model repository.

9.9. Frequency of model promotions

The Model Based Environment assumes that models are used to analyze and document the requirements, design and implement the database and improve efficiency and quality of the database maintenance in production. The efficiency of the team that works on analysis, database design and implementation depends on the stability and efficiency of the model promotion process.

One of the challenges for the data team is a frequency of model promotions and potential impact that every promotion can have on other teams involved in the SDLC.

Coordination of model promotions is necessary since it will have significant impact:

- *vertically* on other streams within the system development life-cycle (application coding)
- *horizontally* on other related[258] systems impacted by model modifications

As the model goes through the life-cycle phases, frequency of model promotions decreases. While a significant number of modifications are required in the development environment, the production environment requires relatively infrequent modifications.

The model life-cycle starts with the conceptual model that is a foundation for the logical model. As mentioned before the conceptual data model represents a model that outlines the major subject areas. Being relatively static in nature, the conceptual data model will change only if there is a radical change in business. Therefore the assumption is that the conceptual data model will go through a very limited number of modifications once it is designed and approved.

The frequency of logical model modifications depends on its stage in the SDLC. During the analysis phase, the logical data model is modified due to refinements in business and data requirements. Once the logical model is signed off and the first-cut of the physical model is produced the frequency of modifications will significantly drop. The logical model modifications are usually a result of:

- *new or modified business requirements*
- *physical model modification with a business nature*

Industry accepted practice for data modeling recommends that modifications to the physical model must go through the logical data model. Typically this poses a challenge for the following reasons:

- *logical and physical data models might be significantly different.* In case of a *data warehouse,* the standard is to use denormalized *star* or *snow-flake schema* design while the logical data model remains normalized. Keeping the logical and physical models in balance would be complex and time consuming

---

[258] The downstream systems

- *physical data model modifications are frequently urgent in nature.* Sometimes the modeler is forced to introduce modifications with limited testing, performed prior to implementation due to the fact that an urgent problem has to be solved quickly. There is no time to go through the regular modeling process and update the logical before the physical model. Performing modification directly to the physical data model should be discouraged but the reality of real life forces us to make exceptions
- *some modifications might not directly impact the logical data model* (e.g. adding an in-line constraint, implementing certain performance optimization alternatives such as materialized views)

Instead of going through the logical and then the physical data model, for simple modifications the modeler might choose to modify the physical data model directly and then, on regular cycles, retrofit the modifications to the logical data model. The assumption is that the introduced modifications will not change the business rules stated by the logical model.

After completion of the design and coding phase, the testing phase commences. As the model approaches the production environment, frequency of modification decreases and handling of each modification becomes more formalized. It is rare that in development environment modifications require a formal change request. However for the testing and production environment change requests are required. Each modification has to go through the review and approval process before it is implemented in the model.

To summarize, provided below is the table with frequency of modifications depending of the current SDLC phase (Table 30):

Model	Modifications frequency
Conceptual data model	• *infrequent*
Logical data model	• *frequent during analysis* • *infrequent afterward.*
Physical data model	• *frequent during design and coding.* • *infrequent afterward.*

Table 30: Model modification frequency by SDLC phase

The following factors will also influence the frequency of model modifications:

- *quality of business requirements*—imprecise, high-level business requirements will result in a constantly changing logical data model, triggering cascade modifications in the physical model
- *quality and level of details in the design documentation*—unclear design documentation or lack of architectural blueprint will result in frequent model modifications during the design phase
- *development methodology used*—rapid development methodologies tend to increase the number of model modifications. Model modifications almost always trigger the application code change.

9.10. Model demotion process

The model promotion process defined steps for model state transition from the analysis through the development, testing all the way to production. Functional errors or performance related problems may require the database modifications to rectify the problem. Every modification has to be recorded in the physical model before implementation.

For any required modification a thorough impact assessment has to be performed prior to modifying the physical data model. The preferred way is to always update the logical before the physical model, but practically when pressed by time, the modeler will opt to synchronize the logical data model after the physical model has been modified.

DEFINITION: *Model demotion is the process of preparing the model for modification due to a reported problem.*

The process is applied when there is a database modification required to fix a problem discovered in production or testing environment. The required modification is a result of a reported problem that needs to be fixed. Fixing a problem reported in production environment has a different priority compared to a problem reported in the testing environment. Problems found in the production database take higher priority and reaction by the team responsible for the problem solution has to be swift.

The test model demotion process will be first explained for fixing the problems reported in the testing database. The following illustration depicts the process (Illustration 198):

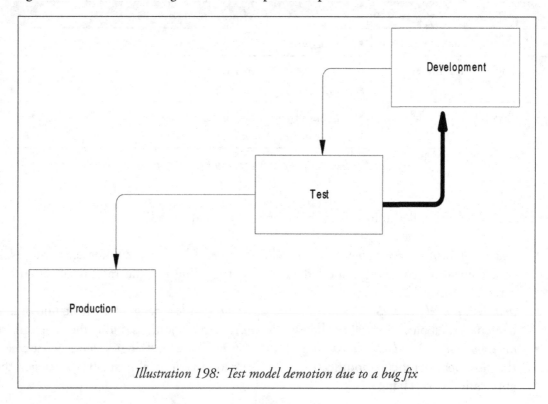

Illustration 198: Test model demotion due to a bug fix

During the testing phase, the physical model and database are frozen (static) so that the testing team can perform the testing in isolation. When the problem[259] is reported in the testing phase, the test data model has to be demoted to the development grade model for bug fixing. Considering that the development can be in progress, it is required that the modeler performs a comparison between the testing and development models and an impact analysis of the test model re-integration into the development model.

Two scenarios are possible:

- a defect is isolated to an area that is not currently impacted by development
- a defect impacts an area under development in the development model

When the comparison of the testing and development models shows no differences in the model's area that requires modification due to a bug fix, the development model can be modified accordingly. After the bug fix in the development model, the development model is promoted to the testing model.

If the defect correction requires modification of database objects not impacted by current development, the testing model can be downgraded to the development grade model

Fixing the problem when the impacted area of the testing data model is already being modified in the development model is far more complex. In that case the modeler has to perform an impact analysis to understand lateral effects that integration of the testing model might have on the development model prior to demoting the testing model to the development.

Handling the problem in the production environment is more complex due to the fact that the production environment is populated with data and might be under constant use. When fixing the production problem the model demotion process requires the existence of an environment where the demoted data model can be implemented into the database so that the support team can perform the necessary modifications. The following diagram illustrates the database layout that will be used to support the demotion process:

---

[259] The term "bug" is common in the industry

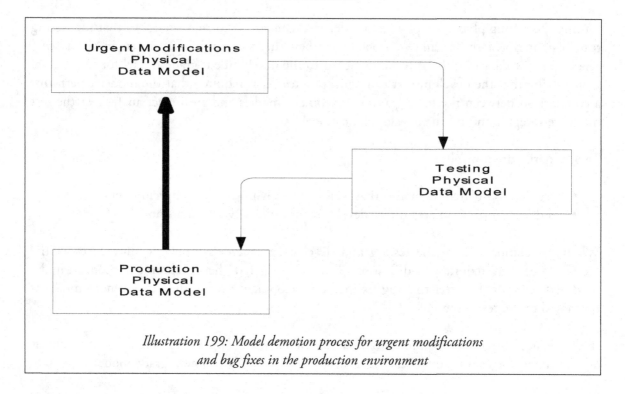

Illustration 199: Model demotion process for urgent modifications and bug fixes in the production environment

Shown here are the physical models for production, testing and urgent modification databases. The database for urgent modifications is in-line with the latest production data model. This database is isolated and intended for production bug fixes only. The production database is demoted to the *urgent modifications database* with the same version so the required modification can be done in this specialized environment. Fixing any production problem requires the following procedure (from the model perspective):

- the production model is compared to the model of the database for urgent modifications. These two models must be the same
- impact analysis of the solution for bug fix is analyzed based on the model
- physical data model for urgent modifications database is modified
- the model is compared with the database and the delta script is created to modify the database for urgent modification
- once the problem is fixed the script is promoted to the testing database and urgent modification database data model is promoted to the test database model
- the solution is tested and the testing database model is promoted to the production model while the script is scheduled for implementation into the production database
- after the script is implemented in the production database, the model is validated against the production database and if there are no differences the process is deemed completed

Urgent modifications tested and subsequently implemented in the production database have to be incorporated into the development database. This step is performed via production and regular development model integration. Integration of these modifications into the regular development model is not an easy or simple task because the development database might have a structure that is used for new development with modifications that are inconsistent with the current modifications performed in the production model (database). Careful impact analysis is required before the production model that went through the modification, is integrated with the current development model.

CONCLUSION

Models, as a concept, are used to comprehend the complexity of the world around us. Data modeling, as a discipline, extensively use models to structure and analyze the data and relationships presenting a business system using a standardized technique. All data models serve the following purposes:

- to document and validate the data structures and business rules
- to implement them consistently in the database
- to validate the model implementation in the database

The data model contributes to better understanding of the business on one side, but more importantly it increases the productivity and quality of work of the Data team. Having a data model is not sufficient if the model is not implementable, therefore the goal is to create a model that will include all components for successful implementation in the database.

CASE tools have their limitations but this should not discourage you, the data modeler, to use them to the full extent. While designing the data model, the modeler is also creating a standard documentation that supports the database design and implementation. One of the major advantages offered by the CASE tool is automated model comparison against the database. Having a lengthy DDL script implemented in database discourages even the most enthusiastic database administrators to perform thorough and comprehensive script deployment validation.

I hope that this book provided you with an overview of all the elements required for successful data model design and implementation using the CASE tool PowerDesigner.

BIBLIOGRAPHY

Core Features Guide, Power Designer 15.1, Sybase, Inc., One Sybase Drive, Dublin, June 2009 (Document ID: DC38093-01-1510-01)

Data Modeling, Power Designer 15.1, Sybase, Inc., One Sybase Drive, Dublin, June 2009 (Document ID: DC38058-01-1510-01)

Physical Database Design, 4th edition, Morgan Kaufmann, April 4, 2007

Data Modeling Made Simple with PowerDesigner, Steve Hoberman and George McGeachie, November 1, 2011

Data Modeling Theory and Practice, Graeme C. Simsion, March 1, 2007

Data Modeler's Workbench, Steve Hoberman, John Wiley and Sons Inc. New York, 2002

Physical Database Design, 4th edition, Morgan Kaufmann, April 4, 2007

Oracle Database Reference 11g Release 2 (11.2), Oracle Corporation, September 2012 (ID: E25513-03)

Oracle Database Administrator's Guide 11g Release 2 (11.2), Oracle Corporation, December 2011 (ID: E25494-02)

Understanding DB2: Learning Visually with Examples, 2nd edition, Raul Chong, Xiaomei Wang, Michael Dand and Dwaine Snow, IBM Press, December 29, 2007

DB2 for Linux, UNIX and Windows Database Administration: Certification Study Notes, Roger E. Sanders, MC Press Online, LLC, November 2, 2011

Oracle Flexible Architecture, Oracle Corporation, (part number B32002-11), 2010, 2011 <http://docs.oracle.com/cd/B28359_01/install.111/b32002/app_ofa.htm#i633068>

Financial Services Data Model, IBM Corporation, 2006 <ftp://service.boulder.ibm.com/software/data/mdm/pdf/BDW_GIM_2006.pdf>

IBM DB2 for Linux, Unix and Windows, IBM Corporation, 2012 <http://publib.boulder.ibm.com/infocenter/db2luw/v9r7/index.jsp>

Oracle Database SQL Language Reference 11g R2, Oracle Corporation <http://download.oracle.com/docs/cd/E14072_01/server.112/e10592/ap_keywd.htm>

ABOUT THE AUTHOR

Vladimir Pantic has been in Data Modeling and Physical Database Design for over twenty five years. He graduated from the University of Belgrade and worked in Information Technology with companies across the industries of Investment Banking, Insurance, Health Care, and Forestry in Europe, North America and Asia. He has guided these organizations in practicing disciplined logical and physical database design while following rigid processes. This book is an effort to help the data modelers be more efficient in their day-to-day work by providing the basic guidelines of how to use the models to optimize the modeling process.